Withold Bonner and Arja Rosenholm (eds.)

Recalling the Past - (Re)constructing the Past

Collective and Individual Memory of World War II in Russia and Germany

Aleksanteri Series 2/2008

Recalling the Past – (Re)constructing the Past

Collective and Individual Memory of World War II in Russia and Germany

ISBN 978-952-10-4098-6
ISSN 1796-3192

Gummerus Printing
Jyväskylä, Finland 2008

Table of Contents

Introduction

Memories and scholarly exploration on memory have become a significant part of contemporary cultural studies. Having been influenced by social and political changes especially in Europe both recalling and forgetting, play a significant role in constituting identities by nations and communities. Major changes in cultural and political orders in Russian and German societies in relation to the sense of memory in the societies' connective structure, were put forward as an orientation for the seminar held in December 2006 at the University of Tampere, Finland under the title of *Recalling the Past – Collective and Individual Memory of World War II in Russia and Germany.* World War II has been one of the most important events and highly emotive topics in German as well as in Russian and Soviet history. Over 60 years after the end of the war the recalling of the wartime experiences is significantly gaining in importance. Eyewitnesses and survivors of the war are passing away and, therefore, we are at the turning point from communicative to cultural memory. On the level of cultural memory history is being re-negotiated. A re-evaluation of recent history has emerged in both countries. As a consequence it has been possible to discuss forbidden and "forgotten" subjects, as certain phenomena of war and occupation in both countries: for instance the siege of Leningrad, anti-semitism and the Holocaust, the fate of P.O.Ws, and forced alien workers during and after the war, life and death at the front and the "home" front, the different situation of men and women, female soldiers' quest in the Red Army, raping of women as a mass phenomenon in the occupied parts of Germany.

In Russia, as pointed out by Boris Dubin in the sociological survey of the Analytic Centre of Juri Levada for the selected years in the period from 1989 to 2003, "[...] the very centre made to fixate the sense of the [Soviet Russian, A.R., W.B.] collective history, is the victory in the *Great Fatherland War* [...]", while, simultaneously, the negative evaluation of such pre-war events as collectivisation, hunger and repression sank noticeably.[1] The myth of the "victory in war" in Russia is a binding element which blurs the boundary between past and present, it had grown into the central symbol of the power of the Soviet history, and delivered sense to the whole Soviet order under the Brezhnev legitimization, the period when the myth was being created. And, according to Lev Gudkov, the revival of the interest in recalling the war in Putin's Russia shows a function of these reminiscences as feeding stability and legitimacy of the master narrative – as an integral element of the connective culture "transposing" memories of the totalitarian into a post-totalitarian culture and society.[2]

Russia has seen a wealth of studies into collective and personal historical memory over the last years; there are conflicting models including the tradition of a monolithic and heroic recalling of the Great Patriotic War and a critical focus upon the tragedies during the war. On the German side the discussion on the WWII has been linked since the 1980s, especially since the unification of the old Federal Republic and the GDR, with the question on whether the Germans can be seen not only as perpetrators, but as victims of the war as well, suffering from Allied bombing, expulsion from the East or looting and mass rape by the Red Army soldiers.[3] Milestones in this ongoing controversial debate were for instance popular TV series on the expulsion of Germans from the East or

---

1 Dubin Boris (2005), Goldene Zeiten des Krieges. Erinnerung als Sehnsucht nach der Brežnev-Ära, Kluften der Erinnerung. Russland und Deutschland 60 Jahre nach dem Krieg. In *Osteuropa. Neprikosnovennii zapas.* 55 Jhg/Heft 4–6, 219–234, here pp. 221–222.

2 Gudkov, Lev (2005), Die Fesseln des Sieges. Russlands Identität aus der Erinnerung an den Krieg. In *Osteuropa. Neprikosnovennii zapas.* Vol. 55, Issue 4–6: Kluften der Erinnerung. Russland und Deutschland 60 Jahre nach dem Krieg. 56–73, here p. 59, see also Gabowitsch, Mischa et al. (2005), Vergangenheit ist mehr als eine Geschichte. In *Osteuropa. Neprikosnovennii zapas.* Vol. 55, Issue 4–6: Kluften der Erinnerung. Russland und Deutschland 60 Jahre nach dem Krieg, 5–7, and the Russian volume in *Neprikosnovennii zapas.* Debaty o politike i kul'ture (2005), 2–3 (40–41).

3 See for the German debate for instance Niven, Bill (ed.) (2006), *Germans as Victims. Remembering the Past in Contemporary Germany.* Houndmills, Basingstoke and Hampshire, Palgrave Macmillan, or Schmitz, Helmut (ed.) (2007), *A Nation of Victims? Representations of German Wartime Suffering from 1945 to the Present,* Amsterdam – New York, and the special edition (Vol. 59, Issue 2) of *German Life and Letters* from 2006 on "Cultural Memory, Hybridity and Identity in German Discourses since 1990" including Assmann, Aleida (2006), On the (In)Compatibility of Guilt and Suffering in German Memory. Ibid., 187–200.

the Allied bombing of Dresden, Jörg Friedrich's book *Der Brand* on war in the air, the exhibition *Flucht, Vertreibung, Integration*, first presented in the *Haus der Geschichte* in Bonn vs the BdV's (League of Expellees) campaign for a *Centre Against Expulsions* in Berlin in a privileged location in the neighbourhood of the Holocaust memorial, the travelling exhibition *Vernichtungskrieg: Verbrechen der Wehrmacht 1941–1944* on war crimes committed by the regular German army or the novella *Im Krebsgang* by Günter Grass on the sinking of the *Wilhelm Gustloff* transporting thousands of German refugees. Although the abandonment of the binary perpetrator / victim opposition is to be welcomed, we agree with Aleida Assmann, who sees in the Holocaust, the recognition and working-through of German guilt, the framework into which all the other memories have to be integrated.[4]

As our volume shows, some more or less monolithic discourses of official and collective memories have been challenged by conflicting fragments, private and alternative memories mediated in oral histories and their exploration being of growing interest for scholars from various disciplines. Reflections upon various memories, traumas and collective taboos take place in scholarly writings which focus on how post-totalitarian national identities in Germany and Russia have been re-constructed in the process of memory re-formation. The scholars ask how the past is made present and what is re-constructed as (significant) memories to become an integral part of personal and national self-identities. Accordingly, dealing with processes of memory – both on micro- and macro levels – the authors pay attention to time, place and media as integral categories of the memory process, as well as hierarchies in agency legitimated to carry on the particular memories.

One of the objectives of our multi- and interdisciplinary volume is to examine the fractures, interactions and intersections of private and collective memories in different times and places in different texts, such as fiction, autobiographic writing, movies, songs, monuments, oral history and "official" historiography, to ask what and how the past is remembered. Thereby the scholars also focus on the question on how, in which ways the reconstructive working of the memory is anchored in cultural conventions of national imagery production, i.e. what are the

---

4 Assmann 2006, 198. See also Schmitz 2007, 15.

topoi which are taken up and reproduced by reconstructing the memory of the past. The comparative character of the volume also pays attention to parallel changes in Russian and German societies and contributes to the discussion on whether and how meanings arising from the common history of war – or, rather, constructions of experiences – differ due to contexts and cultural backgrounds. While focusing on "official" and "private" memories many articles in this volume seem to conform what e.g. Forest, Johnson and Till have criticized as an inadequate "elite-public dichotomy", and accordingly, pinpoint the "[...] mutual interactions among multiple publics and elites, differing in kind and intensity across contexts, [...] combin[ing] to form a complex pastiche of public memory that both interprets a nation's past and suggests desirable models for its future".[5]

The past emerges when we create a relation to it, and it is in the memory where the past is reconstructed. New beginnings and restaurations are always in need of past represented here by the WWII as one of the central constitutive memory elements of German and Russian identities, both for the self-image and the one given by others. A common feature among the scholars of the volume is their interdisciplinary understanding of memory, that the process of recalling is always intertwined with a multiplicity of discourses, with political interests and cultural models merging into a politics of memory. The concept has a social-constructivist impetus while following the central idea of Maurice Halbwachs[6] that memory is socially constructed; memories – also those of personal character – emerge through communication and are framed by social groups, as other scholars,[7] too, have pointed out. There are different terms for memory – collective, individual, political, national etc. – used in the articles. The constructivist approach to memory utilized in most

---

5 Benjamin, Forest, Johnson, Juliet and Till, Karen (2004), Post-Totalitarian National Identity: Public Memory in Germany and Russia. In *Social & Cultural Geography*, Vol. 5, Issue 3, 357–380. They write that "[...] the battle over whether and how to remember the past in Russia remains sensitive and complex, yet far more circumscribed than that in Germany". p. 369.

6 Halbwachs, Maurice (1966), *Das Gedächtnis und seine sozialen Bedingungen*. Berlin, Luchterhand, and Halbwachs, Maurice (1992), *On Collective Memory*. Chicago and London, University of Chicago Press.

7 See for instance Fentress, James and Wickham, Chris (1992), *Social Memory*. Oxford, Blackwell.

of the articles comes close to what Jan and Aleida Assmann have called "cultural memory", *kulturelles Gedächtnis.*[8] It is oriented toward the "external dimension" of human memory implying that the recalled substance, the question of structure and the permanence of memories is not so much an issue of inner capacities but rather more externally conditioned, i.e. socially and culturally directed.[9] That the categories given to the memory by locus, time and hierarchy are overlapping both in the memory process and in the debates of the articles, correspond to the integrative character of cultural memory which integrates various areas of memory such as the mimetic memory, the memory of things and the communicative memory.[10] Cultural memory is not only mediated selectively but is to be found in differentiated and concrete objectifications like traditions, rituals and symbolically codified words, images, music, dance etc. The authors pay attention to the social character of memory by its spatialization, the historical time when the memories come to the surface, the medium via which the memories are given their form, and, not least, to the special bearers of the cultural memory by asking who has the right to own memories and speak them out.

In a sense the articles contribute to a productive tension between two ways of approaching the memory narratives; the post-modern way to recall and tell the past without fixing it on a continuous and unbroken master narrative on the one hand, and the processes of memory reformation on the other hand affected by symbolical representations and dominant conceptualisations of the nation. It is left to the responsibility of the scholar to debate with the interpretative side of the memory, what is recalled, told and what is passed over in silence and why.

To study memory and commemoration is to be closely connected with the implicit question which also brings the articles into a common area, binding scholarly interest with ethical categories; a common question is how individuals and societies overcome traumatic experiences like wars with violence and suffering, what individuals and nations do with their memories, of which some are overburdened, some missing altogether from the public consciousness. Being conscious of the selectiveness,

---

8 Assmann, Jan (2005), *Das kulturelle Gedächtnis.* München, Verlag C.H. Beck, 18ff.

9 Ibid. 19–20.

10 Ibid. 20–21.

discursiveness and value orientation of all kinds of memory processing, the authors debate the question of truth. The authors show the imbalance between commemorialization and forgetting, the battle of forces over what has been debated in public and what has been kept in silence and told in privacy. The authors show that and how conflicts like wars do not come to an end by peace declarations but go on on various "fronts of memories"[11] left over to be fought by the next generations. Exploration of various memories delivers an important cultural space where to deal with and work through crises, conflicts, and traumatic experiences.

As there are different modalities of memory that can be separated from each other only analytically, as memory is a crossroads where different sciences coincide, as it is of great importance to know whose memories are in question, as the process of recalling is always structured by time and place of its occurrence, and as this process takes place in different media, the articles in the volume are ordered according to criteria inevitably overlapping each other, but helping to create contexts where varying scientific focuses investigating different modes of memory can communicate with each other.

Places of Memory

Places have always played an important role in the process of recollection. Spaces in question can be "holy" places participating in the construction of the hierarchical national cultural memory, as it is still – and in a problematic way – the case with the city of Stalingrad / Volgograd, as Elena Trubina demonstrates in her article *"You See Now Just How Small All of You Are". Rhetoric spaces of Volgograd.* On the other hand the same space, playing an important role in the construction of the cultural memory and identity building in one country, may constitute a blind spot in another one, being completely or at least partially repressed from collective and individual memory. This happened to the siege of Leningrad in German historiography and autobiographic texts by

11 Peltonen, Ulla-Maija (2003), *Muistin paikat* [Sites of Memory – On Remembering and Forgetting the 1918 Civil War in Finland]. Suomen kirjallisuuden Seura, Helsinki, p. 308.

former German WWII participants, as it is shown by Katrin Paehler in *The Wrong Grad, the Wrong Victims: (West) German Historiography on the Siege of Leningrad.* The way the time of war is represented in the cultural memory, in Russia as well as in Germany, tends to turn life at the home front into another blind spot, such excluding female experiences which are predominantly connected with the home front. The intention to fill this blind spot gives its special value to *Remembering Everyday Life in 1940–1950s: Femininity, Beauty and Maternity in the Shadow of the War* by Yulia Gradskova, exploring how two aspects of everyday life – maternity and beauty – were remembered by Russian women who were young in the 1940–1950s. The distinction between front and home front was fundamentally blurred during WWII, in the first line due to the Holocaust and other atrocities committed by German occupying forces against the civilian population in the USSR. In the final phase of the war, the German home front turned into the front line where the German civil population suffered mass looting and rape. Among others, since the 1980s these incidents gave ground for the re-negotiation of German collective memory, according to which Germans were to be seen as victims of the war as well. In *Forced Interculturality during War Times. Russians and Germans in Texts from the German Diary Archive, Emmendingen*, Elisabeth Cheauré explores to what degree autobiographical texts by German soldiers and civilians reflect the collectively anchored image of the enemy 'Russian', as transported through the discourse of the time, and how the collective image of the 'Russian' influenced the individual's experience in real encounters.

There are other places, counter-sites in which the real sites that can be found within the culture, are simultaneously represented and contested. Such heterotopias, as Foucault calls these places, are for example, cemeteries and prisons. Therefore, it is not incidental that memories by female Russian survivors of WWII, excluded from the official discourse of recollection, find their voice during a journey by these women to the graves of their husbands, as can be seen in the paper by Kirsi Kurkijärvi on the novel *Remembrance Day* by Russian author Natalia Baranskaia, titled *Dialogues with War in Natalia Baranskaia's "Remembrance Day".* As Withold Bonner shows in *The endless Process of Reconstructing Memories: Captivity and Anti-Fascist Re-education in Texts of Franz*

Fühmann, the prisoner camp and Antifa-School in the Soviet Union, to which Fühmann returned over and over again in his texts, was turned by him into a heterotopia, another space, from which the author contested the official antifascist narrative of the GDR, according to which the East German state had nothing to do with the fascist past.

The importance of space is not limited to the places that are remembered. As can be seen already from the article by Kurkijärvi, space is of equal significance in which the recollection occurs. For this site determines the audience, at which the recollection is directed. Such an impact of space and altering audience on the reshaping of memories and vice versa can be clearly seen from the contributions by Sveta Roberman as well as by Liliana Feierstein and Liliana Furman. While the former demonstrates in her paper *Red Army WWII Veterans in Israel: Mobilization of the Combat Past and Negotiation of Belonging to a New Homeland*, how the past serves as a resource in migrants' negotiations with the new host society, the latter explores in *Memory under Siege: Jewish Veterans of the Soviet Army in Present-Day Germany* the tensions, generated by the memories of this specific group of immigrants in German society as well as in Jewish communities.

Media of Memory

Although it is a common place that the past can be recollected in very different media, the advantage of this section lies in the attention it directs to the vast variety of cultural representations that are in use for constructing memories and to their specific performances, as there are museum exhibitions, autobiographical texts, posters, songs and movies. In her contribution *From Memory to History: Displaying World War Two in the German Historical Museum*, Robin Ostow shows how the exhibition, heavily influenced by the discussion in the 1980s–1990s on the reconstruction of German cultural memory, offers the public a centralized, top-down narrative of two thousand years of German history, told by an omniscient narrator, rather than displaying the diversity of German experiences. The diversity, omitted in the museum, might be found in autobiographical testimonies by participants and eyewitnesses of the war. Kobi Kabalek demonstrates in *Immediate Memories: Written Experiences of the Nazi Past in Occupied Germany, 1945–1949*, how the diaries, for example by Ruth Andreas-Friedrich, written during the Nazi-era and published short after the end of World War Two while conveying individual experiences, try at the same time to participate actively in the re-negotiation of the German collective memory. Although diaries claim to present an "unmediated" proximity to the past, they prove to be already constructed retrospective articulations of past experiences. As for autobiographical texts by Elena Rzhevskaia, who – as an interpreter in the Soviet army – was part of a secret group of Soviet intelligence officers finding the burnt remains of Hitler and Goebbels, Arja Rosenholm shows in *Reflections on a Meeting: Elena Rzhevskaia Meets Marshal Zhukov*, how a marginalized and unauthorized discourse holds the power to disrupt authorized versions of experience. Rosenholm points out that while becoming integrated with the collective memory, the woman writer at the same time writes her own exclusion, for the text making her well known is a voice for a great man.

Movies have had an important impact on the construction of cultural memory of World War II. According to *Alexei A. German's Estranging View of the Great Patriotic War* by Christine Engel, *Poslednii poezd* by the Russian director Alexei A. German deconstructs the usual heroic narrative and rejects the patriotic pathos, typical for so many Russian films on this subject. Engel's close analysis of the movie's visual language emphasises its great number of close-ups, which show that there can be no overview of the war.

Another mode of recollection which had a strong impact on the construction of collective memory concerning World War Two in the USSR, was the huge number of songs that were composed during the war. In *Lyric and Legacy, Melody and Memory: World War II Songs and the Shaping of Memory and Identity* Suzanne Ament shows that multiple layers must be considered in order to define and comprehend why these songs had such a long-lasting effect on society. As recent experiences show, these songs were again in use by the Putin-administration in order to foster a sense of collective identity that would incorporate the Soviet past. In his article *"Despite it All, We've Won": Chechen War and Military Songs* Serguei Oushakine focuses on the use Russian veterans of the war in Chechnya made of World War II songs, given the Russian public amnesia concerning this forgotten war. It is against the background of the incomplete symbolic exchange between the veterans and the state, as well as between the veterans and society, that ex-combatants created a new socio-symbolic context by reclaiming the legacy of Russia's previous wars and re-appropriating them for their own public interests and rituals.

As these songs on the war in Chechnya are placed in the context of the legacy of World War II songs, there had already been previous approaches to place Soviet wartime posters into a historical context. In *History and Metahistory in Soviet World War II Posters* Helena Goscilo shows, how for example medieval Russian epic heroes were used to ensure the power of the multicultural Soviet Army. It is this historical perspective and the tendency to self-citation within these posters, that Goscilo is concentrating on.

Hierarchies of Memory

As already could be seen in the previous section, various modalities of memory do not coexist side by side. For different reasons – in Germany as well as in Russia – contemporary collective and individual memories of the Second World War seem to be incompatible. As for contemporary Germany, Peter Carrier explores in *Political and Ethical Contexts of Collective Memories of the Second World War* the ethical assumptions underlying three approaches to understanding the impact of memories of the Second World War: the political institutional production of memorial narratives, the conversational transmission of memory in family institutions, and the transmission of memory in educational institutions.

The hieratic cultural memory, based on specific fixed points, marked as important and kept alive through cultural forming (texts, rites, monuments) and institutionalised communication (recitation, visiting, viewing) comprehends the tendency to strongly influence, if not to exclude and suppress deviant aspects of memory. What applies for the cultural memory in general, applies even more for the "political" memory as employed in the Soviet Union and continued in today's Russia. In *Two*

Different Wars? World War II as "Second Imperialist War" and "Great Patriotic War" in the Russian-Soviet Tradition Tobias Privitelli explores how the perception of World War II in Russia is still divided into two periods. The article attempts to demonstrate to what extent the official Stalinist interpretation of World War Two has conditioned the Russian public discourse during the last 60 years. It is – among other motives – the impact of the official cultural memory that has interfered with the systematic examination of cooperation by Soviet citizens with the German occupation authorities, as can be seen from the article by Olga Baranova, titled *Collaboration by the Soviet Citizens with the Nazi Occupation Authorities during the Great Patriotic War: How the Issue Was Represented and Treated in Soviet, Western and Post-Soviet Russian and Belarusian Historiography.* The exclusion of specific experiences during and after the war from the cultural memory is subject of the paper by Beate Fieseler, too, with its focus on the presentation of disablement in Soviet films between 1944 and 1959. In *The Wounds of War: Experiences of War-Related Disablement in Soviet Feature Films* Fieseler shows, how disablement is downplayed in these movies in different ways.

In *Remembrance of Things Past: Soviet Histories and Jewish Memories* Zvi Gitelman inquires as to what extent Soviet authorities knew about the systematic extermination of their citizens of Jewish nationality during the German occupation. How did they interpret some of the information to their own citizens and what were the motives of Soviet Jews fighting in the Red Army during World War Two, as remembered by Jewish veterans? Again it is the connection between the presentation of the war in the Soviet media and the motivation to volunteer for the Red Army, which was of crucial importance in the case of Soviet child soldiers, as examined by Olga Kucherenko in *Fiction and Reality of War through the Eyes of Soviet Child-Soldiers.*

The participation of female soldiers in the Red Army was another dark spot in official Soviet historiography. It was not until perestroika that women veterans started to talk about and publish their war experiences. As already insinuated by the title of Roger Markwick's paper, *"A Sacred Duty": Red Army Women Veterans Remembering the Great Fatherland War, 1941–1945*, those women veterans encountered difficulties in their attempts to inscribe their recollections into the official heroic cultural memory of World War II in the Soviet Union / Russia. In his article, Markwick concentrates on what surviving women veterans choose to remember and what they choose to forget. If the participation of women in the Red Army was a taboo in Soviet cultural memory, so it was the fate of Soviet POWs, surviving imprisonment in German camps. *Between Pride and Bitterness. The Fall of Sewastopol in 1942 in the Memory of Soviet Female Prisoners of War and Survivors of the Nazi Concentration Camp Ravensbrück* by Ramona Saavedra Santis explores, how female Red Army veterans from the battle of Sewastopol, later transformed into a symbol of Russian heroism, deal with their memories they had over decades adjusted to the official version of the "Great Patriotic War".

The conference and volume would not have been possible without the financial support of many organisations. We thank and acknowledge the contribution of the Academy of Finland, the Tampere University Foundation, the Kordelin Foundation, the Aleksanteri Institute, the German Embassy in Finland and the School of Modern Languages and Translation studies of the University of Tampere. We also thank Sirje Lällä for technical editing and Sirpa Randell for her work on the layout of the text.

Arja Rosenholm
Withold Bonner

Tampere, 18. 10. 2008

Places of Memory

Elena Trubina

"You See Now Just How Small All of You Are": Rhetorical Spaces of Volgograd

The legacies of war continue to affect cities long after the war. During the war years, some cities are destined to become places for collecting the nation's energies and defeating a foe. After the war, determined to rebound, they become reconstruction sites. One of these cities, Stalingrad, in the history of the twentieth century metonymically stands for a turning point in the war in Europe as well as for the cruelty of contemporary warfare. Stalingrad (renamed Volgograd in 1961) keeps attracting visitors from many countries, mostly from Germany and Russia. What do these visitors see when they come? With its Stalinist architecture and the imprints of war, the city, for some visitors, seems like a time machine, and it is not by chance that the educated locals readily joke that, "[w]e are still the most Soviet city that one can find in Russia." They mean not only that the city's urban fabric was almost entirely defined in the first decades after the Second World War, but the fact that, due to its role in Soviet history, the city has a considerable number of Stalin's supporters. Many of its cultural practitioners see it as a site of patriotic memory of Soviet traditions, which seem to be the only ones available.

The sense of the city one gets as one joins a guided tour through present-day Volgograd is rather ambivalent. This fleeting experience, through which memory comes into existence at a given time and place for a particular audience, can be a useful way to deal with a location that seems to encourage one kind of utterance and performance and to discourage another. The notion of rhetorical space that I use to designate this phenomena, drawing on the work of Lorraine Code,[1] is meant to emphasize the variety of city sites and visual artifacts that together produce a set of imperatives defining what can be said about the city and how it should be seen.

The circulation of the memory of the Second World War, both within and beyond the national narrative, becomes today more and more complex. On the one hand, people, especially the young and middle-aged, increasingly are exposed to diverse and contradictory impulses usually associated with globalization. On the other hand, the nation-state is determined to keep its hegemony of producing and reproducing the official narrative of that very particular historical event. The war in general and the Stalingrad Battle in particular continue to be used as a source of legitimacy for the government and a source of pride for the populace whose history is so problematic and troubled that victory in that war seems a single, untainted accomplishment. The politics of memory and commemoration are produced through the spaces of museums and memorials, the design of monuments, the contents of official speeches and excursions, and the meanings of public ceremonies. What interests me in particular are the social dynamics and political repercussions underlying the activities of young people. What are the reasons that all the sanctimonious patriotic clichés and activities of the Soviet era, after being transmitted through high-school education, become so unreflectively reproduced? Whether one thinks of this phenomenon in terms of collective unconsciousness, social inertia, the conservatism of municipal authorities, or even genius loci, the nature of the peculiar imperatives the reconstructed city imposes on its inhabitants and the version of its identity it promotes appear worthy of reflection.

It is girl teen-agers who give one of the most peculiar performances that help sustain Volgograd's patriotic identity. They take part in the daily honor guard ceremony at the Eternal Fire memorial, which makes one think not only about the implicit significance of gender relations for the construction of history and cultural memory but about the everyday life of the memorials. It is one thing to witness a parade or fireworks on Victory day with the subsequent emotional atmosphere, and quite another to be exposed to or to take part in a patriotic ceremony amidst mundane life. I was curious to know how the training for the guards is organized, and it turns out that a special education center exists in Volgograd whose aim is to promote the patriotic upbringing of Volgograd's youth. It is called Post Number One, referring to a particular episode of the Young Communist League's activities in the 1960s when the league's members in Volgograd were mobilized to be honor guards at the Eternal Fire in the Square of the Fallen Fighters. Since then, only the best high school students receive the right to be on guard. The schools take part in this ritual in turn. Still, I wanted to know if there is a queue among those who wish to work as such, or is it a compulsory obligation? The girls on duty said they are not supposed to talk till they come back to school after performing the ritual. I am someone who does remember not just how difficult it is to stay still for a half of hour while fulfilling my own guard duty (as a university student, by the Eternal Fire in my city) but having that uneasy feeling of both reverence and doubt: if someone asks why I am here, what will I answer except that I was ordered to do so? But I do belong to a different generation and see that times have changed radically. Why do girls and not soldiers perform today this honorary duty? Why make these twelve-year old girls repeat the steps we all know belong to military parades rather then let them enjoy the salsa? A performance that could draw attention to the repeated gestures of devotion and loyalty reveals that this repetition is not identical to its imaginary source, and that it generates reactions more ambivalent than it purports to induce.

In sketching the troubled history of modern social urban studies, the urban scholars, Ryan Bishop and Gregory Clancey, observe that "the City" acquired "a heroic status in both capitalist and socialist storytelling"[2] after the Second World War. One of the reasons for the theoretical neglect or silencing of urban catastrophes was the prevalence of the overarching progressivist narrative, according to which cities were supposed to be places of order and not the places of catastrophe. This model of the city as hero was most impressively exemplified by the Russian government's deployment of Battle of Stalingrad as a vehicle of socialist ideology. The victory-related triumphalism became the very foundation of the Soviet state.

In Stalingrad-Volgograd, three meanings of reconstruction can be differentiated. First, a physical one; second, a reconstruction of the Soviet Union's national identity; and, third, trauma recovery. While the first two meanings of reconstruction became combined in the predominant rhetoric, the third ended up being almost totally suppressed. While triumphalism pervaded the whole public space, while all the city sites were mobilized to highlight patriotism, victory, and courage, little was done to work through the traumatic dimension of the city's history during and after the war. Nowhere in the published accounts of the final years of the war and the first years after it can one find any attempt to theoretically assess the fact that the destruction of institutional and individual life in Stalingrad was so fundamental that no aspect of social or personal life was left unaffected. The cynicism of the state propaganda expressed itself in the fact that the eye-witness accounts of the atrocities committed by the enemy, which were heavily promoted during the war to evoke affective response on the part of Soviet citizens, were shut down after the war was over as if the people's suffering did not matter unless it could be used against the enemy[3] or to serve as proof of the people's loyalty to the regime.

After World War II, a pattern of narrative was established in which the city's history was subsumed under the monumental celebration of the nation-state on a global scale. An imposing commemoration site was built in Stalingrad in 1967, one of nearly 70,000 war monuments that had been built all over the USSR. Mass construction resulted in stylistic affinities: most memorials are hierarchical figural compositions surrounded by plates with names. By now, many of these monuments have lost their function as spaces of rhetorical power and only come to life, so to speak, during the mass commemoration ceremonies on Victory day. Russian researchers of the memorials of the Second World War note that there is one universal obstacle anyone looking for these memorials in post-Soviet Russia would face: "Everybody has seen them and knows they exist, but there are few who could tell where exactly they are located."[4] On the other hand, since the war memorials are often located in the central city, they become the locals' promenade places and their functions thus tend to shift towards quotidian public places.

There are a few memorial and monumental places in the city that are devoted to the Stalingrad battle: the Stalingrad Battle Panorama-Museum, the Pavlov House, and the Mamaev Hill memorial. The Panorama allows visitors to view the entire field of combat, the Pavlov House is a burnt-out shell of the building where Soviet soldiers defended themselves for two months, and the Mamaev Hill memorial was built twenty years after the battle. These historical monuments work as rhetorical artifacts that wouldn't serve their purpose without curatorial zeal. The city narrative that is performed during the guided tour is composed from the sites designed to educate, to honor, and to instill a feeling of unity with those who gave their lives. These are the places where people have come for generations to reflect on who we are and to remember the nation's sacrifices. The image of the city that the texts of the tour reproduce is one of a unique place with unique inhabitants that many enemies tried to conquer but always failed.

The victory becomes an emblem and a common signifier of the city's identity. This explains the immersion of both the city's authorities and the locals in particular accounts of the past that have, since 1943, been invoked by the state as a way to strengthen national identity. In these accounts, a complete German defeat by the Soviet forces is interpreted as proof of the superiority of the Soviet way of life, the "failed prophesies" trope figures as rejoicing at the fact that Hitler's delusions proved wrong while the courage of Soviet soldiers and civilians was endless and awesome. The hundreds of thousands of casualties and the ruins of the city are turned into figures in that narrative as the price we had to pay for victory. The "failed prophesies" trope gets applied not only to the battle itself but to the reconstruction of the city. After the Stalingrad battle, so the narrative goes, visitors from the West advised the local authorities to give up the idea of rebuilding the city since it would be a lot cheaper to build a new city from scratch. But the local Communist party committee and the people of Stalingrad were determined to bring city back to life. The city was destroyed but we've rebuilt it. For a distant listener, it is almost impossible, in this version of the story, to disentangle where the benevolent influence of the Communist party ends and where civic participation begins.

It appears that the narrative has not been revised since the late 1980s. The young tour-guide, who readily reproduces in her speech all the rhetorical devices and the dominant narrative of Soviet times and enthusiastically reproaches those in the group who dare to express their doubts with regard to her words on the pretext of "insufficient respect towards the memory of soldiers," makes one think of the difficulties of producing rhetorical means better suited to the present-day audiences' needs and tastes than those worked out in Soviet times.

What I think differentiates the Soviet politics of memory is that the collective memory after 1945 was not divided into particular generations. The distance from the war increases, but the discursive renderings of those events that would be characteristic of a second, a third, and now a fourth generation haven't become prominent parts of the public discourse. There is a sense in which it is only when exposed to the versions of the past that too obviously belong to the past era that visitors to the city and its numerous patriotic sites begin to feel a discrepancy between the time they live in and the rhetoric that has been promoted. The striking example of this discrepancy and of what might be called the many-pacedness of historical change were the final words of my tour guide: "Together, we just have visited one of the greatest war memorials in the world. You see now just how big is our Motherland (she pointed her finger toward the main statue of Mamaev's Hill) and how small all of you are."

Nowhere do what John Gillis calls a state "bureaucracy of memory"[5] and John Bodnar the "dogmatic formalism"[6] of official memory find their expression more strikingly than in these narratives and the very itineraries of these tours. The city markets itself as predominantly a "hero-city." Both on the official site of the city and in the tourist agencies' brochures, it is named the "hero-city Volgograd." (And this is the title that the city, indeed, received from the Soviet authorities). The legacy of the Stalingrad Battle is considered not as a challenge to present-day Volgograd but as an important symbolic resource and a major tourist attraction. The city's marketing efforts thus nicely coincide with the conservative war memory discourse and the orthodox official interpretation of World War II. One might think that in order to attract today's more diverse and demanding audiences, to the predominant narrative some others could have been added, given the obvious difference in meaning that this war has for the different generations. However, not only is this not the case, but we see the young cultural practitioners eagerly participating in reproducing the old stories.

According to one rhetorician, "[d]isplays are rhetorical because the meanings they manifest before situated audiences result from selective processes and, thus, constitute partial perspectives with political, social, or cultural implications."[7] In Volgograd, by virtue of its location amidst the so-called red belt of Russia, the conservative rhetorical space was created and, while excluding more problematic discourses, especially those focused on traumatic city history, it encourages certain speakers and promotes conventional narratives.

Let me now cite the reactions to the tours given in Volgograd that can be found in the live journals of those young Russians who shared their travel experiences on the Web. One of those who recently visited Volgograd writes as follows:[8]

> The speech our guide delivered was monotonous both in terms of its inflections and its meaning. All its contents could be predicted from the onset since it only transmits the historical stereotypes everybody's familiar with: all German soldiers are cruel cowards, all Soviet soldiers are heroes who are eager to give their lives in the heroic acts, and all the battle is the conflict of good and evil. The Soviet soldiers thus are transformed into half-gods, totally different both from those who lived then and who live now. And war history, rather than being a realistic narrative, turns into mythology with the heroes carefully selected.

It would be surely too naive to reproach numerous Volgograd tour guides for drawing this Manichean picture instead of providing the visitors with a more subtle and balanced version of the events in question. In fact, what gets performed in these speeches is the same strategic forgetting of the traumatic pages of the war that threatened to undermine the legitimacy of Stalinism that was undertaken during the first few postwar decades. We may better understand what caused such a reaction on the part of a visitor if we read the brochures the Stalingrad war museums provides to their visitors. Here is a fragment of the Stalingrad Battle-Panorama Museum's advertisement:

> Against the background of the military operations, the artists are resurrecting the legendary heroic deeds of Stalingrad Battle – a signalman Matvei Putilov, who connected the ends of the torn wires in his mouth, a junior sergeant Nikolai Serdukov, who covered the embrasure of the enemy's gun with his chest, a pilot Viktor Rogalskii, who performed a air-ground ram attack, a nurse Anna Beschastnova, who saved the lives of thousands wounded soldiers by carrying them out of the battlefield, a Red Army soldier Mikhail Panikhakha, who jumped at the enemy's tank and caught himself on fire.

The uneasiness this description causes has to do with the fact that today we see differently the value of a single human life and, left to our private thoughts, ask ourselves uncomfortable questions about what we would do under these circumstances and don't have answers. I believe that what makes the expression of the memory of the war in the city's space deficient is that the rhetorical space we find ourselves in is too heavily ritualized. It precludes discussion and seeks to impose on visitors a passive acceptance of the version of history that seeks to promote the smallness of each of us in the face of the larger-than-life preoccupations of the state. However, what makes things even more complicated is that even if a charismatic leader of today decides to uncompromisingly disentangle the city's history and the deeds of his symbolic father, the very cultural history and tradition of imagery would preclude him from fully succeeding.

Volgograd's rhetorical spaces are paradoxical in many ways. Perhaps the most difficult paradox is that the unique national narrative of courage and resilience is bonded to a territory that remains a blood-drenched and bone-filled ground to an extent that exceeds human imagination because of the symbolic meaning its name had, not only for Stalin himself, but for many on the battlefield.

Endnotes

1 Code 1995.
2 Bishop and Clancey 2003, 66.
3 Dobrenko 1993, 262–273.
4 Konradova and Ryleeva 2005, 139.
5 Gillis 1994, 3.
6 Bodnar 1994, 75.
7 Prelli 2006, 11.
8 http://hitch-hiker.livejournal.com/30809.html.

References

Bishop, Ryan and Clancey, Gregory (2003), The City as Target of Perpetuation and Death. In Bishop, Ryan, Phillips, John and Yeo, Wei Wei (eds.), *Postcolonial Urbanism: Southeast Asian Cities and Global Processes*. New York, Routledge, 63–86.

Bodnar, John (1994), Public Memory in an American City: Commemoration in Cleveland. In Gillis, John R. (ed.), *Commemorations: The Politics of National Identity*. Princeton, Princeton University Press, 74–89.

Code, Lorraine (1995), *Rhetorical Spaces: Essays on Gendered Locations*. New York, Routledge.

Dobrenko, Evgenii (1993), *Metafora vlasti*. Munich, Verlag Otto Sagner.

Gillis, John R. (1994), Introduction: Memory and Identity: The History of a Relationship. In Gillis, John R. (ed.), *Commemorations: The Politics of National Identity*. Princeton: Princeton University Press, 3–24.

Hitch-Hiker, Artyom (2005), Po Dorogam RF. Volgograd. Chast 2. 30 Oct. 2005. Message posted to: http://hitch-hiker.livejournal.com/30809.html (Last accessed Oct. 27, 2007).

Khudozhestvennaia panorama "Razgrom nemetsko-fashistkikh voisk pod Stalingradom". Retrieved 27 Oct. 2007 from http://panorama.volgadmin.ru/panorama.html.

Konradova, Natalya and Ryleeva, Anna (2005), Geroi i Zhertvy. Memorialy Velikoi Otechestvennoi. In *Neprikosnovennyi Zapas*, Issue 2–3, 134–149.

Prelli, Lawrence J. (2006), Rhetorics of Display: An Introduction. In Prelli, Lawrence J. (ed.), *Rhetorics of Display*. Columbia, SC, University of South Carolina Press, 1–40.

Katrin Paehler

The Wrong *Grad*, the Wrong Victims: (West) German Historiography on the Siege of Leningrad

The German blockade of Leningrad, which lasted nine hundred days and led to death of about one million Soviet citizens, most of them civilians, is undoubtedly the most glaring blind spot in the German discourse on World War II, despite recent attempts to shine a light on it.[1] For a country that takes pride in and is frequently praised for its attempts to address its Nazi past – however dubious some of the efforts may have been – this negligence raises interesting questions, namely, why this has been the case for so long, and why and how this situation is changing.

Two self-images have defined postwar West German society.[2] First, Germans like to see themselves as victims, initially as victims of Nazism, now as victims of World War II in general.[3] Second, Germans like to think of the *Wehrmacht* as a "clean" military that existed and operated in isolation from the political system it served, uncompromised by ideological warfare. Ordinary soldiers were regarded as pawns of the political and, to some extent, the military leadership, making them victims as well. While as the symbol of civilian suffering is Dresden, the soldiers' symbol is Stalingrad. This comforting notion of a shared German victimhood, encompassing the home and the front alike, was and still is at the core of West Germany's historical consensus, dissenting voices notwithstanding.[4]

Consequently, the German blockade of Leningrad was not a topic that suggested itself for in-depth historical investigation, as it would have called into question West Germany's (and then unified Germany's) consensus. In the outskirts of Leningrad, German soldiers could not be considered victims. Moreover, the blockade of Leningrad was not the doing of the SS – the proverbial "other" on which the military apologists relied after the war. The image of the German soldier as a victim could not therefore be served by studying Leningrad.

There was, however, no way to skirt the discussion of Leningrad completely. How to make sense of the blockade? For many years, three approaches to the topic, sometimes intertwined, dominated West German historiography. Treatment one: Ignore the blockade of Leningrad as much as possible or treat it as a sideshow to a war that largely happened elsewhere. Treatment two: Assign responsibility as far away from the German military as possible. And treatment three: Argue that any war in any form is terrible and that blockades, while particularly unfortunate, constitute an accepted form of warfare. Far removed from the actualities of the war, these approaches fulfilled their purpose – preventing German soldiers from being cast as perpetrators.

Very few German memoirs focus on the siege of Leningrad or the northern front, but the existing pieces have a lot in common: authors, publishing houses, and overall narratives. Frequently, these memoirs are billed as military histories written by "witnesses."[5] The books' additional purpose is to commemorate the German soldiers who fought there; in effect, authors erect memorials for themselves.[6] Treating the blockade of Leningrad as a side story, the books focus either on the Volkhov front or on the later retreat of the army group while stressing the "honor and value" of the German military. Much is made of the presence of non-German soldiers among Nazi Germany's troops, and this emphasis is clearly intended to suggest the overall righteousness of the cause and its pan-European appeal, thus making it less "Nazi."[7]

The focus on the Volkhov front draws the readers' attention to the particulars of the warfare there. Soon defined by static trenches, this front resembled the Great War rather than the lightening war of the new Germany. Comparatively poorly equipped, the soldiers regarded themselves as fighting both "our fathers' war" and "the poor men's war." The environment, consistently described as jungle-like and forbidding, becomes a significant element of the narrative, leaving the reader to contemplate the savages whom the underequipped German soldiers must have encountered in this jungle. German soldiers were apparently on a civilizing mission.

The blockade of Leningrad is uniformly blamed on Adolf Hitler, who, ignoring military-strategic knowledge and necessities, defied military reason.[8] This then turns the German military there into an underdog, encountering massive Russian formations and the fanatic resistance of Leningrad's civilian population. Consequently, even the encirclement of the city becomes praiseworthy, as it was established and maintained under difficult circumstances.[9]

The blockade as such leads these authors to energetic attempts to square the circle. Leningrad becomes a fortress, fiercely defended by its fanatical civilians.[10] One author likens the situation in Leningrad to Berlin in 1948.[11] An outrageous case of comparing apples and oranges, its gist is clear: All blockades are equal. Consequently, there is no need to dwell on the details of this particular blockade. The authors' tone is emphatically dispassionate:

> During the first weeks and months of the encirclement, the civilian population suffered substantial deprivations. Food and water became scarce, additionally, there were constant air raids and artillery attacks. Due to the forceful shortening of the food rations the first starvation deaths happened in November, a month later 59,000 starved were counted and beginning in January, one calculated that 3500 people died daily of exhaustion, starvation, and hypothermia.[12]

Cause and effect are gone in this description, as are those responsible. Similarly, starvation deaths are not attributed to the blockade, but to the decisions within the city. The situation inside the city had nothing to do with what the German military was doing outside it.

Conversely, the authors focus on improvements inside the blockaded city while neglecting German efforts to destroy them, as in the case of the "road of life," which crossed the frozen Lake Lagoda.[13] Overall, the implication is that while undoubtedly bad, the situation in the city improved tremendously over time; civilians were evacuated while soldiers were brought into the city. This, in turn, ties into the image of Leningrad as a "fortress." Stressing that "[...] it needed the full ruthlessness of a dictatorial system to supersede the living and dying of hundred-thousands of citizens, women, and children," one author effectively blames Stalin for the deaths.[14] This conjecture fits into his later assertion that this was a war against Bolshevism and not against the Russian people.[15]

These accounts create a narrative that all but ignores the blockade or downplays it beyond recognition. Instead, the authors attempt to celebrate German soldiers while trying to find them a place in the postwar German narrative consensus. This is a difficult task, as these soldiers' experience does not fit in with the normative image. Thus, a different, somewhat fractured image of victim, defender, and civilizer is created. Not the most compelling picture, it still worked: While not pure victims, the soldiers were not perpetrators either. Leningrad was not their responsibility.

A very similar view is perpetuated in the *Landser Hefte* – dime, literally "grunt," novels that were, and still are, in fairly wide circulation. They present the war as an adventure and the soldiers as heroes and victims. Unsurprisingly, few of the *Landser Hefte* are set around Leningrad. Scholars have shown that the issues that were set in the area give no place to city as such at all; locations are interchangeable.[16] In addition, it is worth noting that only a few titles even mention Leningrad, even when the story is set in the general area.[17] The jungle imagery and its implications discussed above are by far more prominent – for example, in an issue entitled *In den Urwaldsümpfen vor Leningrad* [In the Jungle-Swamps before Leningrad]. Even if locations appear interchangeable, the notion of master race engaged in a civilizing mission is palpable.

Scholarly writing on World War II in the postwar period presents a different problem. The 1950s and 1960s were defined by a high-brow version of these popular accounts. Ferociously defending the image of a clean and apolitical German military, former military leaders set the tone: Victories were theirs, but defeats were Hitler's, making them and their men innocent victims of Hitler's decisions. Not surprisingly, decisions regarding Leningrad were attributed to Hitler and differences of opinion between Hitler and his military leadership were emphasized.[18] By the 1970s, however, a new generation of historians came into their own in Germany; they focused their investigations on complicity between Nazi Germany's political and military leaderships. The military was no longer regarded as an apolitical institution without ideological designs.[19] Still, Leningrad remained on the margins of public perception. The flagship of this approach was the multivolume *Das Deutsche Reich und der Zweite*

Weltkrieg.[20] The fourth volume, published in 1983, dealt with the German attack on the Soviet Union. Out of several hundred pages, some thirty focus on Leningrad. The discussion is divided into two sections: "The Attack on Leningrad" and "The Soviet Perspective."

"The Attack" is best described as straight military history, focused on overall decisions and paying scant attention to ordinary soldiers. It traces the advance of German army and eventual "wide" encirclement of the city. It then details the military planners' decision-making process. This account strongly suggests that the military leadership in the Northern Sector was more concerned with the developing siege than the military leadership in closer proximity to Hitler. It describes a sometimes vaguely contentious back and forth about various and similarly horrendous options, which ultimately excluded the notion of occupying the city, as this would have entailed feeding its population. Apparently, those involved were taking their clues from Hitler's Order no. 35 of 6 September 1941, which stated that a surrender of the city was not to be accepted.

Despite Hitler's order – and similar orders originating with the German High Command (OKW) – military planners in the Northern Sector kept deliberating on what to do if the city were to surrender. Concerned that German soldiers would find themselves firing on starving women and children, military commanders in the field remained vaguely unsettled; helpfully, the army leadership suggested the use of landmines. Commander-in-Chief of Army Group North, Wilhelm Ritter von Leeb, advocated suspending the "encirclement," if the city should surrender. The outcome would be the same, but more palatable to the Leeb and the army: "A majority of the people would die, but at least not before our eyes."[21] In the end, the discussions never came to a real conclusion. More pressing decisions had to be taken elsewhere, and the blockade became the status quo. This is very much a military history of old – unconcerned with the effects of war on civilians. Yet it clearly establishes that the relationship between Hitler and his generals was largely collaborative, despite occasional differences in opinion. And clearly, all options considered for Leningrad were gruesome.

"The Soviet Perspective" is initially persuasive with its reliance on Soviet scholarship, but turns disconcerting in its judgment. A military history as well, the section focuses on the mood, preparations, and mobilization within the tightly encircled city under constant artillery attacks. Only determined discipline and threats, the author stresses, made ordinary Leningraders stay under these circumstances.[22] This sound overview ends with a dubious and misplaced moral judgment:

> However tragic these developments were, moral condemnations of the German troops lack every basis, as even nowadays [note the passive-aggressive use of the German "*immer noch*," translated as even nowadays] the siege of and artillery attack on a defended city and fortress belongs among the common and non-debated methods of warfare.[23]

Subsequently, the author compares Nazi German and Soviet warfare, drawing attention to Soviet "sieges" of Breslau, Königsberg, and Berlin. This comparison goes to the heart of the matter: Was there anything unusual about the blockade of Leningrad? The answer is yes and the examples given support this contention. [24] A blockade is meant to lead to the occupation of a city, not to the death of its inhabitants. The blockade of Leningrad thus was very much outside of ordinary warfare.

While this study did not construct a clean German military, the war's realities were not its focus either. Neither the situation of the civilians inside the city nor the role of the German soldiers surrounding it becomes clear. Indeed, despite the role of some of its leadership, the German military still maintains a modicum of innocence, mainly because its soldiers remain invisible in these accounts.

Far-reaching plans for the occupation, ethnic cleansing, and overall resettlement of Eastern Europe under German occupation have moved to the forefront of the scholarly inquiry in Germany during the last decade.[25] Initially focused on the Holocaust, this new line of inquiry also drew attention to the involvement of military and civilian agencies in these plans. The most recent investigations evaluate the blockade of Leningrad in this context. Thus, Jörg Ganzenmüller describes the blockade in different terms: not as a military operation gone awry, but as a calculated attempt by Nazi Germany's elites to kill millions.

Cutting through the multitude of ad-hoc military considerations, Ganzenmüller shows that the blockade of Leningrad was decided before any strategic decisions were possible. In late July 1941, Leeb noted that the city was to be enclosed but not be taken.[26] In fact, Hitler had already made a comment to the same effect three weeks earlier: "Moscow and Leningrad are to be razed to ensure that there won't remain people we will have to feed in the winter."[27] Ganzenmüller convincingly shows that OKW clearly understood this directive. Consequently, later notations and military option papers, formerly regarded as reactions to the strategic situation, take on a different meaning. The decision to lay siege on Leningrad was not taken out of military necessities, however ill-conceived, but was a premeditated crime. "The destruction of Leningrad and the annihilation of its people came to be a priority, even before any military goals."[28] The military leaders, for their part, redefined this decision as borne out of military necessity, even if this was clearly not the case. This was, as Goebbels put it in his diaries, to be a "city drama... unprecedented in history"... and it was planned as such.[29]

Nazi Germany had clear plans for the occupied Soviet Union, during the war and thereafter. The territory was to feed the occupying army and Germany proper. The plan was as simple as it was murderous. It divided the Soviet Union into two economic zones, "surplus" and "substitute." Those living in the latter, which consisted of the "forest zones, including the Western industrial centers of Moscow and Petersburg," were seen as "useless eaters."[30] Consequently, "umpteen million people will starve to death," as a May 1941 memo phrased it.[31]

Indeed, German economic planners expected to starve approximately thirty million people; Leningrad would have brought them 10 percent closer to their goal.[32] As Ganzenmüller convincingly suggests, German postwar plans for the territories already factored this in. In the Leningrad area, two hundred thousand Germans were to be settled – the exact number of people estimated to live in the city after the successful war.[33] In other words, there would be no Russian city, there would be no Leningrad. The blockade of Leningrad was a premeditated, ideologically-based war crime planned by German elites.

The extent and ultimate intent of the starvation plans has become the new investigative focus. In his study of the 18th Army as an occupational force around Leningrad, Johannes Hürter takes a more cautious approach, arguing that it did not arrive as "an ideologized murder machine."[34] Rather, Hürter suggests that the decision to starve the city came as a surprise, ruining the 18th Army's plans for occupation. While Hürter is highly dubious of an overarching hunger plan for the entire eastern front, he regards the decision to starve Leningrad to death to be the catalyst for the particularly ruthless occupation policies of the 18th Army.[35] Devastatingly, he surmises the mindset: "Why should one bother with several hundred-thousand people in a poor area if superior authorities let a city of millions starve?"[36] In other words, while the command of the 18th Army or ordinary soldiers might not have been happy with the decision regarding Leningrad, they quickly and efficiently adapted.

Scholarship has made a strong case that the blockade was an ideologized, premeditated war crime. However, older interpretations still dominate the public discourse and memory, creating a schizophrenic dichotomy between the scholarly and the public that is unlikely to be bridged completely anytime soon. But some progress can be found if one looks hard enough. Guido Knoop, author of many well-received public television documentaries on German history, is often ridiculed as the sanitizing TV history teacher of the German nation. However, his programs are actually a good litmus test as to what it acceptable. In 1991, he authored a multipart documentary that dealt with the German invasion of the Soviet Union.[37] One part addressed Leningrad, and its storyline went roughly like this: The inhumane siege was largely Hitler's responsibility, but the military leadership also had some role in it. Military necessities drove many of the decisions, but the decisions were inhumane. At the same time, the program detailed the situation of the Leningraders during the blockade, inviting German viewers to empathize with them. German soldiers, on the other hand, were barely discussed. In short, there is now a victim without a perpetrator, but at least we got one thing right. And there is always hope.

Endnotes

1 Ganzenmüller 2005a; on the historiography, see Ganzenmüller 2005b, 135–47; Jahn 2004, 12ff; Hürter 2001, 377–440; Ganzenmüller 2000, 179–194; Rambow 1995.

2 For a few thoughts on East Germany, see Ganzenmüller 2005a, 367–68 and Ganzenmüller 2005b, 144–46.

3 Most recently: Niven (ed.) 2006.

4 A good example on dissenting voices and their reception is the 1995 *Wehrmachtsausstellung*. There is a vast literature; see, for example, Heer et al. (eds.) 2003.
5 Pohlmann 1962; Haupt 1976; Haupt 1980. Unfortunately, I was unable to review Walter Charles de Beaulieu 1961. A number of German publications dealing with the Leningrad front have been published since 2000, but their titles and descriptions available online do not indicate a significant departure from the above; Stachow 2001; Schatt 2003; Sasse 2005; Bónya 2006.
6 Haupt 1980, 7; Pohlmann 1962, 8.
7 Haupt 1976 (this book's pages are unnumbered). Pohlman 1962, 8.
8 Haupt 1980, 5.
9 Haupt 1980, 6–7; Pohlmann 1962, 44ff.
10 Haupt 1976; Haupt 1980, 6–7; Pohlmann 1962, 24–25. In effect, these German apologists use the image constructed by Soviet wartime and postwar propaganda for different purposes. See also: Ganzenmüller 2005b, 141.
11 Haupt 1980, 7.
12 Haupt 1976.
13 Haupt 1980, 112.
14 Pohlmann 1962, 43.
15 Pohlmann 1962, 128.
16 Ganzemüller 2005a, 365.
17 *Brennpunkt Schlüsselburg, Zwischen Wolchow and Nowgorod, Im karlischen Urwald, Winterschlacht vor Leningrad, Fernziel Leningrad, Schlacht am Ladogasee, Wolchow Kämpfer, Urwaldkrieg am Ilmensee, Wolchow Front, Stukas über Leningrad, Sturm auf Leningrad, In den Urwaldsümpfen for Leningrad, Zwischen Wolchow und Leningrad.* These titles are taken from www.landser.de.
18 Ganzenmüller 2005b, 138–41.
19 For an impressive historiographical overview: Schulte 1989.
20 Militärgeschichtliches Forschungsamt [MgFA] 1983.
21 MgFA 1983, 553–54.
22 MgFA 1983, 739–40.
23 MgFA 1983, 740.
24 Ganzenmüller 2000, 186.
25 For example, Gerlach 2000.
26 Ganzenmüller 2000, 180. Also, at length, Ganzenmüller 2005a and Jahn 2004.
27 Ganzenmüller 2000, 181.
28 Ganzenmüller 2000, 184.
29 Ganzenmüller 2000, 186.
30 Ganzenmüller 2000, 190.
31 Ganzenmüller 2000, 189.
32 Ganzenmüller 2000, 192.
33 Ganzenmüller 2000, 194. Ganzenmüller cautions his readers that these general plans might not have come to fruition, but stresses the clear intent.
34 Hürter 2001, 379–440.
35 Hürter 2001, 439–40.
36 Hürter 2001, 438.
37 Knoop 1991/1997.

References

Bónya, André (2006), *Ziel Leningrad. Die 4. Polizei-Division 1941 am Feind.* Pour le Mérite.

de Beaulieu, Walter Charles (1961), *Der Vorstoss der Panzergruppe 4 auf Leningrad, 1941.* Vowinckel.

Ganzenmüller, Jörg (2005a), *Das belagerte Leningrad. Die Stadt in den Strategien von Angreifern und Verteidigern.* Paderborn, Schoenigh.

Ganzenmüller, Jörg (2005b), Nebenkriegsschauplatz der Erinnerung: Die Blockade Leningrads im Gedächtnis der Deutschen. *Osteuropa*, Vol. 55 Issue 4–6, 135–47.

Ganzenmüller, Jörg (2000), … die Stadt dem Erdboden gleichmachen. Zielsetzung und Motive der deutschen Blockade Leningrads. In Creuzberger, Stefan et al. (eds.), *St. Petersburg-Leningrad-St. Petersburg. Eine Stadt im Spiegel der Zeit.* Stuttgart, DVA, 179–194.

Gerlach, Christian (2000), *Kalkulierte Morde. Die deutsche Wirtschafts- und Vernichtungspolitk in Weissrussland 1941 bis 1944.* Hamburg, Hamburger Edition.

Haupt, Werner (1980), *Leningrad. Die 900-Tage Schlacht.* Friedberg, Podzun-Pallas.

Haupt, Werner (1976), *Leningrad. Wolchow. Kurland. Bildbericht des Heeresgruppe Nord, 1941–1945.* Friedberg, Podzun-Pallas.

Heer, Hannes et al. (2003) (eds.), *Wie Geschichte gemacht wird. Zur Konstruktion von Erinnerungen an Wehrmacht und den Zweiten Weltkrieg.* Vienna, Czernin Verlag.

Hürter, Johannes (2001), Die Wehrmacht vor Leningrad. Krieg und Besatzungspolitk der 18. Armee im Herbst und Winter 1941/1942. *Vierteljahreshefte für Zeitgeschichte*, Vol. 49 Issue 3, 377–440.

Jahn, Peter (2004), *Blockade Leningrads 1941–1944. Dossiers.* Berlin, Links Verlag.

Knoop, Guido (1991/1997), *Der Verdammte Krieg. "Unternehmen Barbarossa."* Gütersloh, Bertelsmann.

Militärgeschichtliches Forschungsamt (1983) (ed.), *Das Deutsche Reich und der Zweite Weltkrieg. Der Angriff auf die SU*, Vol. 4. Stuttgart, DVA.

Niven, Bill (2006) (ed.), *Germans As Victims: Remembering the Past in Contemporary Germany*. New York, Palgrave Macmillan.

Pohlmann, Hartwig (1962), *Wolchow. 900 Tage Kampf um Leningrad, 1941–1945*. Bad Nauheim, Podzun Pallas.

Rambow, Aileen (1995), *Überleben mit Worten. Literatur und Ideologie während der Blockade von Leningrad 1941–1944*. Berlin, Berlin Verlag, A. Spitz.

Sasse, Hans Heinrich (2005), *Zwei Spätsommer von Leningrad*. Books on Demand GmbH.

Schatt, Otto (2003), *Leningrad und das Baltikum. Der Weg eines deutschen Soldaten im Nordabschnitt der Ostfront 1942–1950*. Schatt, Eigenverlag.

Schulte, Theo (1989), *The German Army and the Nazi Policies in Occupied Russia*. New York, Berg Publishers.

Stachow, Hasso G. (2001), *Tragödie an der Newa. Der Kampf um Leningrad, 1941–1945. Ein Augenzeugenbericht*. München: Herbig Verlag.

Yulia Gradskova

Femininity, Beauty and Maternity in the Shadow of War (1940–1950s)

Und ich lebe noch, ich lebe
Und so war das eben
– is nicht traurig, is ja Wahrheit –
Und ich leb mein Leben.[1]
Wolf Biermann "Ich leb mein Leben, sagt Eva-Marie"

This article is dealing with women's memories of everyday life during the Second World War and in the early post-war years, particularly to the memories of women who spent these years outside of the actual fighting. Looking at war experiences from the perspective of the everyday life of women on the periphery appears to be somewhat problematic. Does their experience of living through the war in outer Russian areas – with an almost "normal life" compared to those who were fighting at the front, living in territories that became battlegrounds or were occupied – really deserve to be included at all in a publication dedicated to remembering the war? Does our interest in the everyday life of women in the outer regions undermine respect for other Soviet people's suffering and heroism?

In the Soviet master-narrative,[2] the war is usually presented as a period when Soviet people heroically defended their peaceful country and showed unanimity against an insidious enemy, a period with chronology centred on battles and military events.[3] Thus, the everyday life of everybody, even those on the periphery, is supposed to be centred on heroic work, news from the front and waiting for those taking part in the fighting to come home victorious. However, we know rather little about what was happening on an everyday level and how it is remembered from the perspective of those who lived in the territories far away to the East from the front line. We know considerably little about women's everyday lives.[4]

Furthermore, in Soviet and Russian historical tradition, the War is clearly limited by victory day – 9th May, 1945. However, according to gender historians, Claire Duchen and Irene Bandhauer-Schöffman, who wrote about post-war Europe from a gender perspective, "[t]he chronology of the end of the war is untidy: we cannot say that it 'ended' on a particular date, nor that peace meant the same thing for the populations of different countries." They claim that, "the lines between war and peace [...] were blurred and the disruptions of war persisted long after peace treaties had been signed".[5] Thus it would also be interesting to take the possibility of this assumption into account in the Soviet context, that is, why the period indicated in the title of this article is extended to after the end of the war.

The aim of this article is to explore how two aspects of everyday life – maternity and beauty – were remembered by women who were young in the forties and fifties. It is based on interviews made for a larger project – a study of femininity performance through maternity and beauty practices from the thirties to the sixties.[6] My informants were born between 1919 and 1947 and were interviewed in Moscow, Saratov and Ufa. As the period covered by the larger project shows, war experiences were not the main interest of the initial project and, thus, the topic of "war" slipped into my research due to stories of my informants who connected many of their life experiences and particular choices with the "war." At the same time, while analysing women's stories it is important to take into account the "situatedness" of memory: in this article, "war" is presented as experienced by people who were living in different geographical locations, were socialized in families with different ethnic and religious backgrounds as well as experienced by people who had different social and professional status at that time.

Collected material shows that in contrast to Western Europe where World War II could be seen as an important step in "the disruption of traditional gender roles,"[7] in Soviet Russia, where this disruption started much earlier but was limited by Soviet ideology, a certain continuity with pre-war interpretations of femininity are also worth noting. These interpretations, however, were contradictory. Together with acceptance of work outside the home as the norm, a woman had to become a mother and to take care of her appearance in order to be a "normal" woman. In the situation of shortages of goods, migrations, extra work and difficulties in having or maintaining stable life for a couple, this was extremely difficult.

Relating War Experience

For many of my informants, the effects of the war are intertwined with other important factors that defined their everyday life at that time – authoritarian rule, communist ideology, post NEP economy of shortages,[8] enforced collectivization. However, it often seems that "war" was a title for encompassing and naming all the problems that turned the period of the forties and early fifties into "hard times." Taking into account my informants' expectations about my and their common knowledge of the master-narrative, the reference to "hard times" could be made even through such a rhetorical question as: "What kind of time was it?"[9]

Some of my informants not only used a "hard time" rhetoric, but took a somewhat critical position toward the State's actions during the war. Thus, B, for example mentioned forced subscription for a "state loan"[10] in the *kolkhoz* in Tatarstan where she worked as a teacher, H, who at the time of the war worked as tractor driver in a Bashkir *kolkhoz*, remembered that "we did not eat enough, but were sending 10 kg of dried bread to the front".[11] On the other hand, Q from Ufa mentioned "their" (her and people around her) "absolute trust" in Stalin at that time.

Most of the informants experienced migrations during the studied period. These included evacuation from big cities in the West to the Eastern cities and villages – the direction from the "war" master-narrative – as well as migrations from villages to the country-side more typical for the pre-war and post-war periods. D and her family's migration from Tula to a small city in the Samara region and back, and C and her family's evacuation from Moscow to Kirov in 1941 and their return in 1943 belong to the first type. J's move from a village in the Saratov region to Saratov to study in 1941 and K's move from a village to Saratov in order to help her sister to nurse a baby and find a work as a nanny in 1944 could be seen as the second. One of the interviewed women, N, experienced job-related migration – as a construction worker in Moscow she was dispatched as a food provision worker and travelled through several regions before she had her first child in Omsk in 1942.

Maternity and the War

How much were reproductive practices and attitudes toward the pregnant body, delivery and childcare influenced by the war? To what extent could women who lived in the "rear" mother as they did in peacetime? In order to analyze women's memories, it is necessary first to review changes and continuities in the legal and discursive context of maternity.

After the abortion was outlawed in 1936, all Soviet women were expected to give birth to as many children as possible. On the other hand, women were expected to work outside the home while labour discipline was strengthened in 1938 and criminal persecution of work absentees came into the fore in 1940. State paid maternity leave started to be shortened before the war (from 112 days in 1936 to 63 in 1938) and it was not until 1944 that the Soviet state made new efforts to help mothers: maternity leave was increased to about 2 weeks compared with 1938 while the supplementary food ration for pregnant and nursing women was doubled. Later, in 1947, over-time work for these same categories of women was prohibited. At the same time, according to the 1944 law, children born outside of registered marriages lost the right to the name of their father and to financial support from their biological father. The mothers could only count on a small state allowance.[12] In spite of serious limitations of maternity benefits, the discourse on "care for mothers and children" that was very strong before the war continued to exist during the whole war period: "The Soviet government always shows paternal care for children".[13]

Only a few of my informants gave birth to their children during the war, but "war" was usually somehow present in the stories about becoming a mother that were referred to at least 10 years after the war was over. The most visible context of maternity for this period was family instability and excessive work by the mother soon after giving birth. Thus, B gave birth to her second child in a village in Tatarstan in December 1941 and soon after that her husband, who was the village school director, was called to the front. B replaced him at his workplace (she was 22 years old at that time) and since then for many years did not take any vacations. Her husband survived the war, but never returned to her or helped to bring up their children.

N who was a 17 year old construction worker in Moscow when the war started, was sent to build defence fortifications near Moscow where she met a paramilitary food provisionary. He suggested they should "make a deal"[14] and he would care for her; soon he made her into his (non-official) "spouse" and work colleague. She was given the status of dispatch worker (*komandirovanaia*) and in this capacity made the travels shown above. After giving birth at the age of 18, N brought her daughter from the hospital to a provisional apartment in Omsk and several months after the child was born, N's "husband" was sent to the front and she never saw him again (about one year later he was killed in combat). Due to the lack of official registration of the marriage N never could receive any state money for the child as a widow of a war soldier.

J who gave birth to twins in Saratov in 1946 first presented her partner as her "husband" and only later said that they were not married officially. J's "husband" left her very soon after J's difficult birth[15] because he found his pre-war family that he thought had perished during the evacuation. Due to a lack of breast milk for both children, J, who started working as an accountant in a housing system 70 days after giving birth (her salary was very low), had to buy a bottle of milk for each baby every day on the black market where it was extremely expensive. As a result of complications of a cold (and, probably, low nutrition) one of her twins died at the age of 11 months.

Finally, D who gave birth to her child in 1954 as a single mother while working as a communication officer in a classified state agency in Moscow presented her surroundings in the post war context as understanding: "My mother also told me: you have reached the age – I was 26 at that time – to have a child. Who can say what your life is going to be!? And the military men whom I worked with [...] told me not to worry [about not being married]."

Another important context of maternity was connected with the fact that childcare was no longer a priority for the state during war time[16] and state nurseries (or milk kitchens) are hardly mentioned by any of my informants. In this situation, the availability of older female relatives together with breast feeding was crucial for a child's survival and wellbeing. Thus, J managed with her twins with the help of her mother who came from the village and moved in with her. It was also J's mother who got blamed when one of the twins died (J: "She did not watch out and the child got a severe cold.").

The case of N is even more remarkable. Around 1944 she left her child at her first "husband's" parents' house in the village (she had never seen them before and her "husband" was killed in combat) and went to Moscow to look for a job. N started working there, then got married to a severely ill war returnee, found a living space for her and her new husband and, finally, brought her child to live with her around 1950.

B, a school director from a village in Tatarstan was less "lucky" with older female relatives' help with childcare and had to lock her small children in at home, leave them with neighbours or bring them along to school.

When battlefields attracted the most attention, medical care for pregnant and delivering women in big cities deteriorated,[17] as interview material shows. The same had happened with information for future mothers.[18] J from Saratov, for example, said that during her first pregnancy in 1946, doctors in the maternity clinic had only observed and measured her, while in the beginning of the 1960s, when her younger child was born, there was much more education about childcare. C who had her first child in Moscow in 1946 also related that she came back home from the maternity ward and "did not know what to do with the baby." At the same time, the general instability of life together with lighter state control over citizens contributed to a flexibility of control over the transference of reproductive knowledge. D, for example, told that in the time of evacuation to the Samara region she and her mother lived in the house of a medical nurse and D had access to medical books where she found information about pregnancy. These factors also influenced control over children's upbringing. According to J from Saratov, she did not seem to have encountered any problems baptizing her children born in 1946. However, when she had her youngest child in 1963 and wanted to baptize her, the family ran into problems.

Nevertheless, interview material shows that together with a lack of information about contraception, pregnancy and childcare, as well as underdevelopment of the childcare facilities, pregnancy and childbirth continued to be seen as a sphere of medical dominance and control. One of the most negative memories about childbirth in the collected interviews refers to the war period and belongs to N who started crying while telling this story:[19] "There was no window, no light, so as not to get bombed. She [a nurse] told me: lie down and exert yourself. [...]. They put me down. They pulled me, fastened my arms and legs, I got so scared! Finally, I gave birth."

Thus, it is possible to conclude that women were encouraged and expected to have at least as many children during the war and post war years as before. These demands and encouragements were shared with the state by parents, friends and women themselves. This positive attitude toward maternity was performed in a situation characterized by a lack of knowledge about contraception and prohibition of abortion. Due to the fact that marriage was difficult to achieve in such a situation of general instability, love relationships like in the case of N or J indicated that children had to come soon. Based on interviews, it is possible to suppose that during the war and post-war years the state's biggest efforts were concentrated on medicalization of childbirth, while it withdrew from other forms of help, first of all from organization of childcare. In the situation of family instability and lack of food and goods, maternity was practised as a difficult "female" occupation, additional to the main one – work for victory and for the state.

War and Beauty Practices

Beauty practices during the war and post-war years were remembered by my informants first of all through the "lack" or "shortages". K (born in 1932) even got angry by my question saying that it was "nothing [no clothes, shoes or decorative artefacts] during that [war] time" and it was impossible to speak about beauty. She recalled that during her adolescent years in a village in the Saratov region, she had no shoes and had to wear her hair short due to the spread of lice. Once K received a pretty dress sent to her by her relatives from the city, but she was still sad because she had to wear it while barefoot. H, who lived in a Bashkir village in the Samara region and got married in 1946 said that, although the marriage ceremony was otherwise completely in accordance with Bashkir and Muslim tradition, she did not even have a headscarf because of the lack of clothing. She had to make baby clothes by cutting the hems off her long dresses for her first children born in 1949 and 1950. A (born in 1932) who lived in South Bashkortostan did not have any shoes to go to school.[20]

During the war and soon after, beauty products were frequently used as important exchange articles: B changed her fur coat for a bucket of potatoes in order to feed herself and her two children and several of my Bashkir informants exchanged most of their traditional decorations for food. On the other hand, valuable decorative artefacts were sometimes given to the state during its collections of "help" for the front from the population. Thus, H's mother gave her grandmother's jewellery to someone from the city who was collecting money for building tanks: "My son is fighting, let her buy a tank." H bitterly concluded that her brother perished in the war.

At the same time, stories about beauty practices during the war period demonstrate not only the difficulties of "becoming beautiful," but also some new aspects that indicate rather flexibility taking place in beauty normativity and growing cultural exchange.

The first is connected to a further and, probably, more rapid destruction of religious or ethnic normativity in villages, including Bashkir and Tatar, where traditional dress began to change before the war with the advancement of *kolkhoz* life and shortages of goods. The city life ideal promoted just in the 1930s,[21] continued to be attractive through the 1940s. Those who were evacuated from Western Russia played an important role in look innovation. Thus, A, for example, told about a teacher evacuated from Leningrad who was teaching them embroidery. She also told about American clothes sent as humanitarian aid to a village boarding school and showed a picture where boarding school boys were pictured in check shirts and girls in red bonnets.

The war and post-war years were a period when "city dress" – a blouse and skirt – became a dream for many Bashkir adolescents, particularly for those from distant villages. H, for example, said that when she went to Samara with her grandmother soon after the war she immediately bought a skirt and blouse, "so much I dreamed (to have them)". For those Bashkir and Tatar young people who moved to the cities in these years, city dress became the only possibility. G (born in 1935 in a railway station in Bashkortostan), for example, who as a good pupil and daughter of a deceased Red Army soldier was invited to continue her secondary studies in one of the best Bashkortostan boarding schools in Ufa, remembered as a good sign how similar the girls in her school looked: "We tried to be outstanding in our studies [not in clothes]." C (born in 1922) who was a student in Moscow in 1943–1946 also saw similarity positively: "We did not look at each other so much". However, as being a part of changes brought about by "Soviet power" the modernization and universality of look were evaluated by my informants rather differently. Thus, G was stressing "not noticing nationality" and O (born in Bashkortostan in 1935) modernization of look. At the same time some other informants carefully indicated their view of a change of dress as a kind of cultural pressure from the side of the Russian speaking centre.[22]

A second aspect is connected with looted (*trofeinye*) goods – clothes, shoes, fashion magazines, films – "brought" from the front. D who was a student in Moscow said that her father brought her a suitcase full of clothes from the front, but she had problems in caring for some of them:

> Something good came from the Germans. All this booty! My father brought them, but we did not even know how to deal with all of it. The students who were at the front, they knew. [...] This synthetic item had to be washed in a special way and we were washing it with soap. I had such a nice dress; I washed it and it lost its colours.

D also noted positively that all the girls in her university who came from territories that were occupied during the war, copied German hairstyles. The tone of her comment indicated that "German" hairstyles were seen as fashionable and desirable. Another informant, A, said that looted clothes could still be bought on Ufa's black market during the years of her university studies in the early 1950s. U, born in 1945 in an industrial city in the Urals, in spite of the fact that her adolescent years corresponded to a time much later than the post-war period, still found it necessary to mention while talking about fashion models, that German booty fashion magazines were still in circulation.

Thus, it is possible to say that women on the outskirts experienced the war and post-war period as destructive to their femininity: while everyday normality demanded from them that they looked nice and cared for their appearance, the war scarcities made them refuse some beauty objects and deprived them of many beauty practices. Yet, at the same time through evacuation, aid and looted goods, new styles of clothes and new beauty ideals appeared to be important.

On the basis of the studied material, it is possible to conclude that war played an important role in the everyday life of all the interviewed women, independent of their age or where they lived. In particular, war made the performance of femininity more difficult with respect to practices of maternity and beauty. However, interview material shows that the everyday life of women in the war and first post-war years was much more complex and frequently guided by a more contradictory set of norms than could be assumed on the basis of the Soviet master-narrative on life centred around "work for victory".

Endnotes

1 "And I am still living, still living, and so it was – it is not sad, it is just the truth – and I continue living my life".
2 According to Ferretti 2005, a dominant opinion about the past.
3 Scheide 2004.
4 Nikonova 2005.
5 Duchen and Bandhauer-Schöffman 2000.
6 For the whole project I collected 21 interviews (all the interviews were tape-recorded and transcribed), to 12 of them I directly refer in this article. My informants were mostly (but not exclusively) Russian and Bashkir women. I selected mostly interviews of my older informants spending war years in the rear area. See Gradskova 2007.
7 Duchen and Bandhauer-Schöffman 2000, 3.
8 Osokina 1997, 199.
9 Archive documents also show that "hardships because of the war" was a common rhetoric used for applications for improvement of mothers' situation even in the 1950s. For example, one woman applying for improvement of alimony regulation in her letter to the Soviet of Ministers in 1955 wrote "The Great Patriotic war has destroyed hundred thousands of family hearths, made many children to be orphans and took away many human lives" – GARF, f. 7523, r.45, f. 217, p. 75.

10 Soviet government was attempting to get additional money for defense of the state through "loans" (*zaimy*) from population. In most of the cases these loans were mandatory.
11 In one case J, an informant from Saratov, also got to discuss her attitude toward "Germans". She said that when German captives were for three days placed at their home, "[w]e did not despise them. Maybe somebody did, but we did not. Some Germans were fascists, but some were just forced. Germans as well as 'ours' have not been in command of themselves".
12 See Engel 2004, 209–230; Gradskova 2007, 279–281.
13 *Rabotnitsa* 1943.
14 He meant the beginning of sexual relationships.
15 It is possible, that J was left by her husband even before she gave birth, it is unclear from the interview.
16 Waiting lists for childcare facilities in Moscow in 1949 were long in spite of the high rate of children's contagious diseases (that sometimes lead to death) contacted in nurseries - GARF, f. 482, r. 49, f. 610, pp. 32–33, 234.
17 My informants from Bashkortostan also described destruction of the traditional system of transference of knowledge about pregnancy and childbirth (through sisters-in-law) in the situation when most of the young men had to postpone their marriages.
18 Information about contraception had actually not been available in the 1930s either.
19 N's experiences of giving birth could be compared with the story of a war medical doctor who remembered her war time delivery as an experience that was more frightening than the front. See Engel and Posadskaya-Vanderbeck 1998, 175–219.
20 Although women from different geographic regions presented "war" through a "lack" of beauty, collected memories, however, leave the impression that "lack" was particularly perceptible in Bashkortostan, probably due to the fact that it was a war period when the traditional way of life got to be dramatically destroyed.
21 See, for example, modern style fashion in Tatar magazine *Azat Khatyn* from 1936 that follows mainly "universal" style. See *Azat Khatyn* 1936, fashion page.
22 Gradskova 2008.

References

Azat Khatyn (1936), Kazan, N 24.

Duchen, Clair and Bandhauer-Schöffman, Irene (2000) (eds.), *When the War was Over. Women, War and Peace in Europe, 1940–1956*. London, Leicester University Press.

Engel, Barbara Alpern (2004), *Women in Russia, 1700–2000*. Cambridge, Cambridge University Press.

Engel, Barbara Alpern and Posadskaya-Vanderbeck, Anastasia (1998), *A Revolution of their own: Voices of Women in Soviet History*. Boulder, Westview Press.

Ferretti, Maria (2005), Neprimirimaia pamiat': Rossiia i voina. Zametki na poliakh spora na zhguchuiu temu. *Neprikosnovennyi zapas*, N 40–41, http://magazines.russ.ru/nz/2005/2/fere8.html (25.9.2008).

Gradskova, Yulia (2007), *Soviet People with Female Bodies. Performing Beauty and Maternity in Soviet Russia in the mid1930–1960s*. Stockholm, Edita.

Gradskova, Yulia (2008), From "Backwardness" to "Modern Culture"? "Beauty" and "Femininity" during the Soviet Cultural Modernization from the 1930s to the 1960s. In Olofsson, Kerstin (ed.), *From Orientalism to Postcoloniality*.Huddinge: Södertörns Högskola, 42–56. http://www.diva-portal.org/sh/abstract.xsql?dbid=1565 (25.9.2008).

Nikonova, Olga (2005), Zhenshchiny, voina i figury umolchania. *Neprikosnovennyi zapas*, N 40–41, http://magazines.russ.ru/nz/2005/2/ni32.html (25.9.2008).

Osokina Elena (1997), *Za fasadom 'stalinskogo izobiliia'. Raspredelenie i rynok v snabzhenii naseleniia v gody industrializatsii, 1927–1941*. Moskva, ROSSPEN.

Rabotnitsa (1943), N 6–7, 10.

Scheide, Carmen (2004), Kollektivnye i individualnye modeli pamiati o "Velikoi Otechestvennoi voine" (1941-1945). *Ab imperio*, N 3, http://abimperio.net/scgi-bin/aishow.pl?state=showa&idart=1054&idlang=2&Code= (25.9.2008).

State Archive of the Russian Federation (GARF), f. 7523, r.45, f. 217 – Komissia zakonodatelnykh predlozhenii Soveta Natsionalnostei. F. 482, r. 49, f. 610 – Ministerstvo zdravookhraneniia RSFSR.

Elisabeth Cheauré

Forced Interculturality during the Time of War. Russians and Germans in Texts from the German Diary Archive, Emmendingen

In the general process of analysis and coming to terms with the trauma of the Second World War, the focus of interest seems to have shifted recently to micro-history. This is the case both of academic research and of artistic activity. This interest in the fate of the individual in extreme situations, in his or her strategies for overcoming trauma and putting this experience into words, is illustrated for example, in Catherine Merridale's impressive book[1] which focuses specifically on the individual soldier. A further example comes from the world of the theatre: in 2007 in Wroclaw (in Poland) the theatre group *Współczeny* caused a sensation with the play *Transfer*, which is essentially a collage of the recollections of ethnic German and Polish people expelled immediately after the Second World War. What is sensational is that these people are on stage themselves and are confronted with the figures of Stalin, Churchill and Roosevelt (played by professional actors). The amateur actors, who play themselves, so to speak, are all over 70, and they read texts from their own letters from the front, for example, or describe the rape they experienced. The Polish people recount their partisan activities or scenes in which Jews were shot, Russian soldiers committed acts of brutality and other similar dreadful episodes.[2]

There can be no doubt that these texts have given rise to genuine interest and emotion among the public, and to increasing academic and artistic treatment. Clearly, what fascinates, moves and affects us at the same time is the fate of the individual. These fates make it possible – if it is at all possible – to grasp the trauma of war, expulsion and flight. There are manifold questions which can be asked of the various types of texts from the genre of autobiographic writing (letters, diaries, memoirs), and only a few aspects can be touched on in a short article. Thus, one of the central questions will be whether the text of a single person can be of relevance or significance in the larger scheme of things, i.e. whether a single voice can speak meaningfully for collective experience.

A further important question, as I see it, is an ethical one. Do we, the post-war generation, who are fortunate to have been spared such traumatic experiences, have the moral right to approach these very personal documents with an analytical, even critical, eye, and to measure and judge them according to quasi-objective criteria? I have asked myself this question a number of times while working on the texts I have selected, and I have not yet really found an answer. Before I explore the first problem, i.e. the theoretical and methodological considerations, I would like to present the material that my argument is based on.

I work with texts that are unpublished. They are texts whose source needs to be explained. They are from the so-called *Tagebucharchiv*, or German Diary Archive, in Emmendingen, an archive founded in 1998 in the small town of Emmendingen in the southwest of Germany near Freiburg. In it the diaries, memoirs, letters of ordinary people are systematically collected, archived and where possible reviewed according to content. It is the only place in the German-speaking world where the private accounts of people's lives are preserved in an appropriate manner. The model for this undertaking is in Italy, which set up a diary archive quite some while ago. The Emmendingen Archive is somewhat unique: the sort of texts that were normally collected and preserved systematically, were written by state officials or prominent figures. But the Emmendingen archive collects the personal texts of contemporary witnesses, written at least initially without any intention of having them published.[3]

But it is precisely the direct, personal expressiveness of the texts which sheds light on the history of everyday life and the history of mentality. Such texts make everyday life in specific spaces and specific times come alive. These texts can be seen as a type of 'history from below'. They form a medium which allows the reconstruction of the experiences, the thoughts and the feelings of individual people, especially in relation to collective memory (in the sense that Maurice Halbwachs uses the term) and thus to the discourses of their time. In the diary archive there are several thousand texts from roughly two centuries, and among them a number of diaries and memoirs about the Second World War. The question of the significance that can be assigned to autobiographical texts such as letters, diaries and memoirs can perhaps be best approached through the model of Aleida and Jan Assmann. As is well known, they distinguished between communicative and cultural memory, a distinction which is not meant to suggest a bi-polar model but a continuum.[4]

Modern wartime autobiographies, as we know, began as a mass phenomenon in the First World War. The individual texts are particularly interesting with regard to their autobiographical claim to the truth. Cultural memory, on the other hand, as manifested for example in academic, historiographic representations or in the state's cultivation of memory, passes on a universal interpretation of the war experience that goes beyond the individual and contributes in part to the mythification of this experience. It is also clear that there are a number of interesting formal features or characteristics of autobiographic writing. These typically take the form of everyday, informal communication and they are in contrast to the formal constraints and aesthetic conventions of cultural memory with its special forms of ritual representations and clear patterns of the narrative genre. However, there can be no doubt that these individual memory texts are influenced by the discourses of cultural memory, by stereotypes and by clichés. In the specific case of the autobiographical war memories, they are influenced by the politically stirred up propaganda discourses about the 'enemy', in this case 'the Russian', in the collective sense. In ideologically-blinkered Nazi Germany, the other, the stranger or foreigner, and alterity served to provide an argumentative base for the construction of a German identity as Übermensch, the superior race. In order to marginalise, stigmatise and ultimately wipe out the 'other', old and new myths from cultural memory were summoned up and used to legitimise war, murder and the destruction of entire peoples.

After reading a good many autobiographical everyday texts in the Emmendingen Diary Archive, I found one question increasingly pressing, namely the interdependence between cultural memory and real, individual experience. I have thus looked at these texts in the light of the following questions:

- Do these texts reflect the collectively anchored image of the enemy 'Russian', as transported through discourse of the time, and if so, in what way?
- How did the collective image of the 'Russian' influence the individual's experience in real encounters?
- Were these images confirmed or corrected through the encounters with Russians?
- And, how finally, were the encounters, which were frequently traumatic, treated in narrative form?

I want to apply these questions to three currently unpublished texts. Two texts are from women, a young girl and a young woman, and the third from a German soldier. More precisely we are dealing with the following texts:

1. The first text (No 717): Here we have the letters, postcards, and notes of a soldier by the name of Gottfried G, who was born in 1910 and thus in the Campaign in Russia from the age of 29 to 32. Gottfried G's letters were collected retrospectively together with a few pages of autobiographical text by his son as *Mein Kriegstagebuch* (My War Diary). Gottfried G himself has been missing in action since 1942 and probably fell during the Battle of Stalingrad. In the case of his text, which I think is most revealing for our subject, the ethical questions I mentioned at the start of my talk are particularly relevant.
2. Erna L, (No 562) in a record written long after the war (1970), described her flight from Silesia as the Red Army moved forward over a period lasting from January 1945 to January 1946. The writer was between 20 and 30 years old at the time. It is a text that still has a traumatic effect on readers today, for the suffering described is truly unbearable.
3. Christa R (No 735/I, 1–2) was born in 1929, and was thus 16 years old at the end of the war. In her diary she describes above all the mood of the civilian population before and during the invasion of the Red Army in Berlin in 1945. Christa R later became a secretary and also recorded the fall of the Berlin Wall in 1989–90. In the case of her text the question of genre or text type is raised, for there are a

number of indicators suggesting that the original diary entries were revised to produce this manuscript.

What is striking about the first text, the memoirs of Gottfried G is that the author, who was in fact a trained teacher, had a keen, even ethnographic interest in the areas and culture that he 'marched into' as a soldier. This makes his text a particularly rewarding source of descriptions of the German-occupied Russian territories (for example, he lists the prices of everyday goods), and also of how the 'foreign', the 'other', 'alterity' was perceived. The text shows all too clearly how the stereotypical ideas about Eastern Europe, the Slavic peoples in general, and the Ukrainians and Russians in particular, influenced this individual's perception. "'The Russian' loves music. It is usually the women who play the guitar and sing to it. Every family gives full reign to expressing its artistic talents – paper ornaments, painted flowers [...]."[5]

Furthermore, those images of Slavs (and in particular the Russians) as politically underdeveloped and without any culture anchored in the cultural memory, are reactivated through the massive political propaganda and employed to justify personal behaviour and military actions. "The people here are hardworking, clean, good-natured, [and] politically so apathetic that they would never think of independence. Germany is just the right thing for them. They are lazy and like a quiet life."[6]

The allusions in a paradigmatic text to 'the Slavs' are more than apparent, and are repeatedly activated as the subtext of other passages. These are the stereotypes that the German philosopher and Romantic writer, Johann Gottfried Herder, developed first of all in his famous 'Chapter on the Slavs' in his work *Ideen zur Philosophie der Geschichte der Menschheit* (On the Philosophy of the History of Mankind; 1784–1791). Doubtless under the influence of western European historiography, Gottfried G maintained the master discourse that Slavs had the passive mentality of slaves, a mentality which allowed the individual soldiers of the German Army to feel as if they were even saviours or a type of aid worker in an underdeveloped country. Gottfried G's text also shows an interesting tendency which needs to be checked against other comparable texts: in the period of the successful advance of the German Army on Russian territory, the ethnographically exact descriptions of everyday life in Soviet Russia and the lives of the civilian population with a tendency to being objective. There is even a sign of some understanding for the special circumstances of Russian life. At times Gottfried G even reflects on his experience of foreignness, usually when he encounters women. For example, after a detailed description of a house with all its dirt and its utterly 'bovine' female inhabitants who run a very rudimentary household, he adds a reflective dimension:

> There they sat on the couch, chatting and gossiping. Could it be that they are more content than our women? What a lot of fussing and polishing and washing goes on in our households![7]
>
> It is easy to look down on the strangeness here: the women and girls dress like grandmothers. One has to imagine some of them in western European clothes to do justice to their beauty. Their historical circumstances demand a certain sort of clothing. They wear headscarves for reasons of hygiene, if you have ever seen the amount of dust that a single wagon stirs up. There are no roads. [...] People go barefoot here because of the dreadful roads, and because they are poor.[8]

Paradoxically, however, the dreadful roads are made out as the reason why the Russians are able to put up such fierce resistance to the invaders: "Everything goes more slowly on Russia's roads; I am convinced that the collapse of this paradise of misery, simplicity and indifference would otherwise have happened long ago."[9]

The ironic air of superiority ('this paradise of misery', 'this splendid country') is evident not just in single turns of phrase, but is also quite explicit in Gottfried G's description of the country and its inhabitants, for example in his description of the cultivation of the land. Here his superior stance becomes an agenda: "What a lot can be made of this fertile area once the German with his talent for organisation arrives. The tomatoes rot on the vine here because people don't bother to tie the plants to stakes."[10]

This superior attitude becomes even more unbearable when coupled with the blatant looting and theft practised by soldiers of the German *Wehrmacht*. It is striking that these actions were apparently regarded as so normal that only the outcome counted: the loot (for example, a pair of glasses, a watch) that could be sent home to the family. The actual looting raids are either omitted or described euphemistically and thus can only be reconstructed from the subtext. Here are a few examples:

> Sent off another package on 27th August. I recommend boiling the handkerchiefs before use. I had them washed, but the lazy people here only use cold water and not even much, at that. [...]
>
> I haven't found a shop here which had anything to sell. You have to 'pinch' even the matches off the people. [...]
>
> We get our own supplies, so to speak. In the villages that is quite easy. We have polished off quite a few chickens. [...]
>
> The only necessary physical activity is in the form of raiding chicken coops. Pigs and rabbits are also 'bought' this way.[11]

The narration of experiences alters when those of war are clearly harder to endure and the narrator's situation becomes especially intolerable, whether through military disasters, fleas, lice or lack of food. Accounts of impressions of everyday life in Russia and the habits of the rural population become increasingly aggressive in this context. It is no longer possible to detect even a trace of 'objective interest'.

> It has got me now, too. That's right: in Russia you get to know the country and the lice. The people don't wash themselves either. They must be immune from these parasites.[12]
>
> This time I got stuck with horrible quarters. The stable door is also the front door of the house. Then there's the kitchen. I don't know what stinks most – the two cows or the scabby children. Finally, there's the living-room with the bed. We two radio operators sleep in the bed, while the lady of the house, so charming, and her husband, a giant of a man with the typical broad Slav face, make a bed for themselves on the dirt floor with a fur coat, which no doubt is full of lice. You can hardly move in the room because grain is stored in every corner. The Russian people are too lazy to build barns. If they had just one trunk to put things in it would produce a little order. It is awful that we have to have dealings with this riff-raff. If you attack filth you get yourself dirty, as the saying goes. When are we going to be freed of all this filth?[13]

This appears to be only one of the narrative strategies for coping. There are other passages which construct 'the Russian' by making him the foreigner who cannot be overcome by the 'normal' means of war. He becomes the ultimate foreigner or other, and thus leads to a type of 'blind spot' in the perception of the observer/narrator. The following laconic text is typical of this process: "One can only weaken the Russian, but never destroy him. He leaves behind very little, he takes everything with him."[14]

I find the text of the soldier Gottfried G so interesting because it allows one to see so clearly the superior stance, anchored in western European cultural memory, towards the Slavs. This superior attitude is without question intensified and consolidated through Nazi propaganda, as one can see in the following description of a Jewish family.

> [I am living] in a 'proper' house (with a tin roof, wooden floor, petroleum lamp, clean room with a table, chairs and a bed) [...] This dwelling, which is for once not as awful as the other hovels, belongs to a family of Jews. So they have managed to get on in the world here as well. I got them to wash my clothes, and they begged for a piece of 'Breut'. Unlike the rest of the Ukrainians they can even speak German, the rogues.[15]

The text of Gottfried G is recounted entirely from the perspective of a *Wehrmacht* soldier who sees himself as a member of the *Herrenmenschen*, the master race, and thus attributes the passive role of the victims to the Russian population. The texts by the two women completely reverse these roles. Here it is the German civilian population which is now helpless in the face of the soldiers of the Red Army.

The two texts from Erna L and Christa R, both civilians, are particularly informative with regard to the well-known brutal actions of the Red Army soldiers towards German women in particular.

In Erna L's text, an account of her flight from Silesia, there is a great deal about the murdering, alcohol orgies, and above all the mass rape carried out by Russian soldiers. Her narrative strategies show a number of similarities to the text of Christa R, which is an account of the entry of the Red Army into Berlin. For example, the brutal acts of rape are described by Erna L either in a matter-of fact manner at times ('Frau Lüttmann was raped by two Russians on the short trip to the cellar.'), or euphemistically, ('Frau Lüttmann had to endure a great deal of humiliation.') or even in almost poetic formulations ('We will now bear our shame together.').[16] Detailed descriptions are often directly juxtaposed with the open confession that she was unable to find words for what happened:

> Just before dawn a great tall man turned up, said he was a Jew, dragged off my wedding ring. I resist him with all my strength. With his gun against my back he pushes me along in front of him. I resist with all my strength. He goes into a different cellar. The Jew locks me in with two big dirty Russians. I cannot write down what follows. Then the Jew comes himself as well. I leave the cellar, broken from so much brutality and fall into Frau Lüttmann's arms, weeping. She pushes me into the coal cellar where the daughters are.[17]

Whereas the first encounters with the Russians and the trauma of multiple rape is described in detail, the following records, which apparently were the result of revised diary entries, become briefer and more laconic. It is precisely through the brief narrative sequences that the incredible serial character of the brutal acts becomes credible and tangible. Here are a few examples to illustrate the point:

> The afternoon is dreadful. The house has become a brothel. They have their will of us with their guns at our breasts. In the room next door lies my dead husband. [...][18]
>
> The girls were taken away again. It is dreadful. [...] The hunting of women continues. The nights are terrible. [...][19]
>
> The Russians are given schnapps. Awful things happened in the village again. We are spared. [...] We endure yet another dreadful night.[20]

This general manner of recounting serial rape is only departed from once, to describe the rape of an eleven-year-old girl. Erna L's memoirs can be read as a confirmation of the Nazis' propaganda to scare the population about the Russians. Russians appear in her text as raw soldiers with no culture and no inhibitions and to whom all sense of morality and civilisation is foreign.

The last author I want to present wrote a text called *Eine Jugend in Kriegs- und Nachkriegszeit* (My Youth During the War and After), in which she described her experiences in the war and post war events from 1939 to the end of 1944. She extended these memoirs with diary entries for the year 1945. This diary is particularly interesting, even though, as I mentioned, one has to assume that it was revised at a later date. Fear of the Soviet Army soldiers was stoked by Nazi propaganda – this is obvious from the entries – but at the same time the diarist was sceptical, for mistrust of propaganda was widespread in March 1945: "Goebbels and the newspapers say that the Russians will murder and rape. But the enemy radio says the opposite. You don't know what to believe."[21]

But the real encounter with Russian soldiers proved the propagandist right: the Russian soldiers behaved as brutally as the German population had been warned they would. The author, barely sixteen at the time, leaves the traumatic experience of the actual rape as a blank in the text. The following are some extracts from the text:

> 27th of April. Two terrible days are over [...]. The day before yesterday it finally happened. Artillery fire, strafers, bombs, this time all of it in Russian, on Dahlem and Zehlendorf. We stayed in the cellar the whole time and didn't dare to go outside. Shortly before noon I saw three soldiers in strange uniforms through the window. The first Russians! [...] A little later there was banging on the house door. Two Russians! One of them was quite good-looking and was very friendly. They asked about German soldiers and weapons. Then they searched everything and pointed at Mummy and seemed to be saying 'Mother and daughter'. They took my binoculars, looked through them and handed them back. Could it be that the Russians are reasonable people, after all? [...] Right afterwards the next ones came. One of them with a wounded eye and a Mongolian appearance dragged me out of the room. Mummy pleaded with him but was thrust back. I thought my heart would stop beating as the ghastly man first went into the cellar with me and then upstairs into a room. I wanted to resist but he immediately started to wave his pistol around. Down in the cellar the Russians had also caused havoc. Fraulein S was threatened by a soldier saying 'Uri, Uri', watch, watch, so she dug my watch out of the wastepaper bin and gave it to him, but she was raped anyway. When the Russians left, Mummy and I had

> to think quickly whether I should play 'sick old woman' or 'retarded child'. Taking the child's role was easier for me, at only 15. So I plaited my hair and removed my artificial front tooth. When the next Russians came I lay on a mattress and whimpered like an idiot at them through the gap in my teeth. Mummy, who was doing an 'old lady' act, kept on saying 'djetzko chorro'. That was supposed to mean 'child sick' in Polish. At any rate the Russians always left us after that; one of them even gave me a piece of bread. But Frau H and Fräulein S had to have a second turn.[22]

It is striking that, by means of the narrative structure of omission and euphemism ('have a second turn'), the author of the text conveys the incredible brutality of the Russian soldiers most compellingly. Amazingly enough, there are also a number of passages in which 'the Russian' is associated with precisely those traditional clichés which appear to be anchored in the cultural memory: that is, strong emotionality, a certain kind of childishness and crudeness.

> The soldier ordered us to sit down and he introduced himself as "Me First Lieutenant, Commissioner, 23 years". We had to admire a photo of a pretty young girl he claimed was his wife. Then suddenly he sat down at the piano and began to sing, while we had to clap and dance. He laughed and found it a huge joke to watch us all hopping around, frightened.[23]
>
> They are as delighted as children if someone speaks their language![24]

Summary

The texts from the *Tagebucharchiv*, or German Diary Archive, in Emmendingen are without any doubt authentic, individual descriptions of the conflicts between Germans and Russians in the Second World War. The narrative treatment of the traumatic experiences can be regarded as a form of coping or overcoming strategy. However, the really traumatic events are frequently marked by omissions or can be read in the subtext. The texts also show that clichés and stereotypes about the other, the enemy, 'the Russian' that were anchored in the collective memory have a strong influence on individual memory and thus on the individual autobiographical texts.

Endnotes

1 Merridale 2005. See also (about World War I) Richter 2005; Scherstjanoj 2005.
2 Gnauck 2006.
3 URL: http://www.tagebucharchiv.de (28.12.2007).
4 Assmann 2007; Assmann 2000.
5 Emmendingener Tagebucharchiv. Fond N° 717. p. 89. All quotations from archive texts have been translated by the author.
6 Ibid., 74.
7 Ibid., 124.
8 Ibid., 74–75.
9 Ibid., 78.
10 Ibid., 80.
11 Ibid., 92; 101.
12 Ibid., 91.
13 Ibid., 99.
14 Ibid., 83.
15 Ibid., 76.
16 Emmendingener Tagebucharchiv. Fond N° 562. p. 5.
17 Ibid., 5.
18 Ibid., 7.
19 Ibid., 8.
20 Ibid., 11.
21 Emmendingener Tagebucharchiv. Fond Nr. 735/I, 1–2. p. 7.
22 Ibid., 10.
23 Ibid., 12.
24 Ibid., 11.

References

Assmann, Aleida (2007), *Geschichte im Gedächtnis. Von der individuellen Erfahrung zur öffentlichen Inszenierung*. München, Beck.

Assmann, Jan (2000), *Das kulturelle Gedächtnis. Schrift, Erinnerung und politische Identität in frühen Hochkulturen*. 3rd edition. München, Beck.

Gnauck, Gerhard (2006), Vertriebene erzählen Führerwitze. In *Die Welt* (Hamburg), 21.11.2006.

Merridale, Catherine (2005), *Ivan's War: The Red Army 1939–1945*. London, Faber and Faber.

Richter, Sonja (2005), Der Krieg als Fremderfahrung. Das Rußlandbild in den Feldpostbriefen des Soldaten Friedrich Grelle (1914/15). In Eimermacher, Karl and Volpert, Astrid (eds.), *Verführungen der Gewalt. Russen und Deutsche im Ersten und Zweiten Weltkrieg*. München, Wilhelm Fink, 1003–1029.

Scherstjanoj, Elke (2005), "Vot ona, prokljataja Germanija" – Da ist es, das verfluchte Deutschland. Rotarmistenbriefe vom Frühjahr 1945. In Eimermacher, Karl and Volpert, Astrid (eds.), *Verführungen der Gewalt. Russen und Deutsche im Ersten und Zweiten Weltkrieg*. München, Wilhelm Fink, 1031–1957.

Kirsi Kurkijärvi

Dialogues with War in *Remembrance Day* by Natal'ia Baranskaia

In this article, I explore the role of dialogue in Natal'ia Baranskaia's (1908–2004) novel *Remembrance Day* (*Den' pominoveniia*, 1989) and its connections with the representations of women's memories of the war and trauma. Natal'ia Baranskaia started her career as a writer only after retiring in her sixties. Her most well known publication *Week Like Any Other* (*Nedelia kak nedelia*, 1969) broke new ground in the frankness with which it handled Soviet women's lives. *Remembrance Day* approaches the conditions on the home front during the Great Patriotic War similarly from a woman's point of view,[1] and portrays the lives of seven women before, during and after the war. The frame story that serves as the beginning and end of the novel, depicts the protagonists on the 25th Remembrance Day travelling from Moscow to the south of Russia to visit the graves of their husbands and sons who have died in the Second World War. The year is 1979.[2] Few of the protagonists have met each other during the war. The novel brought new, fresh material into literature, which had before existed mostly only through oral history. Even as a fictional work, the novel was even at the time of its publication, considered sociological evidence of women's lives during the war. To this day *Remembrance Day* maintains its position as one of the most comprehensive fictional works about women's life during the Second World War in the Soviet Union. Baranskaia viewed *Remembrance Day* as the acme of her creativity, but the majority of critics and readers speak of her as the author of *Week Like Any Other.*[3]

In this article, lack of dialogue, in another words silence, is mostly seen as a manifestation of trauma, and dialogue and memorizing as means of working through a trauma. However, it should also be asked whether silence is a survival strategy in the early phase of a trauma. I will deal with trauma in psychoanalytical terms as a belated, repetitive experience.[4] The repetition of the trauma indicates the way the past experience returns persistently, causing emotional stress that one did not necessarily experience at the moment of the event, i.e. belated. Dominick LaCapra aptly condenses the dynamics of memory and working through of a traumatic experience in his book *Writing History, Writing Trauma*:

> Through memory work, especially the socially engaged memory work involved in working through, one is able to distinguish between past and present and to recognize something as having happened to one (or one's people) back then which is related to, but not identical with, here and now.[5]

LaCapra distinguishes "working through" from "acting out" in which the past is relived as if it were fully present rather than presented in memory. In this sense, working through is taking distance from the experience and seeing the future self as not haunted by the traumatic experience.[6] In other words, in the process of working through, the traumatic experience becomes part of the self. Consequently the manifestations of dialogue and recalling in *Remembrance Day* can be seen to represent the working through of the trauma(s) of war. In *Remembrance Day*, dialogue has two dimensions. First there is the dialogue between the seven female protagonists of the novel, and secondly the dialogue that forms between the representations of each protagonist before, during and after the war. This is what I call "the dialogue of the self." It answers questions of how one was living and what kind of a person one was before the war, how the war affected the protagonists' life stories and what kind of a role the wartime experiences have in their present day lives when the war is far away in the past and the women of the novel are elderly. The trauma of war is also hidden in the three representations of the self that are all penetrated by the war experience and that represent how one's life became broken in the war.[7] The representations of the self before the war have a naïve and idyllic stamp on them, whereas wartime is characterized by the fight for survival, and the time after the war by loss.

Dialogue is understood through Bakhtinian conceptualization of dialogue where also the self forms and renews itself through constant dialogue:

> The dialogic nature of consciousness, the dialogic nature of human life itself. The single adequate form for verbally expressing authentic human life is the open-ended dialogue. Life by its very nature is dialogic. To live means to participate in dialogue: to ask questions, to heed, to respond, to agree, and so forth. In this dialogue a person participates wholly and throughout his whole life: with his eyes, lips, hands, soul, spirit, with his whole body and deeds.[8]

The dialogue between the seven female characters of the novel is confirming their right to the memories they have of the war. They have all been positioned at "the less important" home front that brings up important and difficult topics such as rape, relations between Russian women and German soldiers and the failures of the Red Army in the beginning of the war and how they affected the civilian population. These are not the stories that would have been included in the official narratives of the war and for that reason the women of the novel share them only among those who have had a similar experience. In actual fact, both women's memories from the home front and the front lines were excluded from the discourses of war that were dominated by male heroism and the victory.[9] After the war women's experiences in the army and at home did not fit in with the positive reinterpretation of the events. A female soldier was often a powerful symbol of many things (failure, shame, challenging patriarchy etc.) and at the end of the war, they were sent home where even their presence in the army was denied. Many returned home trying to keep their history in the army in secret. The "home front" was not always sympathetic to their stories either. It was believed that all the women who had been to front had been prostitutes and were not considered suitable to become wives or mothers.[10] The joy of victory was not shared with women *frontoviki*.

At the same time the Soviet Union offers a unique example of women's mobilization to the armed forces, most of the Soviet women were still positioned at the home front during the war. The history of Soviet women's war efforts at the home front is no less impressive than the one at the front. The German Army proceeded rapidly towards Moscow after war had been declared and some 80 million people were left in the occupied territories where women had to face threats of violence, rape, and deportation and forced labour. Approximately 100 000 women joined the partisan movement or were involved in other underground activities. No less than 25 million people were evacuated beyond the Urals. At the home front women and girls were mobilized to different fields of industry and to agriculture. The heavy work was combined with harsh wartime labour regime that was controlled by the NKVD: not attending work could lead a civilian to a military tribunal. Soviet women at the home front had to survive on extreme food rations: by the end of the war the living standards had fallen to the level of the 1920s.[11]

In *Remembrance Day* the dialogue of the self represents how the women are looking for their memories in the collective memory of the war and are reluctant to tell the story that does not follow the official storylines. In the process of the stereotypization of memory[12] few narratives depicting the experience, here of war, came to represent many.[13] At the same time, however, generational change, time (distance to the events and the experience, and also as a result of working through) or, for example, change of power, can alter the content of the "acceptable" memory. All these elements can interrupt the stereotypization giving room to new kinds of memories of the war. As Jan Assman notes: "No memory can preserve the past. What remains only is that "which society in each era can reconstruct within its contemporary frame of reference".[14] It should also be noted that "[...] war is a gendering activity, one that ritually marks the gender of all members of a society whether or not they are combatants"[15] and this gendered "ritual mark" is connected to the stereotypization of memory. The stereotypical narratives of the Second World War were, and still are produced and renewed also through literature. The male dominated canon of war literature focuses on the depiction of the front line and places in the centre of the narrative a male protagonist, most often a soldier. Boris Vasil'ev (1924) depicts Soviet female combatants in his novel *And the Night Was Calm* (*A zori zdes' tikhie...* 1969). But where are the women of the home front and how did they experience the war? To these questions Natal'ia Baranskaia wants to give an answer in her novel *Remembrance Day.* Baranskaia notes in an interview that she wanted to write particularly about women at the home front, and she adds: "If I can express one tenth of my feelings about the war and my experiences during the war in my novel, then I will have succeeded, then people must understand what our war was, and they will understand how it lives in our emotions."[16]

Silence and Speaking Out

In Soviet society, literature played a significant role not only in supporting and propagating the official party line, but also in paying attention and introducing the most sensitive questions to the public. Literature was often the first forum to bring forward topics that had previously been censored most severely. *Remembrance Day* was published in 1989 when *perestroika* and *glasnost'* had already been in force for several years and actually were at the very end of their road. During *perestroika*, literature played a particularly important role in the cultural and social discussions about the past. Literature was exceptionally closely linked to the cultural and political debates of the time and it had a relatively large impact on preparing people for the new politics in comparison, for example, to political science or historiography.[17] *Perestroika* also affected the politics of memory and it was one, if not the most important force, to interrupt the stereotypization of the memory of the Second World War and to allow the publication of such works as *Remembrance Day.*

For the protagonists of the novel the purpose of the trip to the graves and to the memorial service is to work through the trauma and the war experiences. The narrator implies in the frame story that the atmosphere concerning attitudes towards talking about the experiences in war has changed. On the 25th Remembrance Day something has changed from the past years. Until this, people have mourned in secret, the narrator relates: "Until this moment of collective memory and common sorrow, every one bore their trauma in solitude and cried alone in the night."[18] Historically, however, at the time of the events of the frame story, women's "collective memory, [...] common sorrow" represented in *Remembrance Day* could not be published or discussed publicly. In the Soviet case, the grand narrative of the victory and its centrality in the recalling of the war was in contradiction with any negative or bitter memories of the war. The characters in *Remembrance Day* are unwilling to talk about their experiences in war and, therefore, the act of recalling takes place in the unconscious of the sleeping protagonists. The reluctance to talk and recall are reiterated throughout the novel by many of the characters marking the traumatic nature of the war memories:[19]

> Aksinia did not like to recall the war.[20]
>
> The first years after the war Lora did not like to remember.[21]
>
> And how I got the announcement of Vanechka's death – I don't want to recall it now.[22]

The paradox of trauma as a recognized absence is presented here in the expressions of dislike and unwillingness to recall the events. We can also look into the absence of dialogue, recalling and eventually the lack of the symbolic (words[23]) through the concept of latency that follows the trauma. The recognized absences (reluctance to talk and recall) in *Remembrance Day* can be seen to indicate to the period of latency, which takes place both on the individual and collective level.[24] On the other hand, however, the novel underlines the moments of silence, both repressive and positive, emphasizing the ambiguous nature of silence that can be seen as a repressive block that prevents the trauma being treated, or as an important phase of the working through process and surviving. The protagonists of *Remembrance Day* already know each other's memory of the war and because of that, words are not always needed. The women share the memory of the war that is represented as a positive force for the characters in the novel. The knowledge of what life was like at the home front during the war is what unites them, and it is also the reason why they are now travelling together on the train. While they are sitting in the compartment together, one of the female protagonists Nonna Romanova bursts into tears and tells them about the feeling of guilt she has experienced after remarrying. The narrator states that the women are understanding and do not judge her, but suddenly Nonna realizes from the silence that nothing should be said now: "[...] a sudden silence descended, and she felt that now you should not say anything."[25] The narrator depicts also Maria Nikolaeva's reluctance to talk on the train, and appeals to the protagonists' unarticulated unanimity on the issue: "Maria Nikolaeva, of course, was not against guests. Only now she did not want fall into enquiries and conversations to which people on the road are very often prone. But no one was looking for a conversation."[26] The journey to the graves has just started and an open dialogue between the protagonists cannot yet take place.

Dialogues between the Self and War

Representations of the self are also part of an endless process of dialogues: "He (a person) invests his entire self in discourse, and this discourse enters into the dialogic fabric of human life, into the world symposium".[27] Consequently, the representations of the self of the characters in *Remembrance Day* form a dialogic level. A journalist travelling on the same train with the women asks them to say a few words about themselves and begins the dialogue of the self: "Please, tell me a few words about yourselves [...]".[28] This is an invitation for the protagonists to describe who they are now 34 years after the war from which arise further questions of where they come from and why they are now together on the train. When the train departs the women fall asleep and the narrative turns into a description of their lives before, during and after the war. It is these three representations of the self that form the dialogue of the self. The narrator of the novel speaks on behalf of all the protagonists, but gives way to their voices as well. Even though the narrator of the novel clearly identifies with the characters of the novel, her point of view to memorizing and speaking differs from the others. The narrator's point of view reflects that of a war writer in relation to recalling and talking about the experiences of war. She stresses the importance of memorizing and talking from the very beginning, while the protagonists of the novel comment several times that they wish they did not have to say or remember anything. In *Remembrance Day*, the narrator takes on the responsibility to speak out and work through, as does the writer of the novel, Natal'ia Baranskaia.

Memory connects the characters of the novel to the experience of war and forms a conversation between the representations of self before and during the war and at the time of narration of the frame story on the 25th Remembrance Day. The narrative structure of the novel looks into the experience of war from the individual's angle from the "present" towards the "past". This sets the perspective and tone of the novel, which directs its gaze into war from the retrospective view through recalling. The pre-war era plays a major role in the women's stories. We look at the events that take place before the war from hind side with the knowledge of the coming war, and peace as well, that are already introduced in the frame story. Maria Nikolaeva's story begins with a depiction of a perfect summer day just before the beginning of the war. It is the crystallization of the life and of oneself prior to the war:

> Masha sits on a summer cottage chair made out of straw, on the edge of an open field under the only leafy tree there, a young linden, which cast a faint, lace-edged shadow. Next to her, in a carriage sleeps her ten-month-old son, Mitjusha, who's been rocked to sleep. [...] Silence. Not a single sound. [...] And Masha is nodding in some sort of a limp bliss, a deep peace in which one's body and soul rests.[29]

A man brings the message of the war to the scene of sweet motherhood and naïve unawareness. Maria's husband, Nikolai, rushes in announcing the beginning of the war: "Masha, war has broken out, Germany has attacked us."[30] Nikolai leaves for the front and Masha stays alone with the children, following the most common representation of women in war where they stay at home waiting for the soldiers to return from the front, perhaps most obviously manifested in Konstantin Simonov's popular wartime poem *Wait for Me* (*Zhdi menia*).[31] But *Remembrance Day* stays with Masha and she tells a story, not of waiting, but of moving, dislocation and transformation. A fur coat that Masha has got from her husband in the time of peace becomes a borderline between the life before and after the war: "A fur coat, a fine squirrel fur coat. Now it was just a piece of cloth. You could wear it in the day and cover yourself with it in the night. On the road you could place it under your head."[32] War changes the meaning and purpose of things for Masha. Luxury material, symbolizing femininity, is transformed into a multifunctional everyday item and a tool for survival for evacuation.

Another protagonist in the novel, Aksinia, points out the difficulty to memorize not only the wartime, but also the times before the war underlining the changes in her perception of life and the self in the context the war: "It is difficult to recall the war. And what was before the war, that is also difficult to recall."[33] The war has changed her understanding of herself not only after the war, but also before it, challenging the continuity of the self. The representations of the self before, during and after the war, as clearly separate chapters, manifest the fragmentation of the self by the traumatic experience. Aksinja also describes how the memory of the war has a will of its own – it forces her to remember the war, supporting the Freudian understanding of trauma as a repetitive experience:[34] "The war recalled it itself. It was reminded of itself like a throbbing ache of old scars that make you remember the wound."[35]

The Beginning of Dialogue

At the end of the novel an outspoken conversation emerges between the protagonists bringing forward their common wish not to experience war ever again. The women sit on the train returning back from the graves and the memorial service, when one of them pronounces a wish, according to the narrator, the words that they all have in mind: "Let us hope there will never be another war."[36] One of them states that women are against war: "We, women, are against war [...]".[37] What unites the women is their memory: "This is our memory[...]".[38] They consider it to be common to them, "our memory", even if it includes a variety of experiences. The purpose of the trip was to work through the experience of war and finally, to take a distance from it. The protagonists are all reluctant to talk about the war, but on the other hand the experiences and memories of the war are the reason they are together on the train travelling to the cemetery. The narrator of the novel knows their memories and can, therefore, help them in the recalling process. When they depart from Moscow for the graves, there is one more woman travelling with them, the dark lady. She is the grief that the protagonists of the novel see and recognize in each other. The continuous sorrow and feeling of loss is the outcome of the war from the women's point of view and it is in contradiction to the great stories of heroism and victory. When the women arrive at the graves, the lady in black is at a distance from them: "The woman in black also stepped out of the train with all the others, but she stayed at the side, walked behind. [...] From time to time she was lost from sight – where she went, they did not know."[39] The purpose of the trip was to recollect memories and console themselves, which is materialized at the end whereby the constant sorrow in the form of the dark lady, disappears. Even though the stories the women reluctantly told were not complete, the result was that the dark lady was no longer in their midst: "But where is our fellow traveller – the Black Lady? She has left this conversation."[40] It becomes evident that the dark lady has gone now that open discussions have begun.

Endnotes

1 Kelly 1994, 397, 400.
2 Barker 2002, 287.
3 Ledkovsky, Rosenthal, Zirin (eds.) 1994, 56
4 LaCapra 2001, 81.
5 Ibid., 66.
6 Ibid., 21–22.
7 When the most central protagonist of the *Remembrance Day*, Maria Nikolaeva, finds out about the beginning of the war and her husband leaves for the front the narrator states bluntly: "Just like that on a sunny summer day their life got broken." (Baranskaia 1989, 6). [Translation is mine]. The trauma in *Remembrance Day* is the life stories of the women that depict "the oscillation between a crises of death and the correlative crisis of life" through the descriptions "of the unbearable nature of an event" and "of the unbearable nature of its survival". (cit. Caruth 1996, 7). It should be noted that *Remembrance Day* is a survival story.
8 Bakhtin 1984, 293.
9 Read more about the contradiction between women's experiences in war and the official narratives of war in Svetlana Aleksievich's book *War's Unwomanly Face* (*U voiny ne zhenskoe litso*, 1985). The book can be uploaded in Russian from Aleksievich's website (http://www.alexievich.info/booksRu.html). One of the interviewees is suggesting that Aleksievich should talk to her husband, who knows "the names of the commanders and generals" (p. 21 in the aforementioned web publication).
10 Moll-Sawatzki, 2003, 25.
11 Erickson, 1993, 51–59.
12 In connection with the stereotypization of memory Liljeström (2004, 40) quotes Primo Levi: "a memory evoked too often, and in the form of a story, tends to become fixed in a stereotype... crystallized, perfected, adorned, installing itself in the place of the raw memory and growing at its expense".
13 Liljeström 2004, 39–40.
14 Assman 1995, 130.
15 Joseph 2003, 64.
16 Monks 1988, cit. 33, 32.
17 Marsh 1995, 1–2.
18
18 Baranskaia 1989, 6. All translations are mine, K.K.
19 LaCapra writes in the *Writing History, Writing Trauma* (2001, 22) that people that are traumatized by extreme events "may resist working through because of what might almost be termed a fidelity to trauma, a feeling that one must keep faith with it."
20 Baranskaia 1989, 21.

21 Ibid., 186.
22 Ibid., 140.
23 See Aleksievich's *War's Unwomanly Face* (http://www.alexievich.info/booksRu.html). Many of the interviewees tell, that they have no words to describe their experiences and memories of the war (see for example p. 128 in the aforementioned webpublication).
24 Stewart 2003, 113–114, Caruth 1996, 17.
25 Baranskaia 1989, 13.
26 Ibid., 11.
27 Bakhtin 1984, 293.
28 Baranskaia 1989, 6.
29 Ibid., 15–16.
30 Ibid., 16.
31 Nikonova 2005, 5.
32 Baranskaia 1989, 88.
33 Ibid., 97.
34 Caruth 1996, 2.
35 Baranskaia 1989, 21.
36 Ibid., 244.
37 Ibid., 245.
38 Ibid., 247.
39 Ibid., 254–255.
40 Ibid., 260.

References

Baranskaia, Natal'ia (1989), *Den' Pominoveniia*. Moskva, Izd. Sovetskii Pisatel'.

Assman, Jan (1995), Collective Memory and Cultural Identity. *New German Critique*, No. 65, 125–133. Translated by John Czaplicka.

Bakhtin, M. M. (1984), *Problems of Dostoevsky's Poetics*. Manchester, Minnesota, Manchester University Press.

Barker, Adele Marie and Gheith, Jehanne M. (2002) (eds.), *A History of Women's Writing in Russia*. Cambridge, Cambridge University Press.

Caruth, Cathy (1996), *Unclaimed Experience: Trauma, Narrative, and History*. Baltimore and London, The Johns Hopkins University Press.

Erickson, John (1993), Soviet Women at War. In Garrard, John and Garrard, Carol (eds.), *World War Two and the Soviet People*. London, St. Martin's Press, 50–76.

Joseph, Tiffany (2003), "Non-Combatant's Shell Shock": Trauma and Gender in F. Scott Fitzgerald's *Tender is the Night*. *National Women's Studies Association Journal*, Vol. 15 Issue 3, 64–81.

Kelly, Catriona (1994), *A History of Russian Women's Writing 1820–1992*. Oxford, Clarendon Press.

LaCapra, Dominick (2001), *Writing History, Writing Trauma*. Baltimore and London, The Johns Hopkins University Press.

Ledkovsky Marina, Rosenthal, Charlotte and Zirin, Mary (1994), *Dictionary of Russian Women Writers*. Westport, Conn., and London, Greenwood Press.

Marsh, Rosalind (1995), *History and Literature in Contemporary Russia*. Houndmills, Basingstoke, Hampshire and London, MacMillan Press Ltd.

Stewart, Victoria (2003), *Women's Autobiography, War and Trauma*. Basingstoke, Palgrave Macmillan.

Monks, Pieta (1988), Natalia Baranskaia talking with Pieta Monks. In Chamberlain, Mary (ed.), *Writing Lives, Conversations Between Women Writers*. London, Vigaro Press.

Moll-Sawatzki, Andrea (2003), Dobrovol'no na front? In Jahn, Peter (ed.), *Masha+Nina+Katjusha, Frauen in der Roten Armee 1941–1945. Zhenshchiny-voennosluzhashchie*. Berlin, Museum Berlin Karlshorst Ch. Links Verlag, 21–27.

Nikonova, Ol'ga (2005), Zhenshchiny, voina i «figury umolchania». *Neprikosnovennyi Zapas* N 2–3(40–41). http://magazines.russ.ru/nz/2005/2/ni32.html.

Withold Bonner

The Endless Process of Reconstructing Memories: Captivity and Anti-Fascist Re-education in Texts of Franz Fühmann

In one of his prose texts, Franz Fühmann[1] (1922–1984), one of the most important GDR authors, together with Christa Wolf and the playwright, Heiner Müller, quotes Baudelaire who stated that in order to comprehend the soul of a poet, you have to pick out from his works the word that occurs most frequently. The word reveals what he is obsessed with.[2] The word Fühmann is obsessed with is clearly *Wandlung*, change, metamorphosis. Without mentioning his name, Fühmann quotes more than once the German poet, Gottfried Benn:[3] "By all means take on the task of a partial function, but see that you fulfil it meticulously. …"[4] The partial function that Fühmann had to take on, was the change that – did not take place, took place, started, continued, was intensified? – during his years as a POW in Soviet camps. Over and over again he returned in his works to this place and time. First in *Die Brücke*[5] and *Das Land*,[6] two short prose texts from the early 1950s, then in the poem *Die Fahrt nach Stalingrad*,[7] later on in the screenplay *Die heute vierzig sind*[8] and in *The Car with the Yellow Star. Fourteen Days out of Two Decades*, a collection of short stories first published in 1962,[9] then again in *Twenty-two Days or Half a Lifetime* from 1973,[10] for the seventh time in *Vor Feuerschlünden. Erfahrung mit Georg Trakls Gedicht*, published in 1982,[11] and finally in numerous interviews, among them in the last, given only several weeks before his death.

As Fühmann once stated, he had taken care of his partial function, as far as poetry translation and children's literature were concerned. But the third (which should have been the first), covering the time of change as a POW, was never taken care off satisfyingly.[12] Why was that? How did it come about that the author's main subject never became central to any of his texts? The explanation that the reasons are to be found in censorship and anticipating self-censorship in the GDR, which made it difficult to cover with any satisfaction, the re-education in Soviet camps and Antifa Schools,[13] is far too simple. I agree with Fühmann, for whom self-censorship and taboos were not simple opportunistic acts. "Every taboo in literature is raised by the writer himself, and it only becomes taboo by my acceptance of it myself, and it is only then that it becomes a literary problem."[14]

For me the problem is rooted in the difficulties to understand the complicated and contradictory process of changing: When did it start, when had it come to an end? Did it even ever start or come to an end? And most important: What does change mean? What made understanding that difficult, was the fact that this constant individual process of recalling the past was inevitably and inseparably overlapped by the official cultural memory,[15] which had declared already in the Antifa School how this time had to be remembered.

While in the short prose sketch bearing the symbolic title *Die Brücke* German POWs learn that they have the same interests as their Soviet guards, *Das Land* reflects on the controversial reception of the land reform in the Soviet Occupation Zone by the inmates of a Soviet POW camp depending on their class position. *Die Fahrt nach Stalingrad* praises the humanity of the Soviet people, who – in contrast to the Germans – do not kill their prisoners. Instead they see the POWs as seduced and give them the chance to start a new life. In *Die heute vierzig sind* a former worker, nowadays manager of a GDR company, recalls military service at the Eastern front, followed by imprisonment and anti-fascist re-education before his release to the socialist GDR.[16]

Out of the fourteen short stories from *The Car with the Yellow Star* one deals with May 8th 1945, the date of the capitulation of the German *Wehrmacht*. Three deal with the time of imprisonment in a Soviet camp in the Caucasus, while the last one treats the first days of the released POW in the Western sectors of Berlin and in the GDR. Although all these stories take place in their original settings and use a great deal of autobiographical material from the author's life, told by a first person narrator, they seem to disassociate themselves from a closer relation with the author. The reasons are to be found in the stories' pedagogical impetus, typical for this phase of GDR literature. The stories cover the role of the Red Army exactly the way they should be told according to the GDR cultural memory. The message for the reader is obvious and follows the former texts: The Soviet soldiers do take prisoners rather than executing the German soldiers; they do not treat them inhumanely. From story to story the first person narrator is transformed from a fascist soldier into a socialist and supporter of the new order. This process has reached its end in the last story, where the protagonist makes it all too clear that he belongs to the GDR. It is in *this* story where the transformation has come to an end, that the word "change"[17] is mentioned explicitly for the first time.

About ten years later, in *Twenty-two Days or Half a Lifetime*, things are seen differently. This book marks a turning point in the author's creative process. What was supposed to be "small, jolly, easy, lively travel prose"[18] about a trip to Hungary, turned out to be something very different; the balance sheet of half a lifetime. "All of a sudden I discovered that I wrote in order to make something clear to myself, especially in relation to my past, which I had completely overcome, as I thought by then."[19] This meant first of all a revision of the understanding of the process of change, which itself became the object of metamorphosis, thereby questioning the cultural memory of what had happened in the Antifa School. A hitherto static understanding of metamorphosis became transformed into an increasingly dynamic one. It is here for the first time that we can relate to a work by Fühmann as being what Salman Rushdie states about metamorphosis: "Stasis, the dream of eternity, of a fixed order in human affairs, is the favoured myth of tyrants; metamorphosis, the knowledge that *nothing holds its form*, is the driving force of arts."[20]

It is not by chance that the questioning of the cultural memory was put into the form of a diary. It turned out to be adequate for what was developing during the process of writing. Where something that seemingly had been dealt with, turns out to be problematic, where new findings are opening up in the clash with old ideas and where the author does not know what his book is aiming at, it is in fact the diary that is offering itself as a specific mode of autobiographic writing. Diaries can be characterised by their more diffuse form and discontinuity, a lack of formal cohesiveness, which makes them resistant to the telling of a continuous plot establishing order, as it was demanded by the kind of socialist realism to which Fühmann had been obligated for many years. "[...] the discourse of the diary is particularly open to a series of coterminous and contradictory subject positions", as Felicity Nussbaum points out.[21]

Over and over again Fühmann examined the change, and came to the conclusion, that the new Paulus was much closer to the old Saulus than he had assumed.[22] He tried to approach the process of change through various formula and metaphors. He discussed whether a locomotive on a turntable, which hitherto had gone on the track A-B and had been changing to track C-D, had gone through a change. Finally the engine metaphor was transferred to a person, who is "turned around" by the secret service: "[...] that would correspond to the image of the locomotive on the turntable. Someone has worked for A against B; now, 'turned around,' he works for B against A. Can this be called a change?"[23]

The more one relates these displeasing formula and pictures to a life within Fascism and Stalinism, the more they start to make sense. Wasn't it so that many belonging to Fühmann's generation, who had believed in Fascism and who had all of a sudden lost their track after its defeat, tried to get as soon as possible onto the right track again? And wasn't it so that the POWs, who had been trained in Antifa Schools, had – at least partly – been just turned around?

In his comments Fühmann stated that he had found his way into the new order via Auschwitz. As execution of his change he had considered putting himself at the new order's disposal as a tool, whose own will was extinguished. But where the new Paulus resembled in many respects the old Saulus, it might then be that continuity could be found in the old Saulus as well; in other words, had he already shown traces of the new antifascist Paulus?

Fühmann did not go that way. In fact it was in the opposite direction that he constructed himself in the position of one hundred percent fascist and asked himself the question of what he would have done if he had been sent to Auschwitz. In his answer he stated that he would have functioned there as well as all the others and he, too, would have done his "duty".[24]

As far as this point is concerned, the understanding of change remained partly static. This seems to correspond with the contents of the lectures at the Antifa School. As Fühmann put it, he had to condemn the person to death that he once had been. And as he recollected, some of the prisoners, after certain lectures, executed the former fascist inside them by committing suicide.

As the author states in his last interview, at the time when he wrote *Twenty-two Days* he still believed that he did not have the right to criticise his society. "You are someone who defended Auschwitz, and they are the ones, who freed Auschwitz, and therefore you should just shut up. [...] I couldn't get away from this relationship of guilt, before I had completely made sense of my past."[25] – In other words, was this a confession of his own guilt in front of the leading politicians of the GDR, who had found their way from exile and persecution to power? This would mean acceptance of the antifascist narrative, the founding discourse of the GDR[26] as well as the moral superiority of the communist re-migrants, whose doctrine was contaminated by Stalinism. But the literary text was more ambivalent than the interviews presuppose. It contained elements, which started to break up the official antifascist narrative. Where especially someone, who had just been turned around from Fascist to Socialist, was fitting in that well to build up the new order, what did it tell about it? And when Fühmann pointed out that he had found his way into the socialist society via Auschwitz, he posited a clear difference to the official antifascism in the GDR, where the victims of the holocaust had always been second degree victims.[27]

Another 10 years later, in his tremendous essay *Vor Feuerschlünden. Erfahrung mit Georg Trakls Gedicht* on the important impact the poetry of the expressionist Austrian writer had had on his life, Fühmann returns again to the Antifa School near Moscow. The narrative is centred on the examination of the lessons held by Michael Janzen, professor of philosophy. This encounter with Janzen had already been dealt with in *Twenty-two Days*, and was something which would continue to bother him until his death. The recollection of these lectures is extremely contradictory. On the one hand there is a deep and ongoing gratitude for the initiation of the process of change. On the other hand there is the increasing critique at the re-establishing of a binary world, a new split into two, black and white, bad and good.

As Fühmann recollects, in the beginning of captivity and after he had learnt about Auschwitz[28] he had come to the conclusion that after the mistaken belief in Fascism, he would never again participate in any political action. At that point the unwavering one-sided Janzen-lectures gave support to those who had lost their way and offered a path out of the past.

The uncompromising break with the old convictions had to be the departure towards something new, the radical change of the society into a new and socialist order, which – as implemented in the basic antifascist discourse of the GDR – would make fascism forever impossible. And those who had been cursed by the people of the world would build up this new society. It was in this context that the recollected self understood the meaning of fairy tales: the hero being released from his transformation into a wolf. But as he recollects, Fühmann remarks: fairy tales are black and white, too. And as he states, this totally dual view of the world, was just the complement to the world view which had governed the POW's way of thinking before.[29]

At the end there is an insight, which in *Twenty-two Days* – at least partially – had still been rejected. The becoming of man is not taking place in succession, it is rather the concomitance of contradictions. "You lose nothing of what you once have been, and you have been, what you are only to become."[30] Where the old world view was partially surviving even after the change had taken place – or better: was beginning – at the Antifa School, the unfolding of new insights must already have started at a point of time, where the author of *Twenty-two Days* still constructed himself as hundred percent fascist. "The points of rupture stepped out abruptly, consistencies remained unnoticed for a long time, they seemed to be the unthinkable per se, but continuity is to be found already in the person in question: The one who is changing, is at the same time remaining the same [...]."[31]

Finally in 1984, in his last interview, Fühmann again returns to the lectures given by Michael Janzen, who is now mentioned with his real name. The author shows a growing distance to the doctrine, as it had been taught at the Antifa School. As he sees it now, isolation and indoctrination in the camp were complete, and people moved in narrow, restricted circles.[32] There is not much sympathy left for the Janzen-lectures, which Fühmann now recalls as "superb demagogy".[33]

It is not a coming-of-age novel that is constructed here, a Bildungsroman of a former POW, who is step by step replacing the official, cultural memory of Fascism and World War II as it was imposed already at the Antifa School, with his private, individual memory. On the contrary, it seems that Fühmann never left the site of the prisoner camp and the Antifa School, when he gets back to them over and over again in his poetry and prose, whether fictional or factual.

One explanation is that it became impossible to separate private and cultural memory precisely from each other. On the one hand the recollection of the past undergoes a perpetual metamorphosis that can be characterised by a growing distance to a doctrine, which turns out to be just another religion. On the other hand, there is a continuity of positions to be found as well in the author's very first comments on captivity as well as in his later and last ones. In his last interview he puts it as follows: "I was not shot, not slain nor beaten. [...] The hunger was awful, but there was a scorched country. We too were bearing the blame for Auschwitz, and they who had freed Auschwitz, who had not killed us, who taught us German history, who sent us to school, they were the Russians."[34] The same gratitude can already be found in an early letter that Fühmann wrote in 1949 from the Antifa School to his sister: "[...] here I have experienced that much care, that much goodness, that much humanity and generosity, so that I asked myself in the beginning over and over again: How can it be possible? Why don't they give back the same as what these Hitler criminals have inflicted on humankind and above all on these people?"[35] When I wrote with respect to the stories from 1962 that they covered the role of the Red Army exactly the way they should be told according to the GDR cultural memory, it is only one side of the coin: what the first person narrator tells about the Soviet army, corresponds at least in parts with how the author had felt all these years ever since the times of captivity.

Another reason for Fühmann's continuous returns to the prisoner camp and Antifa School is that they became a counter-site, a heterotopia "[...] in which the other real sites that can be found within the culture, are simultaneously represented, contested and inverted."[36] First of all, time seems to have come to a complete standstill, as it happens in sites where people are locked up for a long time and where one has to return over and over again even after one's release. Heterotopia turns into heterochronia. It starts to function when men arrive at a sort of absolute break with their traditional time, as it is the case in a POW camp.[37] Then, the heterotopia of the Antifa School is creating a "real" space that is other, as perfect, as meticulous, as well arranged as the fascist world had been messy, ill constructed and jumbled.[38] "Only twice was I actually 'within it,' completely within it, in complete, blissful harmony, and in both cases I was on the periphery: behind barbed wire at the Antifa School [...] and during my time at the Warnow shipyards."[39] The rites and purifications the students at the Antifa School have to submit to[40] lead to nothing but a space of illusion, a site of fairy tales, where the world is divided into black and white, bad and good, as in the lectures given by Michael Janzen, delivering a completely binary worldview, a counter-piece to the worldview which had governed the fascist soldiers' way of thinking before.[41]

For the different representations of the author in his texts, whether fictional or factual, the space of heterotopia turns more and more into a site of deviation, "[...] in which individuals whose behaviour is deviant in relation to the required mean or norm are placed."[42] First, they are constructed as fascists and are therefore contesting the GDR antifascist narrative, according to which people who participated in the building of a new socialist society would be released from their fascist past,[43] while the responsibility for the fascist crimes in post-war Germany was completely shifted to the side of the imperialistic Federal Republic. Secondly, Fühmann and his protagonists remain in a space of deviation, as the confrontation with the holocaust, which took place in the prisoners' camp, remains for them the decisive motivation for their engagement with socialism. "My generation has arrived at Socialism via Auschwitz. All reflection on our change must begin at the gas chamber and nowhere else [.]"[44] This is indeed a deviation from the antifascist narrative of the GDR, according to which Jews were only victims of the second degree. This led to just another deviation, causing Fühmann to take the side of Israel instead of the Palestinians, in opposition to GDR foreign politics. In the end there was a double-bind of taboos that could not be overcome, at the same time disconnecting and connecting the author with the cultural memory, as formed in the Antifa School and later on in the GDR: "By the way, presumably certain positions of my inner censor cannot be overcome, in two different aspects: I could never write anything containing a negative predication concerning the Red Army, and I could never criticise the Jewish state, whatever government might be in power."[45]

Endnotes

1 Fühmann was born in 1922 in Rochlitz – nowadays Rokytnice – in the Sudeten, a German speaking region which was by then part of Czechoslovakia, but had until the end of WWI belonged to the Austrian-Hungarian empire. As the Nazi regime intensified its activities in the Sudeten, Fühmann voluntarily joined the SA at the age of 16. When Nazi Germany invaded Poland in 1939, Fühmann tried to volunteer for the German army, but was not accepted due to his age. After graduating from school in 1941 he was drafted – first to the "Reichsarbeitsdienst" and later on during the same year to the regular army. He served behind the frontlines as signaller in the Soviet Union and in Greece. Wounded during the withdrawal from Greece, Fühmann was sent to a hospital nearby his home town. In early may 1945 he was taken prisoner of war by the Red Army. He was sent to a camp near Nephtigorsk in the Caucasus. From there he was sent in 1946 to the central Antifa School Noginsk near Moscow, among others founded to recruit potential cadres for the administration of the Soviet occupation zone. After the end of the course Fühmann became assisting teacher in Noginsk. Later on he taught in Antifa Schools in Rjasan and Ogre near Riga. When the school in Ogre was disbanded in late 1949, Fühmann became citizen of the newly founded GDR and moved to Berlin. There he joined the NDPD, a party that had been founded in order to attract former soldiers of the "Wehrmacht". As party official he was in charge of the NDPD cultural activities until 1958, when he quit. From that day on until his death in 1984 he lived as a free and independent author. See for further biographical details Tate 1995 and Richter 2001.

2 Fühmann 1984, 61.

3 Fühmann could not mention Benn, because he was in the GDR a persona non grata due to his expressionist poetry and his flirt with the Nazi regime.

4 Fühmann 1980, 58.

5 "The Bridge". Fühmann 1951. The titles of texts not translated into English are given in German. Quotations from those texts are translated by me, W.B.

6 "The Land". Fühmann 1952.

7 "Travelling to Stalingrad". Fühmann 1953.

8 "Those who are forty today". Fühmann 1961.

9 Fühmann 1968.

10 Fühmann 1980.

11 "Facing the Fiery Abyss. Experiencing Trakl's Poem." Fühmann 1982.

12 See Fühmann 1980, 165. See further Fühmann 1983, 372: "What I definitely still want to cover and with the utmost concreteness is the time as a prisoner of war, those extremely important four years. In the meanwhile I've come to the conviction that only I'm able to cover it, for one must have experienced this time, the documentary can't be invented. In the case that I don't do it, this time will vanish into oblivion."
13 For further information on the Antifa Schools for German POWs in the USSR, see e.g. Hilger 2000, 220ff.
14 Fühmann 1980, 182.
15 Cultural memory is characterised by a certain distance from everyday life. It is based on specific fixed points that are marked as important and kept alive through cultural forming (texts, rites, monuments) and institutionalised communication (recitation, visiting, viewing). See Assmann 1988, 9.
16 See also Tate 1995, 60–61.
17 Fühmann 1968, 175.
18 Letter by Fühmann to Hans Richter with date of November 22nd 1975. See Schmitt 1994, 171.
19 Fühmann 1986a, 419.
20 Rushdie 1991, 291; original emphasis.
21 Nussbaum 1988, 129.
22 Without mentioning his name, Fühmann quoted the West-German critic Reich-Ranicki, who had once stated in respect to Fühmann's poetry from the fifties, that what was in question was "pure NS-lyrics from the pen of a man who, without a doubt, didn't want to have anything to do with National Socialism and who hated it from the bottom of his heart. He just had been changed into something else at the Antifa School. Therefore he wrote HJ-poetry with FDJ-key-signature." See Reich-Ranicki 1970, 272.
23 Fühmann 1980, 125.
24 Fühmann 1980, 221.
25 Fühmann 1994, 591–592.
26 For the GDR antifascist narrative see Hell 1997, 1ff.
27 For the hierarchy of victimization in the GDR see Assmann, Frevert 1999, 166–172.
28 The first article in German on the Holocaust was published in 1943 in *Freies Deutschland*, a paper edited by Rudolf Herrnstadt and published by the *Nationalkomitee Freies Deutschland* in the USSR. The paper was directed at German POWs in the USSR and German soldiers on the Eastern front. And it was *Freies Deutschland* too, where the first article in German on Auschwitz was printed. See Liebmann 2008, 197 and 213. According to Uhlig the confrontation with war crimes committed by the German Wehrmacht was one of the ways of re-education directed at the German POWs in the USSR. Uhlig 1998, 49. The latter can be seen as well from the memoirs of former Antifa School teacher Eilderman, who recollects several lessons, when he was talking about crimes committed by the *Wehrmacht*. See Eildermann 1985, 56, 82, 88, 159ff.
29 Fühmann 1984, 44ff.
30 Fühmann 1984, 194.
31 Fühmann1984, 46.
32 Fühmann 1994, 576.
33 Fühmann 1994, 575. In the interview Fühmann mentions as one example how Janzen dealt with rumours about the existence of the GULAG. Once he entered the stage of the auditorium in order to read a note, according to which there should be some kind of punishment camps in the Soviet Union, where people allegedly disappeared. "'Comrades!

I want you to think about this. Did Goebbels tell you: >The Soviet Army doesn't take any prisoners?<' 3000 people shouted 'Yes'. >Have you been told that you will be tortured here?< 'Yes' >Have you been tortured?< 'No!' >Could you ever imagine that you would be allowed to write home?< 'No!' >Are you allowed to write home?< 'Yes!' >And now the print media tell us that here should be a camp, where people disappear. Do you believe that?< A three thousand fold No?" Fühmann 1994, 576.

34 Fühmann 1984, 574.

35 Letter from May 23rd 1949 in Heinze 1998, 48.

36 Foucault 1984.

37 "Suddenly" is one of the keywords, used by Fühmann in order to construct his life-story, as he puts it in a letter from August 22nd 1971 to Kurt Batt from the Hinstorff publishing house: "[...] suddenly a fist grabs me and plugs me into a miles long platoon, trotting its way, and suddenly I am prisoner, wojennoplenny, trotting into something black, uncertain, unknown – and as suddenly as before I come from the work camp to the Antifa School, from the naphta primeval forest to a library with ten thousands of books – there lies my basic experience." Fühmann 1994, 102–103.

38 See Foucault 1984.

39 Fühmann 1980, 83.

40 See Fühmann 1980, 205: "Can one define change as a transition to a different value-system [...], as a process which marks the end of the old value-system and with a purification (self-criticism, confession, atonement, penance, retribution, ritual and so forth) begins the new one? That would explain many strange phenomena in camp".

41 Fühmann 1984, 46.

42 Foucault 1984.

43 As Heukenkamp (2003, 109) points out, Fühmann was very critical of literary figures in GDR prose, who were portrayed as seduced and capable of changing.

44 Fühmann 1980, 173.

45 Fühmann 1983, 382.

References

Assmann, Aleida and Frevert, Ute (1999), *Geschichtsvergessenheit – Geschichtsversessenheit: Vom Umgang mit deutschen Vergangenheiten nach 1945*. Stuttgart, Deutsche Verlags-Anstalt.

Assmann, Jan (1988), Kollektives Gedächtnis und kulturelle Identität. In Assmann, Jan and Hölscher, Tonio (eds.), *Kultur und Gedächtnis*. Frankfurt a.M., 9–19.

Eildermann, Wilhelm (1985), *Die Antifaschule. Erinnerungen an eine Frontschule der Roten Armee*. Berlin, Dietz.

Foucault, Michel (1984), *Of Other Spaces* (1967), *Heterotopias*. www.foucault.info/documents/heteroTopia.

Fühmann, Franz (1951), Die Brücke. *Aufbau*, Vol. 7 Issue 11, 1003–1007.

Fühmann, Franz (1952), Das Land. In Tschesno-Hell, Michael (ed.), *Neue deutsche Erzähler: Geschichten aus unserer Zeit*. Berlin, Aufbau, 192–228.

Fühmann, Franz (1953), *Die Fahrt nach Stalingrad. Eine Dichtung*. Berlin, Aufbau.

Fühmann, Franz (1961), *Die heute vierzig sind. Eine Filmerzählung*. Berlin, Aufbau.

Fühmann, Franz (1968), *The Car with the Yellow Star. Fourteen Days out of Two Decades*. Berlin, Seven Seas Publishers. First published in German in 1962.

Fühmann, Franz (1980), *Twenty-two Days or Half a Lifetime*. Berlin, Seven Seas Publishers. First published in German in 1973.

Fühmann, Franz (1983), Gespräch mit Wilfried F. Schoeller. In Fühmann, Franz, *Den Katzenartigen wollen wir verbrennen. Ein Lesebuch*. Ed. by Hans-Jügen Schmitt. Frankfurt a.M., Büchergilde Gutenberg, 349–384.

Fühmann, Franz (1984), *Vor Feuerschlünden. Erfahrung mit Georg Trakls Gedicht*. Rostock, Hinstorff.

Fühmann, Franz (1986a), Gespräch mit Jacqueline Benker-Grenz. In Fühmann, Franz (1986b), *Essays, Gespräche, Aufsätze 1964–1981*. Rostock, Hinstorff, 408–422.

Fühmann, Franz (1994), Butzbacher Interview. In Schmitt, Hans-Jürgen (ed.), *Franz Fühmann. Briefe 1950–1984. Eine Auswahl*. Rostock, Hinstorff, 572–595.

Heinze, Barbara (1998) (ed.), *Franz Fühmann. Eine Biographie in Bildern, Dokumenten und Briefen*. Rostock, Hinstorff.

Hell, Julia (1997), *Post-Fascist Fantasies. Psychoanalysis, History, and the Literature of East Germany*. Durham & London, Duke University Press.

Heukenkamp, Ursula (2003), Ein Kontrahent des Hoffens. Franz Fühmann und seine Kriegserzählungen. Zeitschrift für Germanistik. *Neue Folge*, Vol. 13 Issue 1, 101–112.

Hilger, Andreas (2000), *Deutsche Kriegsgefangene in der Sowjetunion, 1941–1956. Kriegsgefangenenpolitik, Lageralltag und Erinnerung*. Essen, Klartext-Verlag.

Liebmann, Irina (2008), *Wäre es schön? Es wäre schön! Mein Vater Rudolf Herrnstadt*. Berlin, Berlin Verlag.

Nussbaum, Felicity A. (1988), Toward Conceptualizing Diary. In Olney, James (ed.), *Studies in Autobiography.* New York, Oxford, Oxford University Press, 128–140.

Reich-Ranicki, Marcel (1970), *Deutsche Literatur in West und Ost. Prosa seit 1945.* Reinbek bei Hamburg, Rowohlt Taschenbuch Verlag.

Richter, Hans (2001), *Franz Fühmann: Ein deutsches Dichterleben. Biographie.* Berlin, Aufbau Taschenbuch Verlag.

Rushdie, Salman (1991), *Imaginary Homelands. Essays and Criticism 1981–1991.* London, Granat Books.

Schmitt, Hans-Jürgen (1994) (ed.), *Franz Fühmann. Briefe 1950–1984. Eine Auswahl.* Rostock, Hinstorff.

Tate, Dennis (1995), F*ranz Fühmann. Innovation and Authenticity. A study of his prose-writing.* Amsterdam - Atlanta.

Uhlig, Christa (1998), *Rückkehr aus der Sowjetunion: Politische Erfahrungen und pädagogische Wirkungen. Emigranten und ehemalige Kriegsgefangene in der SBZ und frühen DDR.* Weinheim, Deutscher Studien Verlag.

Sveta Roberman

Red Army WWII Veterans in Israel: Mobilization of the Combat Past and Negotiation of Belonging to a New Homeland

Introduction

When they migrate to a new country, immigrants bring with them their "cultural tool-kits"[1] – their pasts. The return to the past by individuals and groups is not merely the result of nostalgic longing surfacing in the migrants' lifeworlds;[2] nor is it just another venue for the consolidation of diasporic communities.[3] In the current paper, I demonstrate how the past serves as a resource in migrants' negotiations with the host society as a form of symbolic capital mobilized to empower migrants in the social hierarchies of their new countries. In other words, the past serves as a venue for framing projects of belonging to a host country.

All acts of remembrance and commemoration develop around significant events,[4] episodes that encompass critical experiences and bear symbolic meanings for individuals and immigrant communities. As the past is embedded in the present,[5] and the choice of what is to be remembered is determined by its potential relevance to current socio-cultural and historical contexts in host societies, memory of the past is never static.[6] Narratives of the past are constantly reinterpreted in the conjuncture of subjective experience[7] with wider historical and social realities.[8]

The case at the focus of this study is the group of Red Army WWII veterans who immigrated to Israel in the 1990s. Following their migration, this marginalised group of elderly immigrants turned to their combat past as WWII Red Army soldiers, which became their main symbolic capital in their struggle for an identity of belonging in the new country. That struggle took place around arenas of commemoration, rituals commemorating WWII, museums built by the veterans to frame their story, and monuments to Jewish soldiers who fell during WWII. Using examples of veterans' commemorative work, I demonstrate how, by mobilising their combat past, they contest meta narratives in the host country by introducing new narrative frames and heroes. Remembering and commemorating the past, they manage their way in a new country as they construct their projects of belonging.

The Case Study

These elderly people arrived in Israel as part of the massive influx of one million immigrants from the former USSR. In the late 1990s, the number of Red Army veterans living in Israel totalled around 20,000. Migration placed the elderly immigrants in multiple circles of marginality and constrained their social networks. Their lack of proficiency in Hebrew – although most made dedicated, but unsuccessful, efforts to take language courses for immigrants – left them outside the social circles of the host society. In many cases, the different climate exacerbated chronic illnesses. Differences in specialization and language barriers, combined with the critical factor of old age, precluded any possibility of their entering the labour market. Their professional lives, like many other elements of their pre-immigrant lives, became merely nostalgic artefacts. Although they desperately sought urgent self-realization, they mostly found frustration instead. "We are useless people," many complained. The deep pain caused by the elderly immigrants' multiple marginality was particularly intense in light of the prevailing perception that their immigration to Israel was actually a "homecoming":[9] immigration as homecoming grants immigrants automatic citizenship upon arrival, and promises the right to join the national collective as equal and respected members. But the reality they encountered was quite different, and thus a gap was created between the promise of "being one people" and their marginalization as elderly immigrants. On the one hand, the situation was a source of despair, while on the other it sharpened and intensified the immigrants' efforts to achieve equality within the national collective. In challenging the multiple marginalities of the present, the elderly immigrants turned to the symbolic resource of their past.

Out of the "hierarchy of identities" that they could draw on,[10] they chose to emphasise their soldiering identity. In the Israeli political and socio-historical context, the identity of soldiering, and particularly that of combating Nazism, bore potential relevance. The immigrants found themselves in a country with a deeply rooted discourse of militarism that glorifies army service and combat, with military tropes intervening in all spheres of life, and where military service is the main criterion for full citizenship.[11] This Israeli context of militarism framed the elderly immigrants' combat past as a salient episode in their autobiographies.

The Israeli context of Holocaust memory endowed the soldiering narrative with a further special meaning: they had fought in WWII and had defeated the Nazis, thus saving their people from complete physical destruction. Accordingly, the veterans began presenting their defeat of Nazism not only as a struggle for the Soviet motherland, but also as part of the fight for the Jewish people's survival. Indeed, they went one step further and claimed that their combat and victory in 1945 should be seen as laying the basis for Israel's establishment in 1948. The elderly immigrants linked their Soviet war heroics with the narrative of the foundation of the state of Israel.

From their former country, the elderly immigrants had imported the highly developed mnemonic praxis of veteran culture that was shaped and nourished by the Soviet cult of the Great Patriotic War.[12] It enabled the immigrants to organize quickly and, by the mid-1990s, they had developed a flourishing network of veteran organizations and activities in the new country.

The Israeli arena of memory of the 1990s provided fertile ground for the elderly immigrants' struggle. For years, this arena had been monopolized by the state, which defined and controlled the contents of the collective memory. In more recent decades, though, it had undergone a democratization process and become a space far more receptive to the voices of marginalized groups.[13] Entering that arena in the 1990s, Soviet immigrants constituted one socio-ethnic group among many, each searching for a way to tell its own story.[14] Their belonging to a massive immigrant community that was rich in social resources[15] was a crucial facilitating factor for them – both when negotiating with the authorities, and in terms of their acceptance in the Israeli public arena. Below I present examples of the veterans' memory work, and show how they mobilized a narrative from the past to construct texts and spaces of national belonging in the present.

Commemorating the Combat Past

The Veterans' Museums

During the 1990s, a number of museums were created by veterans in towns throughout Israel. Museum material was assembled from books and encyclopaedias, and the veterans' oral narratives were also an important source for exhibits. Veterans, relatives, and friends of soldiers who had perished in the war or died thereafter, would donate precious artefacts – soldiers' photographs, war letters, and medals. The veterans' museums strike the visitor as a garish blend of Soviet and Israeli symbols – flags and war medals (with the colour red predominating) are juxtaposed with the symbols of the Stars of David and the Menorah, as well as Israeli flags. Jewish soldiers who had served in the Red Army, and Soviet Jews' contribution during the war, are central topics in the exhibitions, and the narratives are always related to the participation and combat of the 1.5 million Jewish soldiers who had fought in WWII. In turn, these soldiers' deeds are presented as an instantiation of the centuries-long tradition of Jewish resistance and military endeavour. Accordingly, alongside the veterans' stories other exhibits depict sketches of the Biblical David, stories of struggles against the Crusaders, sketches of Jewish soldiers who had served in Napoleon's army, data about Jewish soldiers, and many other references to various epochs and places. Interweaving myth, memory, and history, the exhibits present a claim of strength and military heroism, and construct a narrative of Jewish resistance and combat valour over the centuries. The veterans' narrative as created in the museums ultimately confronts the Israeli foundational meta-narrative that is built on the contradiction between pre-state exile (*galut*, in Hebrew) and the new era of state sovereignty. In the meta-narrative used to present Jewish life in Diaspora as one of endemic victimization, dependence, and vulnerability, the *galuti* man – passive and weak – is cast as the antithesis of the New Israeli, the *sabra*, the strong, native-born soldier.[16] It was the generation of the sabras – particularly those who reached adulthood in the 1948 War of Independence – whose heroic deeds made the birth of the state possible. They were instrumental creating the state of Israel out of the devastating history of the *galut* and the destruction of the Holocaust, and later in defending it.[17] However, the museums' narrative provides a new vision of Jewish life in the Diaspora, showing it not as a period of weakness and passivity, but rather as one of strength and struggle. The era of the independent state is not depicted as the opposite of exile, but rather as building upon the exilic historical tradition and as being inspired by its values and spirit. The veterans' narrative asserts that it was not only native Israelis who were instrumental in the state's foundation and whose lives were sacrificed for its sake. In fighting the Second World War, they claim, Jewish soldiers also gave their lives for the sake of the future Israeli state.

The Victory Day Parade

The interplay between two dates – victory in WWII and the birth of the Israeli state – framed the main plot in another arena of commemoration – the Victory Parade over Nazi Germany, held in Jerusalem. The first Jerusalem parade of Red Army veterans took place in 1995, close to the date on which the victory is commemorated in the Soviet Union – 9 May. When I attended the parades in the late 1990s, the ceremony was already well-framed and was held with the assistance and support of the Jerusalem municipality. The parades took place in the city centre, with close to 700 participants. The marching veterans wore their Soviet medals, some were in Soviet military uniforms, and held Israeli flags. A rally followed the parade. As an integral part of the event each year, the rally had its repertoire of songs, hymns, and speeches. Songs in Yiddish were mixed with Israeli Hebrew songs, followed by some Soviet Great Patriotic War songs. People rose to their feet for the song about the great battle of Stalingrad. At these moments of triumph and sacredness, the distant battlefields of Stalingrad and Kursk, the walls of Jerusalem's Old City, the Soviet medals, and Israeli flags, seemed to merge into a whole. That motive of wholeness was explicitly articulated in a speech by a participant in the 2000 rally: "Fifty-five years ago we laid the foundation stone for our future and today we see the result: we are celebrating the 52nd anniversary of our home [Israel]. May it be blessed and happy."

The Monuments

In their struggle for memory and recognition, the veteran organizations assigned a crucial role to the setting up of monuments to the Jewish fallen soldiers of WWII. The veterans' monuments were erected in town parks, often near the veterans clubs or hostels for the elderly where many veterans lived. Many of those monuments were fashioned in the form of a tomb, a widely accepted form of commemoration for fallen soldiers in Israel, where the bringing of the body to burial is required by religion. Furthermore, in the Israeli context of the continuing conflict over the land, the military grave comes to signify "sacrificial death", marking out the national territory.[18] Borrowing that monumental form allowed the veterans to achieve two goals. First, the burial place of millions of Soviet soldiers who fought in WWII, among them soldiers of Jewish descent, is unknown. By erecting monuments to them in Israel, the veterans created virtual graves, finally providing a place of burial and memory for the fallen. Thus, religious tradition was fulfilled and a moral debt was paid. Second, the virtual graves also connected the soldiers who died in faraway places to a concrete physical locality and particular national territory: the soldiers' death could thus be signified as a sacrificial death for the Israeli state and nation. The monuments territorialized the memory and sanctified the place. Moreover, by connecting the bearers of the memory to a particular place, they attached the elderly immigrants to the concrete localities of their habitat. Through their pasts, embodied in the monuments, they now belonged to the new country.

Concluding Remarks

This paper has shown how the narrative of the past is mobilized by elderly immigrants in their struggle for recognition in their new country. In the ongoing encounter between the immigrants and the host society, the veterans' narrative is reconstructed: the Red Army Jewish soldiers fighting and sacrificing themselves in the battles of WWII contribute, through victory, to the future Jewish state. Thus, two periods of the elderly immigrants' lives – in the Soviet Union and Israel – become connected through the battlefields of WWII. Through the trope of heroic combat, they construct a narrative of belonging by connecting their war past to the sacred roots of national history – the history of the state's foundation – thus staking a claim to national identity of honour in the present. The case illuminates narratives as "social events" that are always "in process".[19] Reread and reinterpreted in the intersection of individual experiences with wider frames of memory and socio-political realities, the narratives of the past nourish individual and communal projects in the present.

Endnotes

1 Swidler 1986.
2 Boym 2001; Ganguly 1992.
3 Amit 1989; Naficy 1991; Rubchak 1993; Safran 1991.
4 Schwartz 1982.
5 Olick and Levy 1997; Schudson 1992; Zerubavel, 1996.
6 Gillis 1994; Zelizer 1995.
7 Ganguly 1992.
8 Antze and Lambek 1996; Peacock and Holland 1993; White 2005.
9 Golden 2002; Lomsky-Feder and Rapoport 2001.
10 Unruh 1983.
11 Helman 1997; Kimmerling 1993; Sasson-Levy 2002.
12 Merridale 2006; Tumarkin 1994.
13 Azoulay 1994; Ram 2000.
14 Meir-Glitzenstein 2002; Paine 1989.
15 Zilberg and Leshem1999.
16 Almog 2000; Raz-Krakotzkin 1993; Zerubavel 1995.
17 Handelman and Katz 1990; Sivan 1994.
18 Handelman and Shamgar-Handelman 1997.
19 Peacock and Holland 1993.

References

Almog, Oz (2000), *The Sabra: The Creation of the New Jew*. Berkeley, University of California Press.

Amit, Vered (1989), *Armenians in London: The Management of Social Boundaries*. Manchester, Manchester University Press.

Antze, Paul and Lambek, Michael (1996), Introduction: Forecasting Memory. In Antze, Paul and Lambek, Michael (eds.), *Tense Past: Cultural Essays in Trauma and Memory*. New York, Routledge, xi–xxxviii.

Azoulay, Ariela (1994), With Open Doors: Museums and Historical Narratives in Israel's Public Space. In Shermann, Daniel and Rogoff, Irit (eds.), *Museum Culture: History, Discourses, Spectacles*. London, Routledge, 85–109.

Boym, Svetlana (2001), *The Future of Nostalgia*. New York, Basic Books.

Gillis, John. R. (1994), Memory and Identity: The History of the Relationship. In Gillis, John R. (ed.), *Commemorations: The Politics of National Identity*. Princeton, Princeton University Press, 3–27.

Golden, Deborah (2002), Belonging through Time: Nurturing National Identity among Newcomers to Israel from the Former Soviet Union. *Time and Society*, Vol. 11 Issue 1, 5–24.

Handelman, Don and Katz, Elihu (1990), State Ceremonies of Israel: Remembrance Day and Independence Day. In Handelman, Don, *Models and Mirrors: Towards an Anthropology of Public Events*. Cambridge, Cambridge University Press, 191–233.

Handelman, Don and Shamgar-Handelman, Lea (1997), The Presence of Absence: The Memorialization of National Death in Israel. In Ben-Ari, Eyal and Bilu, Yoram (eds.), *Grasping the Land*. Albany, State University of New York Press, 85–108.

Helman, Sara (1997), Militarism and the Construction of Community *Journal of Political and Military Sociology*, Vol. 23, 305–332.

Kimmerling, Baruch (1993), Militarism in Israeli society. *Theory and Criticism*, Vol. 4, 123–141 (Hebrew).

Lomsky-Feder, Edna, and Rapoport, Tamar (2001), Homecoming, Immigration, and the National Ethos: Russian-Jewish Homecomers Reading Zionism. *Anthropological Quarterly*, Vol. 74 Issue 1, 1–14.

Meir-Glitzenstein, Esther (2002), Our Dowry: Identity and Memory among Iraqi Immigrants in Israel. *Middle Eastern Studies*, Vol. 38 Issue 2, 165–186.

Merridale, Catherine (2006), *Ivan's War: Life and Death in the Red Army, 1939–1945*. New York, Metropolitan Books.

Naficy, Hamid (1991), The Poetics and Practice of Iranian Nostalgia in Exile. *Diaspora*, Vol. 1 Issue 3, 285–303.

Olick, Jeffrey K., and Levy, Daniel (1997), Collective Memory and Cultural Constraint: Holocaust Myth and Rationality in German Politics. *American Sociological Review*, Vol. 62 Issue 6, 92–136.

Paine, Robert (1989), Israel: Jewish Identity and Competition over Tradition. In Tonkin, Elizabeth, McDonald, Maryon and Chapman, Malcolm (eds.), *History and Ethnicity*. London, Routledge, 121–137.

Peacock, James L., and Holland, Dorothy C. (1993), The Narrated Self: Life Stories in Process. *Ethos*, Vol. 21 Issue 4, 367–383.

Ram, Uri (2000), National, Ethnic or Civic? Contesting Paradigms of Memory, Identity and Culture in Israel. *Studies in Philosophy and Education*, Vol. 19 Issue 5, 405–422.

Raz-Krakotzkin, Amnon (1993), Exile within Sovereignty: Toward a Critique of the "Negation of Exile" in Israeli Culture. *Theory and Criticism*, Vol. 4, 23–57 (Hebrew).

Rubchak, Marian J (1993), Dancing with the Bones: A Comparative Study of Two Ukrainian Exile Societies. *Diaspora*, Vol. 2 Issue 3, 337–371.

Safran, William (1991), Diaspora in Modern Societies: Myths of Homeland and Return. *Diaspora*, Vol. 1 Issue 1, 83–99.

Sasson-Levi, Orna (2002), Constructing Identities at the Margins: Masculinities and Citizenship in the Israeli Army. *Sociological Quarterly*, Vol. 43 Issue 4, 357–383.

Schudson, Michael (1989), The Present in the Past Versus the Past in the Present. *Communication*, Vol. 11 Issue 2, 105–113.

Schwartz, Barry (1982), The Social Context of Commemoration: A Study in Collective Memory. *Social Forces*, Vol. 61 Issue 2, 374–403.

Swidler, Ann (1986), Culture in Action: Symbols and Strategies. *American Sociological Review*, Vol. 51 Issue 2, 273–286.

Tumarkin, Nina (1994), *The Living and the Dead: The Rise and Fall of the Cult of World War II in Russia*. New York, Basic Books.

Unruh, David R. (1983), Death and Personal History: Strategies of Identity Preservation. *Social Problems*, Vol. 30 Issue 3, 340–351.

White, Geoffry (2006), Epilogue: Memory Moments. *Ethos*, Vol. 34 Issue 2, 325–341.

Zelizer, Barbie (1995), Reading the Past against the Grain: The Shape of Memory Studies. *Critical Studies in Mass Communication*, Vol. 12 Issue 2, 214–239.

Zerubavel, Eviotar (1996), Social Memories: Steps in the Sociology of the Past. *Qualitative Sociology*, Vol. 19 Issue 3, 283–299.

Zerubavel, Yael (1995), *Recovered Roots: Collective Memory and the Making of Israeli National Tradition*. Chicago, University of Chicago Press.

Zilberg, Narspi and Leshem, Eli (1999), Imagined Community and Real Community: The Russian Language Press and Renewal of Community Life among Immigrants in Israel. *Society and Welfare*, Vol. 19, 9–37 (Hebrew).

Liliana Ruth Feierstein and Liliana Furman

Memory under Siege: Jewish Veterans of the Soviet Army in Present-Day Germany*

Listening

Dressed in holiday finery, surprised that their stories still arouse interest, and revealing a trace of enthusiasm about having a listener: that's how we would describe the six Jewish Red Army veterans, including one woman, and one survivor of the Siege of Leningrad who were waiting for us at the interview sites.[1] Many had brought along photos, letters, medals, and official recognitions of achievement. If you're willing to listen to them,[2] they tell their stories, and their voice shatters some of the assumptions on which memories of World War II are based in present-day Germany: above all, the image of the Jew during this time as "eternal victim," passive, helpless, and broken.

For many, this is their second time in Germany. The first time, they told us,

> We were young and came here fighting the 'Nazi Beast'; we were liberators of our own people and others; we opened the gates of the concentration camps, clearing the way for the future. And those of us who never got to set foot on German soil resisted the Nazis in our homeland, survived sieges (Leningrad, Stalingrad), built catacombs and clandestine networks (Odessa), and received the title of war heroes.

And although later they suffered through Stalin's era of terror and anti-Semitism, they were able to maintain their pride: After all, they had

* The authors want to thank Galina Buschkova,Wladimir Georgijenko, Lena Gorelik, Kathleen Luft, Tanja Smolianitsky, and Nadya Yessakova for their help with the interviews, filmed material and the translations.

vanquished the terror of the *nemtsy* – the Russian term for Germans, usually taken to be derived from *nemoĭ*, "dumb" or "mute."

The second time they set foot on this soil, it was to stay. This time they came not as heroes, but within the framework of a legal structure, as *Kontingentflüchtlinge*, or "quota refugees."[3] It is one of history's ironies that a complex political agreement in 1990 allowed Jews from the former Soviet Union to immigrate to Germany. Among them was this group of old men and women who wore on their suits the medals, and bore in their hearts the memories, of a past that was both terrible and glorious.

Our paper seeks to investigate the tensions between identities, history, and memories in this group of Jewish veterans and above all the conflicts these tensions generate in Jewish communities, as well as in the veterans' confrontation with German society and in some of their ways of remembering.[4] This is only a preliminary, qualitative approach based both on interviews and on the observations we made in our years of daily work in Germany's Jewish communities.[5]

Nemtsy, Barbarians: Where is Civilization?

These interviewees are war heroes, and their pride shines forth not only from their medals, but from every face. They consider themselves "invited guests of the German Government," a notion that finds its dissonant point in the dispute that some of them have with a part of the society. When the subject of the treatment of German prisoners of war by the Russian Army comes up during the group interview, Naum, president of the Association of Jewish-Russian War Veterans in Düsseldorf, reacts this way: "Did we invite them, maybe?" in an ironic play of implicit allusions related to his present status in this land and the "reproaches" of some German civil servant.

This interplay of crossed projections exists on many other levels. While a predominant image in German society considers the Russian mindset and culture premodern, based on traditional and hierarchical values,[6] many of these immigrants, who bring with them to Germany an education that is both excellent and cosmopolitan, consider the nemtsy the true "barbarians," although sometimes this image is mixed with one that recognizes classical German culture (Goethe, Schelling, and above all the beloved Heine).

Emigrating implies relinquishing the life and history one has created, one's family and social networks, one's mother language and mindset, a set of codes and conducts. One response to this loss was to create Russian enclaves where people recognize "who's who," and to elevate the Russian culture and language to a superior rank as a way of compensating.[7]

Some of the émigrés, however, have established good relations with their German neighbors. Repeatedly, they emphasize positive features of their life together – a finding that does not agree with the results of other studies.[8] With some Germans, they even talk about the war. Marc, a former officer in the Red Army, told us,

> With my neighbor, for example, we're very good friends and we've talked about the fact that we both fought on opposite fronts, but he's very helpful nevertheless. [...] I do see that there are still people who have a different opinion, but I personally have never had any bad experiences.

The majority reiterate that, as Rosa said, "You shouldn't lump everybody together. Not everybody was a Nazi, and not all Germans are bad." It is a point of view that, curiously, is not shared by many of their children. While those who actually endured those times attempt to see each person as an individual, their children in many cases seem to have a more generalized aversion to what they view as "German." Rosa's son stated, "When I meet someone unfriendly on the street, I always think: this German would have shot me during the war..." The transfer of memory between the generations would seem to generate a specter: Those who either did not directly experience that era or knew it only as children appear to construct a more generalized "enemy" than the old people, who try to differentiate among individuals.

Feinschreiber or on the Rewriting of Identities, Soviet and/or Jewish

All emigration implies readaptation and redefinition of one's identity and history. The arrival in Germany adds a specific complexity: On the one hand, there is a reinforcement of and/or grappling with Jewish identity, which is what makes the visa possible, and at the same time, there is a revival of the memories and traumas of the war. Unlike the Russian Jews who emigrated to Israel, the recent arrivals in Germany are in an upside-down situation. As Jews, they are an absolute minority in German society, but as Russian Jews, they are an absolute majority (about 90%)[9] in Germany's Jewish communities, though they differ profoundly from the long-established communities in their concept of Judaism. Most German Jewish communities define themselves as orthodox, while the Russian newcomers, especially those of the older generations, think of their Judaism as a cultural component.

In old age, the multiple identities of the veterans are activated and deactivated, as these individuals are bearers of a Soviet patriotic legacy and of the traces of a secular Judaism that continued to be transmitted in a culture of the book and a way of understanding the world. This paradoxical identity, not free of conflicts, was indirectly reinforced by the anti-Semitism that lived on in the USSR, where having a surname as beautiful as *Feinschreiber* (the name of the husband of Fanya, one of our interviewees) was punished with the impossibility of being admitted to a university – as was also the case with Fanya's son.

Mosaic or Maccabean Memory?

In the internal field of the Jewish communities in Germany, a mechanism of several memories "in competition" appears to have become established. The narrative of the Jewish soldiers of the Red Army in Germany, though filled with sorrow for the dead, differs tremendously from that of most of the victims who suffered directly under Nazism. The veterans speak of their actions and reactions, whether in the field of combat, medical care, or civil defense. Their words do not reflect the impotence, humiliation, and self-denigration evident in the testimonies of some who survived the camps. Having actively influenced the outcome of the war and having held a military rank put the veterans in a different position from a psychological standpoint.

Naum, the president of a Jewish veterans' association, says that when he proposed to his Jewish community some years ago that they celebrate Victory Day, one leader replied, "But what did the Russians do? The ones who liberated us were the Americans." It is a paradoxical situation, in which the German Jews (somehow in accord with German society) reject the prominent role of the Soviet Army and the idea that in the context of World War II there is something to celebrate. On the contrary, the commemoration traditionally takes place (both in the general public and in the Jewish communities) on November 9, the anniversary of the unleashing of a wave of pogroms: *Kristallnacht*, the *beginning* of the disaster. By remembering the onset of large-scale violence every year, the horror would seem to extend ad infinitum. The veterans, however, celebrate the *ending* and thereby "close" the story and bring closure to the trauma.

The presence of these veterans in the "German" Jewish milieu (the postwar Jewish community was made up almost in its majority of former Displaced Persons, most of them Poles or other Eastern Europeans)[10] revives a past that produces cracks in the community discourse. The Russian veterans break with the Jewish traditional mnemonic community as soon as they start to remember and dramatize other experiences from the war. The conflict derives from the veterans' double affiliation: with *victory* (Russian) and with *victimization* (Jewish), a dual allegiance that is difficult to integrate into the Western Jewish-German community memory.

Thus a competition between memories is set up, a struggle to impose the respective perceptions of the groups. It is a conflict that, as we see it, is not new in the construction of the Jewish narrative, and it refers us to the differences between the Mosaic and Maccabean memories. The traditional story *par excellence* of the Jewish commandment of *zakhor!* (remember!) refers to the Exodus from Egypt.[11] There it is G-d (not man) who plays the leading role, and thus it is that Moses goes almost unmentioned in the Pesach Haggadah. Redemption is not generated by the people, but is bestowed through divine intervention and violence. We remember that "we were slaves" (*Avadim hayinu*, Deuteronomy 6:21), and it is from that status, from impotence and weakness, that we celebrate our liberation. Curiously, the campaign organized by the American Jewish community in the 1960s to press for unrestricted emigration of the Jews from the Soviet Union had this slogan: *shlach na et ami*, "let my people go," the words Moses spoke to Pharaoh in the book of Exodus (8:1).[12]

At the other pole we find the narrative of the Hanukkah celebration, the struggle against Greece and the Hellenized Jews. The Maccabean memory is that of a group of heroes who fought a military rebellion in the second century BCE This memory, however, was later to be blurred by the rabbinic commentaries and turned into a "miracle" story, in which the lights in the reclaimed temple burned for eight days despite the lack of oil. The later rebellions against Rome (66–73 CE and 132–135) left countless dead, but the rabbis, following the same logic, "displaced" this recollection of the armed uprising by favoring concentration of the memory on Pesach and thus on the messianic idea and passive hope for redemption. The decision was a conscious one.[13] As Rosenzweig writes, "We understand the true Jewish ethic only when we realize how many elements that among other peoples found a place in the military ethic have, in this case, sought refuge in the ethic of teaching and learning."[14]

The founders of the State of Israel and later of the *Tzahal* (Israeli Defense Army) merged the Maccabean tradition and the Masada narrative to create a new ritual. According to the account of the historian Josephus Flavius, upon escaping from the siege of Jerusalem in the year 66 (the siege ended in the city's fall in the year 70), the Sicarii held off the Romans for three months and then, with defeat imminent, chose mass suicide over surrender. The contemporary ceremony performed atop Masada culminated in the swearing of the oath that "Masada shall never fall again," *Masada lo tipol shenit*, reaffirming an identification with the model of Jews who were combative and prepared for "martyrdom" to avoid falling into the enemy's hands.[15]

The Jewish veterans of the Red Army (like the partisans, the participants in the Warsaw Ghetto Uprising, and all the other Jewish soldiers who fought in World War II) took up arms and broke with the stereotyped image of the Diaspora Jew found in anti-Semitic caricatures, effeminate and intellectual, *always expecting* an exodus or a miracle: in these Jewish groups the Maccabean memory prevailed.

"Metabolizing" Memory: *fun dor tsu dor*

Although, after the Shoah, the story of the concentration camps was integrated in different ways into many Pesach Haggadot, where we read that "we were not only in Egypt but also in Auschwitz,"[16] the Russian Jews always preserved this memory on May 9, in remembrance of the military victory, not of the "miracle of liberation." Some wearing their medals, the veterans get together at the proper time to commemorate this date. Many Jewish communities feel uncomfortable with this even today, and some go so far as to refuse them a place for the celebration. The gulf between the memories is wide; the official discourse of the Judeo-German community has not incorporated, and finds it difficult to incorporate, the concept of self-defense as a structuring element.

It doesn't matter. The veterans celebrate their victory, building a bridge that links their beloved dead with their grandchildren. The interesting thing is that their way of incorporating the recollection resembles a Pesach Seder[17] and accords with Jewish law: the *literal incorporation* of the memory. *By eating the words.*[18] Marc says, "We meet in the Community Center, a lot of people come. We drink vodka in memory of the dead. And then we make *kasha*, that's a kind of porridge, because we always had that to eat during the war." The times are long past, in the waning years of the nineteenth century, when a popular Jewish song in Yiddish made the rounds in Russia:

> Oy, av haRachamim, shoychen bamrymim
> Du bist a foter iber alle yesomim.
> Beser tsu lernen chumash mit Rashi
> *Eyder tsu esn di soldatske kashe.*[19]
>
> (O G-d of Mercy, who livest in the heavens
> You are the father of all the orphans.
> Better to study Bible and Rashi
> Than to eat the soldier's mush.)[20]

In a celebration in the context of a Jewish community, the vodka could replace the wine, the kasha, perhaps, the matzoh, but the meaning is the same: the incorporation of the memory in one's body, the "metabolism" of the memory. Owing to a linguistic caprice that may resound in the memories of some of our interviewees, *kashe*, the Yiddish name of the Russian porridge, sounds identical to the word for "question" in the phrase for the Four Questions (*di fir kashes*) of the Passover Seder – there are even jokes in Yiddish about it. These questions are the ones traditionally asked by the youngest child on the night of the Seder; they are the opening words for the story of the Exodus, through which we learn "Why is this night different from all other nights?" and the commandment to remember the enslavement, the defeat of the Pharaoh, and the wonder of freedom.

Here a place opens for resignification and negotiation of meanings and rituals between both memories. Although controversial, it opens up the possibility of "readapting" the narratives of the trauma. For the veterans, it has to do with creating a new experience of remembering that transforms the memory itself, since it incorporates the Jewish element, which – previously denied or sublimated – emerges basically in the *present tense*. The particularity of Jewish suffering in the Shoah was a topic that the Soviet leadership denied, and it can be recovered in the new Jewish community environment.[21]

In a valuable attempt to integrate the Red Army veterans into the Jewish narrative, a rabbi from a major Jewish community (Düsseldorf) says in his speech at the 2006 ceremony commemorating the sixty-first anniversary of the war's end, "This day should be a day of celebration in the Jewish calendar." Thus he includes them also in the tradition of Jewish fighters (encompassing the Jewish rebellion against Rome in 66 B.C.E., which brought about the second exile) and classifies the date as a "victory of survival," after which he recites *El Maleh Rachamim* ("O G-d full of compassion," the prayer for the soul of the departed at a funeral and on the occasion of a *yahrzeit*, as well as the traditional memorial prayer for the victims of the Holocaust), and says the mourner's Kaddish for the dead Red Army Jewish soldiers, thereby offering the veterans a feeling of belonging that unifies both experiences of the war.[22] While their memory thus is "Judaized," the veterans offer something to the communities as well; they offer to "heroize" their memory to some extent by inviting them to participate in the victory. The Exodus and the struggle of the Maccabees: Both have their place in the Jewish narrative.

Will the communities also manage to let the memories complement one another, instead of continuing to fight one other?

It has to do first and foremost, as in the Pesach Seder, with passing down the memory to the youngest ones. *Fun dor tsu dor*, from generation to generation. Most of our interviewees stated that they participate actively in the "mission" of passing their experiences along to future generations. Then it is not only that, as written in the Pesach Haggadah, "Every person, in every generation, should feel as if he had been liberated from Egypt," but also that, simultaneously, "Every person, in every generation, should feel as if he had liberated Auschwitz."

The (In)difference of German Society

This restructuring of memories, moreover, is taking place in Germany, where May 8 (9) is neither celebrated nor commemorated, but where World War II and the Shoah are omnipresent topics.[23] The ritual, then, will occur *in private*, almost with embarrassment. It will occur in an environment in which the Red Army has, at least for part of society, negative connotations – an idea that was reinforced in the last few years by the associations of German post-war expellees (*Vertriebene*). It is an environment in which even nowadays the majority of the dialogues refer to the occupation (*Besatzung*), rather than to the liberation (*Befreiung*), of Germany.

Nevertheless, there is a desire to convey *to the public* the lessons of their hard experiences. There is a memory they also would like to leave for German children, because, as they all reiterate, "You can't make distinctions between children. They aren't responsible for what their grandparents did. But they ought to know what happened" (Marc and Rosa). It is a matter of bearing witness. In Germany there are several clubs of Jewish veterans. One of them, the Stuttgart club, with the full support of the local Jewish community, published a book of these memories. That book was awarded a Yad Vashem prize, and last February the German translation of the volume appeared.[24]

But is anybody listening? Mark tells us that he already has visited the Jewish communities several times to tell the children about his experiences. "The children all paid close attention, and they were very interested in the medals." In 2006, students in Berlin did a project in which they interviewed their Russian grandparents and friends and used the material to create an exhibition called "Zwischen Sowjetstern und Judenstern" (Between the Red Star and the Star of David), which was shown in Berlin's Centrum Judaicum in 2007 but had a low impact outside the community area – and met with little interest from the press or other mass media.[25]

As for the German schools, on the other hand, "they suggested it to me, but so far no invitation has been forthcoming," reports Marc. The invitations sent by the veterans are mostly not paid attention to by either German society or German politicians. Nobody bridges the gulf: "We always invite the government officials from Stuttgart to our celebrations in the community, but they don't come." It would seem that some official memories of German society also do not tolerate an image of Jews who are combative and victorious, not merely victims to whom pity is due.

Such deafness or denial[26] contrasts with the tactfulness shown by this Red Army officer toward the memory of the war. On his way to the festivities in the Community Center, he says, "I wouldn't want to wear my medals on the street, because the Germans lost people in the war too, and you shouldn't challenge these feelings."

Levinas' "Glance of the Other": Fragility

This sensitivity to the other person's grief and suffering is something that Marc, a doctor and music lover ("in all the shooting I only listened to symphonies"), reveals throughout the interview. It begins with a story that opens and closes his "memory" about the Germans:

> In my town, Kharkov, after the victory, I saw a camp of German prisoners. Before that I had viewed them only *en masse* as enemies, but for the first time I saw them as human beings. They were digging in the garbage, looking for food, and I saw their eyes: hunger, fear. I brought them canned goods. On the second day I went back there and they were waiting for me, and I gave them more food. The third day I

> didn't go back again, because I was being followed by Russians, since they were afraid that I was a spy. I had to think about this experience before I emigrated, to keep in mind that not all Germans were powerful murderers.

A narrative like this one incorporates an image of the Germans as conquered, hungry, broken. It puts an end to the fascination of power. The Nazi, envisioned as always victorious, with his highly polished boots, turns into a poor wretch. Will the pedagogical discourses of German society, on which the education of the new generation is based, accept an account like this one? Can German society hear these voices and include these testimonies in the narratives of the past?

Breaking the Siege

Most of our interviewees are physicians. Two scenes stick in our mind: Marc drinking coffee with his German neighbor and healing, with words, the wounds in their memories that both men bear from their days on opposing sides at the front. Fanya taking the blood pressure of all the elderly neighbors in the building who need it, taking the pulse of German memory with the Soviet instruments she brought with her to her subsidized housing in Duisburg.

Both are breaking the siege of this memory in their daily life. But they cannot make the final breakthrough alone. To "break the siege" of the suppression of this memory in German society means to be willing to listen to these stories, which surely will deconstruct some of the basic assumptions of the German national narrative concerning World War II, and of the German-Jewish narratives about the Shoah, by incorporating voices as wide-ranging as those of the people who have been, in the same life, both conquerors and refugees in the same foreign country.

Endnotes

1 Our interviewees are members of the Jewish communities in which we work (Duisburg, Düsseldorf, Stuttgart). Six were combatants in the Red Army (Marc was an officer, Mr. F. was deputy commander of a Katyusha division), and one (Rosa) survived the Siege of Leningrad as a textile factory worker. The interviews were held during August 2006: three as individual conversations (Fanya, Rosa, Marc) in the interviewees' homes and one as a group interview in the Jewish community center of Duisburg and Düsseldorf. The material is in taped form, and for this article parts of the interviews were transcribed – these transcriptions remain unpublished.

2 On hearing witnesses to the traumas of World War II, see Laub 2000.

3 Act on Measures in Aid of Refugees Admitted under Humanitarian Relief Programs (Gesetz über Maßnahmen für im Rahmen humanitärer Hilfsaktionen aufgenommene Flüchtlinge), April 12, 1990.

4 On the phenomenon of the veterans from the standpoint of their memories of World War II and the Shoah, focusing on the account and subjective experiences of the prewar period, the war itself, and the post-war years, see Gitelman 2001.

5 Our remarks are confined to communities in the FRG, since the intersection of history and memories with the political culture of the communities located in the former GDR would have to take into account other variables that exceed the scope of our study.

6 See Gladilina 2004, 174.

7 Our data agree on this point with those already cited by other authors, such as Jasper 2004, 137.

8 In a 1999 study, 70 percent of the Jewish immigrants interviewed reported predominantly negative experiences in dealing with Germans. (Jasper 2004, 146).

9 According to the official statistics of the ZWST (Zentralwohlfahrtstelle der Juden in Deutschland/Central Welfare Agency for Jews in Germany) for the year 2005, of the 107,677 members of the Jewish community, 97,700 were immigrants from the former Soviet Union. ZWST membership statistics as of January 1, 2006.

10 "The Jewish community was made up (until 1991; *Authors' Note*) mainly of Polish, Romanian, Czech, and Hungarian Jews, who came to Germany after 1945 to enter refugee camps or found themselves stranded there after emerging from the labor, concentration, and death camps of Eastern Europe. They belong to a Jewish tradition different from that of the German Jews, who today account for about 10 percent of the membership of the community." See Schoeps 1992, 354.

11 On the commandment of *Zakhor*, as well as the relationships between history and Jewish memory, see Yerushalmi 1982 and the critique by Funkelstein 1995. On memory, forgetting, and Judaism, see Yerushalmi et al. 1988.

12 In *Let My People Go: Three Studies on Jewish Emigration from the Soviet Union*, the author summarizes the origins of this movement. See Korey 2001, 185–6. Further, as part of its revitalization plan, the Diaspora Museum in Tel Aviv is marking the fortieth anniversary of the Soviet Jewish movement with a unique exhibition titled "Jews of Struggle: The Jewish National Movement in the USSR, 1967–1989," Dina Kraft 2007.

13 On this displacement of memories concerning Hanukkah, see Levinas 1995.

14 Note from the diary of Franz Rosenzweig, quoted in Weber 1997, 157.

15 For a critique of this narrative and the persistence of the myth, see Ben-Yehuda 1995.

16 The *Haggadah of Pesach* is the account that traditionally is read during the Passover celebration; it deals with the liberation from slavery in Egypt. Traditionally, *Haggadot* have a fixed core, but different editions add songs and stories that "complement" the original with local customs. The account of the concentration camps has been included in many of them since post-war times.

17 *Pesach Seder*: ritual feast held at Passover to remember the Exodus from Egypt and liberation from slavery.

18 In this regard, see the interesting psychoanalytical interpretation by Haddad 2005, Chapter 1.

19 Our emphasis (L.F., L.F.).

20 Quoted in Roskies 1999, 6.

21 Nina Tumarkin asks: "Did antisemitism [...] explain the malignant silence about the Holocaust? Yes and no: ...But I believe that in this case the main explanatory factor has to do with the psychological economy of suffering: from the point of view of Soviet historiography, the German had meted out to all the Soviet peoples a horrible fate: to have granted to the Jewish people an equal or even (in terms of his logic) higher status in the pecking order of martyred nationalities would have vitiated somewhat the Soviet claims on behalf of their own victimization, and was therefore impermissible." Tumarkin 1994, 50.

22 Source: Documental video of Wladimir Georgijenko.

23 "Remembering is not so much a matter of calling up an internal image, stored in the mind, as of engaging perceptually with an environment that is itself pregnant with the past." Tim Ingold, *The Perception of the Environment. Essays in Livelihood, Dwelling and Skill*, London and NY, Routledge, 2000. Cited in Cappeletto 2005, 8.

24 Klub Veteranov Vtoroy Mirovoy Voiny [World War II Veterans' Club] 2006, *Zhivaya Pamiat* [Living Memory]. Stuttgart.

25 The exhibition was organized by students of four schools of different religious orientations: Canisius-Kolleg, Jüdische Oberschule, Evangelisches Gymnasium zum Grauen Kloster, and Gottfried-Keller-Gymnasium, so that Jewish and non-Jewish students took part in it. They interviewed 13 veterans of the Red Army.

26 On the historical "deafness" of some pedagogical discourses (above all the discourses of school texts) about World War II concerning the Jewish and gypsy voices, see Kolinsky 1992, Schweiger 1998, Leo Baeck Institut 2003, Feierstein 2008 and in print.

References

Ben-Yehuda, Nachman (1995), *The Masada Myth: Collective Memory and Mythmaking in Israel*. Madison, University of Wisconsin Press.

Cappelletto, Francesca (2005), *Memory and World War II: An Ethnographic Approach*. Oxford, Berg Publishers.

Feierstein, Liliana Ruth (2008), Die Reise nach Jerusalem. Darstellungen von Juden, Judentum und Israel in deutschen Schulbüchern. *Text und Kritik*, Summer 2008, 103–114.

Feierstein, Liliana Ruth (in print): Von Schwelle zu Schwelle. Randgänge(r) der Moderne.

Funkelstein, Amos (1995), *Jüdische Geschichte und ihre Deutungen*. Frankfurt, Suhrkamp.

Gitelman, Zvi (2001), Internationalism, Patriotism and Disillusion: Soviet Jewish Veterans Remember World War II and the Holocaust. In Roth, John K. and Maxwell, Elisabeth (eds.), *Remembering for the Future. The Holocaust in the Era of Genocide*, Vol. 3. Hampshire, Palgrave, 296–308.

Gladilina, Natalya, and Brovkine,Vadim (2004), Sprache und Identität. In Schoeps, Julius H., Grözinger, Karl E., Jasper, Willi, and Mattenklott, Gert (eds.), *Russische Juden und transnationale Diaspora*. Menora 15: Jahrbuch für deutsch-jüdische Geschichte. Potsdam, Philo Verlagsgesellschaft, 151–185.

Haddad, Gerard (2005), *Manger le Livre: Rites alimentaires et function paternelle*. Paris, Pluriel.

Jasper, Willi (2004), Transnationalismus. In Schoeps, Julius H., Grözinger, Karl E., Jasper, Willi, and Mattenklott, Gert (eds.), *Russische Juden und internationale Diaspora*. Menora 15: Jahrbuch für deutsch-jüdische Geschichte. Potsdam, Philo Verlagsgesellschaft, 137–146.

Josephus, Flavius (1994), *The Jewish Wars*. London, Penguin Editions.

Korey, Wiliam (2001), Let My People Go: Three Studies on Jewish Emigration from the Soviet Union. People of the City. Jews and the Urban Challenge. *Studies in Contemporary Jewry*, Vol. XV, 185–192.

Kraft, Dina (2007), *Soviet Jewry struggle goes on display* Article from the JTA (Jewish Telegraphic Agency), 10/30/2007.

Kolinsky, Eva (1992), Remembering Auschwitz: a survey of recent Textbooks for the Teaching of History in German Schools. In *Yad Vashem Studies* 22, 288–310.

Laub, Dori (2000), Zeugnis ablegen oder die Schwierigkeit des Zuhörens. In Ulrich Bauer (ed.), *Niemand zeugt für den Zeugen. Erinnerungskultur nach der Shoah*. Frankfurt, Suhrkamp, 68–83.

Roskies, David G. (1999), *The Jewish Search for a Usable Past*. Bloomington, Indiana University Press.

Leo Baeck Institut (2003), *Deutsch-jüdische Geschichte im Unterricht: Orientierungshilfe für Lehrplan- und Schulbucharbeit sowie Lehrerbildung und Lehrerfortbildung*. Frankfurt.

Levinas, Emmanuel (1972), *Humanisme de l'autre homme*. Montpellier, fata morgana.

Levinas, Emmanuel (1995), The Light and the Dark. In Levinas, Emmanuel, *Difficult Freedom. Essays on Judaism*. Baltimore, John Hopkins University Press.

Schoeps, Julius H. (1992), Jüdisches Leben in Nachkriegsdeutschland. In Nachama, Andreas, Schoeps, Julius H., and van Voolen, Edward, *Jüdische Lebenswelten*. Frankfurt am Main, Suhrkamp Verlag.

Schweiger, Egon (1998), Zur Darstellung und Wahrnehmung der Geschichte und Gegenwart der Sinti und Roma in den Schulbüchern. In: Landeszentrale für politische Bildung BW (Hrg.), *Zwischen Romantisierung und Rassismus. Sinti und Roma - 600 Jahre in Deutschland*. Bonn.

Tumarkin, Nina (1994), *The Living and the Dead*. New York, Basic Books.

Weber, Elisabeth (1997), Denkmäler. Krypten. Zur deutsch-jüdischen Geschichte nach 1918. In Weber, Elisabeth and Tholen, Georg Christoph (eds.), *Das Vergessen(e). Anamnesen des Undarstellbaren*. Vienna, Turia+Kant.

Wolfe, Thomas C. (2006), Past as Present, Myth, or History? Discourses of Time and the Great Fatherland War. In Lebow, Richard Ned, Kansteiner, Wulf, and Fogu, Claudio (eds.), *The Politics of Memory in Postwar Europe*. Durham, Duke University Press, 249–283.

Yerushalmi, Yosef Hayim (1982), *Zakhor! Jewish History and Jewish Memory*. Washington, University of Washington Press.

Yerushalmi, Yosef Hayim et al. (1988), *Usages de l'Oubli*. Paris, Editions du Seuil.

ZWST (2006), Mitgliederstatistik der einzelnen jüdischen Gemeinden und Landesverbände in Deutschland per 1. Januar 2006. Frankfurt am Main, ZWST e.V.

Media of Memory

Robin Ostow

From Memory to History: Displaying World War II in the German Historical Museum

In 1983, then Chancellor Helmut Kohl announced his plans to build a German national museum. It was to be located in what was then West Berlin, to honor the city's 750th anniversary in 1987. The museum was intended, among other things, as a response to the Museum for German History established in East Berlin by the Socialist Unity Party of the German Democratic Republic. It was also part of Kohl's vision of overcoming the division of Germany and integrating Germany into a unifying Europe.

Kohl's preoccupation with German history and its display[1] can be traced to the late 1970s when both Cold War Germanies began to publicly reappropriate German history, rehabilitating national figures such as Martin Luther, Frederick the Great, and Otto von Bismarck, among others. In 1986, this engagement with history and the tensions that grew out of it crystallized in West Germany's Historians' Controversy (*Historikerstreit*) over whether National Socialism, and specifically the Holocaust against the Jews of Europe, should be understood as a unique result of German history, or rather, as a defensive reaction against the crimes of Bolshevism in the East.[2] The intense public discussion and debates around the planned museum – which Kohl referred to as a "gift to the Germans" (albeit without specifying which ones) – took place against this background.[3] The Christian Democratic government's sponsorship of the project caused concern that, in this museum, the CDU version of German history would be written in concrete. Specifically, many Germans feared that the plan for the museum to display the longer course of German history, from its beginnings through 1945, was a strategy to dispose of the need to deal with Germany's Nazi past.[4] Critics referred to it as a "Chancellor museum" and as a "propaganda shack."[5] Meuschel[6] pointed to the growing lack of confidence in the CDU's economic and social programs in the mid 1980s, and to the regime's inability to respond to the Peace and Environmental movements and the Green party, among other forces. In this context, she saw the museum as part of a policy of encouraging Germans to reconnect with their longer history and to focus on their Germanness as a distraction to avert a crisis of legitimacy of the federal government.

The German Historical Museum was formally established by the federal government and the state (*Land*) of Berlin in 1987. By this time, the word 'national' had been dropped from the name, to allay fears of a nationalist agenda around the museum.[7] Two years later, a design by architect Aldo Rossi was selected, and the cornerstone was laid on a plot of land near the Berlin Wall, which, in the 1940s, had been designated for a "*palais*" for the *Führer*. After the collapse of the German Democratic Republic in 1989 and German reunification a year later, the (East German) Museum for German History was closed. Its staff of GDR curators and historians was dismissed, and the German Historical Museum set aside Rossi's design, and took over the East German museum's collection and its building on *Unter den Linden*. The structure, called the *Zeughaus*, or armoury, had served as a weapons depot and museum for successive German states.[8] It is the oldest building on Berlin's traditional representative boulevard (and parade route). Its foundation was laid in 1695, and construction was completed in 1730. By the late 18th century, the *Zeughaus* had become the largest arms depot in Brandenburg-Prussia. In the 19th century, it morphed into a museum of Prussian, and, after 1871, German history. Its extensive collection was based on military objects (some brought in from other armories) and the spoils of war.[9]

The *Zeughaus* was taken over by the *Wehrmacht* (Hitler's army) in 1939, and integrated into the Nazis' war propaganda effort. Trophies from the invasions of France and Poland were put on display, and Nazi ceremonies were staged regularly in the covered courtyard until 1944–5, when the building was badly damaged by bombs and grenades. The museum was closed by the Allied forces in 1945, but it was restored by the East German government between 1948 and 1965. Already in 1952, the building was reopened by the Socialist Unity Party as the Museum for German History. Its permanent exhibit displayed the history of the workers' movement, its rise to power and the realization of its vision in the GDR.

The German Historical Museum now occupies one of the most splendid buildings in the capital of reunified Germany,[10] a stone's throw from the *Reichstag* (Parliament), and from the city's Museum Island. In this authentic site, with a glorious and burdened history of its own, the GHM is exhibiting Germany's history, including its cultural achievements, some of which are embodied in the building, its opulent dimensions and exquisite architecture. At the same time, though, the museum must distance the current German state – often referred to as the 'Berlin Republic'to distinguish it from the Cold War Federal Republic of Germany – from the military values that the *Zeughaus* has traditionally represented, and from the building's Nazi past.[11]

The structure of the German Historical Museum's permanent exhibit which opened in June, 2006, was laid out by a committee of German historians and museum specialists. The display was organized by the museum's founding director, Christoph Stölzl, a curator close to the CDU and his successor, Hans Ottomayer. The resulting exhibit responds to the Historians' Controversy by situating National Socialism within German history. But it also represents a reaction to the developments in the writing and displaying of German history which characterized the last two decades of the 20th century. History writing in this period was shaped by the concerns and the politics that grew out of the student movement of the late 1960s; it was dominated by local histories, workers' histories, oral and biographical histories. These studies produced accounts that foregrounded the diversity of German experiences, and that gave expression to subaltern voices, and to memories. Much of the focus was on the Nazi regime, its genocide against the Jews of Europe and the need to remember and to learn from these crimes.

By contrast, the German Historical Museum offers the public a centralized, comprehensive, top-down narrative of two thousand years of German history, from the Roman times to 1994.[12] Since most European countries begin their national histories in the Middle Ages, Germany's history, as exhibited in the GHM, is twice as long as the histories of its neighbors. And this long course of history is displayed with 8,100 objects in an area of 8,000 square meters. Due to the evolution and nature of the collection in the *Zeughaus*, a large part of the display is military and aristocratic history.

The GHM's display of World War II is part of this permanent exhibit. The section, called "1933–45: NS Regime and Second World War," is allotted approximately one sixth of the entire exhibition space. Like the rest of the larger display, it is framed by the political debates and historiographical trends of the end of the Cold War, and by the history of the *Zeughaus*. And it is surrounded by the narratives of this war showcased at several other sites in and around Berlin – The Allied Museum in Zehlendorf, The German-Russian Museum Berlin-Karlshorst, The Jewish Museum Berlin in Kreuzberg, the Memorial to the Murdered Jews of Europe, the Topography of Terror, the exhibits at the Plötzensee Prison, the Stauffenberg Memorial, and other memorials, as well. In this rich World War II exhibit and memorial landscape, the German Historical Museum's exhibit represents a German point of view, and provides a comprehensive account of the war as a part of German history. In the words of the guide book,

> A great deal of space is devoted to the darkest period in German history – the twelve years of National Socialist dictatorship. The GHM is currently the only museum in Germany able to provide a broad overview of the political and military history, as well as of the mechanisms and crimes, of the National Socialist state.[13]

World War II, then, is presented at the GHM as history, as events that have been carefully evaluated and reconstituted for the public by experts, not as memories of individuals or groups. The major characteristics and events of the war are related in blocks of text inscribed on pillars – which the museum calls *Meilensteinen*, or milestones – stationed at regular intervals on the main route through the display. The voice of this text is anonymous, distant and omniscient. The language is formal, factual, and unemotional. One excerpt reads: "*Hate and Stigmatization*: The responsibility of the Jews for the war was constantly emphasized [...]The defamation was followed by public stigmatization of Jews from September 1941 on."

The war experiences of individuals are displayed through (usually small) objects – items of daily life, photos, scrapbooks, paintings, and diaries, which are encased in vitrines, and, in this way, distanced from the viewers. Blown up photos, facsimiles and talking heads on tv monitors are deployed sparingly. Computer monitors for accessing data banks and drawers containing facsimiles of documents are built discretely into rear parts of the vitrines, so as not to interfere with the visual effects of the display. In contrast to the displays of World War II in, for example, the Canadian War Museum in Ottawa, The U.S. Holocaust Memorial Museum in Washington D.C., and the Imperial War Museum in London, the exhibit at the GHM has no repainted bombers, no dioramas, no trenches or cattle cars for visitors to enter, and no special effects. It is mostly visual, there's very little sound: the *Frankfurter Allgemeine Zeitung*[14] called it a "Guck-Museum," or museum for looking.

Stölzl's concept was to build the permanent exhibit around carefully chosen, history-bearing objects that he called *Zeitzeugnisse*, or witnesses to history. Most of these objects are authentic and engaging. For example, the end result for Germany and the global import of World War II are dramatized for visitors by a large plexiglass vitrine, situated in the middle of wide open space, containing Hitler's own globe with a (Russian) bullet shot through Berlin. The exhibit of the war begins and ends with grainy newsreels projected over the entrance and exit. As s/he enters the war section, the visitor views newsreel footage of German soldiers lifting up the border gate and crossing into Poland. The exhibit of the war is organized along a fishbone structure. The large course of the war is explained and displayed in the center aisle. To the left, parallel paths lead visitors though installations representing the various aspects of the domestic experience: daily life in wartime Germany; war heroes; the euphoria of Vichy; the allied air raids; foreign workers; workers from the East and forced labor; POWs; total war; the defeat. To the right, parallel paths follow the foreign campaigns, the "war of conquest and annihilation" (*Eroberungs- und Vernichtungskrieg*): the invasion of Poland; the persecution of Jews; the occupation of Norway and Denmark; the war in Western Europe; the war in the Far East; the war in Africa; the war against Britain; the war against Yugoslavia; the general plan East; the war of annihilation against the USSR; Operation Barbarossa; the National Socialist genocide; the advance of the Red Army; flight of the civilian population, and the final defeat.

In his review of the permanent exhibit for *Die Zeit,*[15] Thomas Assheuer notes that, in this section of the permanent exhibit, the somber grey color of the walls suggests a military installation, and effects a change in mood from the museum's display of earlier, more glorious centuries in halls painted in warm, pastel hues. On the left side, the succession of paths is interrupted by a small theater in which newsreels of the beginning and end of the war from the German, British, American, Polish and Russian news services are looped – in the original languages with subtitles in German. This installation is dramatic, loud and polyvocal, breaking the silence and the German war narrative.

The horrors of this war are carefully calibrated for a diverse public. As the visitor follows the fishbone paths leading through the foreign campaigns, the images become more violent. The most difficult material is far back, and often has to be selected on computer screens or sought in drawers built into the vitrines. This layout enables visitors to maintain their own comfort level, as they walk through the exhibit of a succession of gruesome battles and occupations. The Holocaust section is found in the very back corner, towards the end. As Christian Esch[16] points out, it can't be seen from the main route through the war display. No signs point the way, and it is easy to pass it by. It consists largely of text, photos, the oil painting Self Portrait in Hiding, by the Jewish artist Felix Nussbaum (who died in Auschwitz in 1944) and films.

The major Holocaust installation is the wood and plaster model of Crematorium II at Auschwitz, Birkenau, by the Polish sculptor Mieczyslaw Stobierski (1914–98). The original of this model, with 3,000 figures of victims in the process of being gassed, was created in 1947 for the memorial at Auschwitz. Copies were then made for the U.S. Holocaust Memorial Museum, Yad Vashem, and the GHM. White, devoid of sounds or smells, and in miniature, it is something of a ghost. Directly in front of this model, are items from the camp – a can of Zyklon B next to a booklet with instructions on how to use it, a fork, a spoon. Facing it on one side is a vitrine with photos and biographies of individual inmates. On the other side, film footage of the liberation of Auschwitz is projected against a screen. This installation serves as a kind of internal Holocaust memorial, what van Alphen[17] calls a "Holocaust effect," "a confrontation with Nazism or with the Holocaust by means of a re-enactment," in this case, within the realm of art. A Holocaust effect brings the viewer directly into contact with the Holocaust, or some aspect of it, rather than casting her/him as a passive addressee of a narrator.

In the GHM, the wartime role of the *Zeughaus* is quietly acknowledged through the display of three original small photos depicting "the exhibit of booty from Poland in the atrium" (1939), "the exhibit of booty from France in the atrium" (1940) and "the induction of soldiers in the *Zeughaus*" (1941). Particularly striking, although World War II is most often remembered and narrated around larger-than-life leaders – Hitler, Mussolini, Stauffenberg, Eisenhower, Shukow, Truman and Churchill, among many others – the role of individual leaders and the identification of individual heroes and villains is minimized in this exhibit. The defense of Germany against enemy attacks is represented by a large anti-aircraft gun placed in the back, in an open space behind the vitrines. One aisle in the domestic area displays photos of men who were designated as heroes by the Nazi regime. These images of Aryan men of different ages and social classes illustrate the kinds of men who could become heroes. So many names and faces are exhibited, that no one stands out. The Nazis' appropriation of the concept "hero" seems to preclude its use in Germany for representing that era today. By contrast, the DHM's display of earlier centuries includes considerable text and multiple images of figures such as Charlemagne, Martin Luther, Napoleon, Otto von Bismarck, and others, as well.

Even the German resistance is downplayed. The text of the subsection called "The Fragmented Resistance" explains:

> only a comparatively small minority opposed the totalitarian demands made by National Socialist ideology and their brutal implementation. This resistance against the NS regime was carried out by various groups and individuals for political, religious and ethical reasons. However, a unified resistance movement did not form from these isolated groupings.

This display features the groups around Count Stauffenberg, the Scholl siblings and others: the only Jewish resistance group within Germany, the Herbert Baum group, appears in a small photo in the lowest row of the display.[18]

The exhibit of the war ends with film footage of the allied bombing of German cities projected against the wall on the left, followed by photos of the flight from Danzig. A 3.5-minute film clip of the battle for Berlin is looped on a tv monitor on the right, and on the wall marking the exit hangs a copy of Jewgeny Chaldej's iconic photo of soldiers of the Red Army mounting the Soviet flag on the burning *Reichstag*.[19] Grainy newsreel footage of Wilhelm Keitel signing Germany's unconditional surrender in Berlin is projected over the exit. The text, on the wall, to the left reads:

> On 4 May 1945, German troops surrendered in Denmark, northwestern Germany and the Netherlands. On behalf of the supreme command, Colonel Alfred Jodl signed the unconditional surrender of all military forces on the morning of 7 May 1945 in the Allied headquarters in Reims, France.
>
> To honour the contribution of the Red Army in liberating Europe from the NS regime, the surrender was repeated in Berlin-Karlshorst at Stalin's request. There, high-ranking German military officials signed the capitulation document on the night of 8 to 9 May shortly after midnight.

Walking through this exhibit, the visitor must negotiate the contrast between the very powerful display objects and the impersonal, emotionless text which categorizes and clarifies the displays, but refrains from introducing meanings that would make the exhibit a story. The subtitle of Assheuer's review of the entire permanent exhibit sums it up: "history becomes an event of nature." In his words; "The exhibit is discrete, conventional and – informative. It is cool to the point of being devoid of history, and sterile, to the point of being a provocation" (my translation, RO).[20] One installation which captures this tone is a vitrine which serves as a closet with seven different Nazi uniforms on hangers. The uniforms are clean, and hung in an orderly way; but there are no people in them, and they're not presented against a background of meaningful action. They hang in an enclosed empty space.

To this viewer, the DHM's exhibit of World War II is, most of all, encyclopedic. It's comprehensive, it's clear, and all the objects and events are sorted into their proper categories – to the point of making this war seem like an orderly event, obfuscating the chaos it created and became.

The energy in the creation of this exhibit seems to have gone into collecting engaging objects; into organizing the representation of the war along its many, discrete dimensions; into ensuring its completeness and political correctness; and into maintaining a distance between the visitor and the displays. Baudrillard related collecting, displaying and ordering to the need to bring a sense of order to the chaos of history.[21] And in the GHM especially, these activities represent ways of coming to terms with this terrible war and genocide – a process that the Germans call *Vergangenheitsbewältigung*, or "mastering the past."

Anderson[22] identified museums as major sites of nation building. In museums, states display themselves as guardians of the national treasure and the national history. Hajdarpasic[23] describes how the current weakness of Bosnia's government is reflected in its inability to properly care for and exhibit the historical and artistic works in the Bosnian National Museum in Sarajevo. And Crooke[24] explains how the reluctance of Northern Ireland's national museums to display the "Troubles" has led to the devolution of this work to local museums and community centers which represent the issues and events of this conflict from local points of view. Referring to Germany's recent reunification, the GHM's current General Director, Hans Ottomayer, writes: "In the twenty-first century, it is clear that a new beginning is hardly possible without explaining and provisionally dealing with the horror and trauma of the last century with clarity and historical distance."[25] The German Historical Museum has succeeded in exhibiting German national treasures, and clarifying major events and personalities from its past. Opening this museum with German money and with a completely German team of historians, curators and designers is, among other things, an act of sovereignty.

Like the larger permanent exhibit around it, the GHM's display of World War II identifies, displays and categorizes the major events of this conflict comprehensively and correctly. That is Kohl's gift to the (now reunified) German people. But it fails to represent this central trauma of the 20th century as a story. Esch[26] sees this failure as characterizing the entire permanent exhibit. He points out that the two postwar Germanies had master narratives which shaped their histories. In the GDR, it was the road to Socialism, and in the old Federal Republic, it was the way to the West. But, he argues, in the GHM, there is no master narrative. The passion for history – for the deeds and sufferings of people – has been replaced by a passion for beautiful objects. Chakrabarty[27] points out that the musealization of historical objects usually follows and depends on the chaos, destruction and plunder of war, though this relation is rarely acknowledged.

This author would add to Esch's and Chakrabarty's observations, that the GHM's preoccupation with historical and artistic objects also reflects the Berlin Republic's definition of itself as a *Kulturnation*, a 21st century nation held together by a shared culture, as opposed to a shared religion or race. But, in the long run, to bind Germany's inhabitants to each other and to their state, authentic and thought-provoking objects must be anchored in an engaging narrative, a history which they display, refract and (optimally) interrogate. In the German Historical Museum's permanent exhibit, and particularly in the display of World War II, the story which would lend meaning to the display objects, to the enormous destruction and to the suffering and murder of so many people remains to be told.

Endnotes

1 Helmut Kohl studied history before he entered politics. He also established the House of the History of the Federal Republic of Germany (*Haus der Geschichte der Bundesrepublik Deutschland*), a popular museum of postwar German history, which opened in Bonn in 1994.
2 For a thorough documentation of the *Historikerstreit*, see Augstein et al. 1987, and Kühnl 1987.
3 Ehmann 1987, 9; Kurze 1997.
4 Ehmann 1987.
5 *Der Tagesspiegel*, June 2, 2006, 25.
6 Meuschel 1988.
7 *Der Tagesspiegel*, May 30, 2006, 25.
8 For a history of the building, see Kretzschmar 2006.
9 For the relation between museums and plunder, see Chakrabarty 2005.
10 Kurze (1997, 2), notes that, from 1945 to 1989, architecture in the FRG tended to be simple and modest, but in 1990, German reunification brought a return to pretentious representative architecture.
11 The Latin inscription over the main door to the *Zeughaus* reads (in translation) "To honour military actions, to intimidate the enemy, to protect the peoples and confederates, the noble and undefeated King of Prussia Frederick I had this armoury built in the year 1706 as a sanctuary for all weapons of war as well as for the spoils of war and trophies,"

Kretszschmar 2006, 72. On the problem most western military museums have today, of both renouncing militarism and providing comfort and paying respect to the war dead, see Greenberg 2007.

12 This represents a change from the original plan to have the exhibit end with the year 1945.

13 Koschnick 2006, 8.

14 *Frankfurter Allgemeine Zeitung*, May 29, 2006.

15 Die Zeit, June 8, 2006.

16 *Berliner Zeitung*, June 2, 2006, 25.

17 van Alpen 1997.

18 This group was largely ignored in Cold War West Germany because it was Communist. In the GDR, it was remembered, but the fact that it was Jewish was airbrushed out until the very last years of the Honecker regime. It is hung, also in a back corner, in Berlin's Jewish Museum.

19 For a discussion of the history of this photo, see Hütter and Rösgen 2005.

20 "Geschichte wird zum Naturereignes." "Die Ausstellung ist diskret, konventionell und – lehrreich. Sie ist kühl bis zur Geschichtslosigkeit und steril bis zur Provokation." *Die Zeit*, June 8, 2006.

21 Baudrillard 1996; See also Ostow 2003.

22 Anderson 1983.

23 Hajdarpasic 2007.

24 Crooke 2007.

25 "Im XXI. Jahrhundert wird deutlich, dass ein Neubeginn nur schwer möglich ist, ohne klar und in historischer Distanz die Schrecken und Traumata des vorangegangenen Jarhrhunderts darzustellen und ansatzweise zu behandeln." Deutsches Historisches Museum, 2006, 3.

26 *Berliner Zeitung*, June 2, 2006, 25.

27 Chakrabarty 2005.

References

van Alphen, Ernst (1997), *Caught by History: Holocaust Effects in Contemporary Art, Literature and Theory*. Stanford, Stanford University Press, ch. 3.

Anderson, Benedict (1983), *Imagined Communities: Reflections on the Origin and Spread of Nationalism*. rev. ed., New York, Verso.

Augstein, Rudolf et al. (1987), *Historikerstreit. Die Dokumentation der Kontroverse um die Einzigartigkeit der nazionalsozialistischen Judenvernichtung*. München, Piper Verlag.

Baudrillard, Jean (1996), *The System of Objects*. (James Benedict, transl.). New York, Verso.

Chakrabarty, Dipesh (2005), After History, Vergangenheit archivieren, erfahren und zerstören. In Burghartz, S. and Habermas, R. (eds.), *Historische Anthropologie: Kultur. Gesellschaft. Alltag*. Köln, Böhlau Verlag, 121–35.

Crooke, Elizabeth (2007), Putting Contested History on Display: The Uses of the Past in Northern Ireland. In Ostow, Robin (ed.), *(Re)Visualizing National History: Museums and National Identities in the New Millennium*. Toronto, University of Toronto Press.

Deutsches Historisches Museum (2006), *Das Deutsche Historische Museum: Aufgaben und Ziele*. Berlin.

Ehmann, Annegret (1987), *Auschwitz in der deutschen Nachkriegsgeschichte – Einige Aspekte zum Umgang mit einem Erbe*. unpublished ms., 9.

Greenberg, Reesa (2007), Constructing the Canadian War Museum/ Constructing the Landscape of Canadian Identity. In Ostow, Robin (ed.), *(Re)Visualizing National History: Museums and National Identities in the New Millennium*. Toronto, University of Toronto Press.

Hajdarpasic, Edin (2007), Museums, Discourses of Multiculturalism and the Remaking of Public Culture in Postwar Sarajevo. In Ostow, Robin (ed.), *(Re)Visualizing National History: Museums and National Identities in the New Millennium*. Toronto, University of Toronto Press.

Hütter, Hans and Rösgen, Petra (2005), *Bilder die Lügen*. Bonn, Stiftung Haus der Geschichte der Bundesrepublik Deutschland.

Koschnick, Leonore (2006) (ed.), *German Historical Museum Berlin: German History in Pictures and Documents*. Berlin, Prestel, 8.

Kretzschmar, Ulrike (2006) (ed.), *The Berlin Armoury: From Arsenal to the German Historical Museum*. Berlin, Prestel.

Kühnl, Reinhard (1987), *Vergangenheit, die nicht vergeht. Die "Historiker-Debatte." Dokumentation. Darstellung and Kritik*. Köln, Pahl-Rugenstein.

Kurze, Jan-Hendrik (1997), *Das Deutsche Historische Museum im alten Berliner Zeughaus: Wieviel Symbolik eines preußischen Militärdenkamls verträgt ein Ort der Selbstbesinnung durch historische Erinnerung?* Magisterarbeit, Freie Universität Berlin.

Meuschel, Sigrid (1988), Kulturnation oder Staatsnation? – Zur Renaissance der Suche nach Nationaler Identität in beiden deutschen Staaten. *Leviathan*, Vol. 16, Issue 3, 406–435.

Ostow, Robin (2003), Religion as Treasure: Exhibits of Rituals and Ritual Objects in Prague's Jewish Museum. In Lanwerd, Susanne (ed.), *Der Kanon und die Sinne. Religionsästhetik als akademische Disziplin*. Luxembourg, Études Luxembourgeoises D'Histoire & de Sciences, 152–68.

Kobi Kabalek

Immediate Memories: Written Experiences of the Nazi Past in Occupied Germany, 1945–1949*

"A door opened, allowing entrance to a far and yet entirely real world."[1] This sentence appears in Peter Doebel's foreword to the published edition of his late father's diaries from the Second World War. Writing sixty years after the end of the war, Doebel describes how he felt the events emerging from his father's pages, and promises a similar experience to other readers:

> Reading transforms the past into an everyday present – the present of the Third Reich, the Second World War. The reader can witness [*miterleben*, literally: co-experience] the initial certainty of victory, later the increasing hardships [...], and finally the chaos, in which the Reich and the private world of Günter Doebel collapsed...[2]

The publication of the diaries enables Peter Doebel to critically confront the opinions of his father, who, almost until the end of the war, believed Germany would be victorious. His temporal distance from the events and Günter Doebel's death made this confrontation possible. They also seem to explain the sensation of sharing a personal experience of a lost past, which is promised to the reader of the diaries. One may assume, therefore, that people in Germany who wrote about these events and introduced similar texts just a few years after the war ended would not use such language. After all, didn't they experience this war and the collapse of the Reich firsthand?

* I would like to thank Allan Megill, Uli Heikaus, and Jenny Le Zotte for their helpful comments on this text.

But a look at autobiographical literature from the early postwar years reveals a similar promise, in which authors and editors invite readers to share the immediacy of past experiences. More than a mere aesthetic gesture aimed at persuading one to purchase the book, such an invitation applies a cultural form authors thought their audience would recognize and accept. The promise of immediacy is based on the assumption that written accounts of experience have an unmediated proximity with one's personal perception of history and can communicate this experience to the reader.

In what follows, I will examine claims for the immediacy of experience in one autobiographical writing from the postwar period, Ruth Andreas-Friedrich's published diary *Der Schattenmann.*[3] This book should not be viewed as illustrating some "collective" frame common to all of her contemporaries, but as one narration written under specific circumstances that nonetheless draws on general cultural patterns. It offers us, therefore, a starting point for exploring assumptions regarding the connections between experience and writing. I shall do this under four headings: truth, authenticity, immediacy, and memory.

Truth

Ruth Andreas-Friedrich (1901–1977) worked as a journalist and writer in Berlin throughout the Nazi period. She was active in a resistance group known as "Uncle Emil," which gave refuge to Jews, political activists, and others who were persecuted by the Nazis. Andreas-Friedrich tells the story of this group in her diary, which portrays her experiences in the years 1938 to 1945. With the help of friends, the diary was translated into English and initially published in New York in 1947 under the title *Berlin Underground 1938–1945.*[4] Later that year Suhrkamp published it in Germany under the title *Der Schattenmann* (The Shadow Man).[5] The two editions present some different selections from the manuscript, but most of the material overlaps.

The message the diary wishes to convey is stated in the foreword, which carries the date of October 1945. It is supposed to "raise the German people a hairsbreadth from its present low degree in the eyes of the world" by showing that not all Germans in Hitler's Germany were Nazis.[6] In order to make this claim plausible, Andreas-Friedrich must persuade her readers that her account is congruent with "what actually happened." Accordingly, her foreword begins with the words: "This book does not pretend to be a work of art; it is simply the truth [*dieses Buch ist Wahrheit*]."[7] But what kind of truth does she have in mind?

The claim of truth in autobiographical writing as a whole does not always refer to the factuality of events. As Roy Pascal demonstrated, an author may consciously omit and change episodes and details from his or her life story without necessarily damaging the "truth value" of the autobiography.[8] Writers and readers are often primarily interested either in the search for a higher truth, whether expressed in terms of religious belief, philosophical worldview, or existential concerns, or in the author's attempt to explore and expose the inner truth of the self. The truth of "fact" and the truth of the writer's feeling coexist in practically all autobiographies, and diaries are not exempt from this rule. Nevertheless, autobiographers who have a clear political or social agenda will certainly want to claim that their accounts provide credible information. As Katharina Gerstenberger shows in relation to women's autobiographies in turn-of-the-century Germany, the "memoir boom" that started in the late nineteenth century challenged the notion that literary talent was a necessary precondition for writing. Published letters, diaries, and memoirs were supposed to provide insight into history and enable readers to cope with modernity or construct a national identity.[9] Therefore, the writers of these texts found it essential to distinguish their writings from novels and other forms of fictional literature.[10]

Andreas-Friedrich's assertion that her diary is not a work of art but simply the truth follows the same logic. Yet her concern with convincing readers of the truthfulness of her account seems also to stem from the specific context of her writing. Before, and especially after, their rise to power, Nazi leaders portrayed their ideology and actions as part of a campaign to "reveal the truth." Nazi propaganda repeatedly claimed to oppose the plots of "World Jewry" and "expose" Jews as aggressors rather than victims. In addresses to local and international audiences, Joseph Goebbels spoke about the "honest struggle over the truth," which allegedly counters the lies that falsely accuse Germans of committing atrocities.[11] Yet by the end of the war the Nazis' massive propaganda campaigns made the media seem inherently unreliable, and when the Allies arrived on the scene they encountered great difficulties in trying to convince Germans to accept the "rumors" of atrocities as true.

In her diary, Andreas-Friedrich frequently discusses the struggle over truth during the war. She sees the problem not only in people's lack of reliable news, but also in the long-term effects of Nazi propaganda: "The mischief, falsification of history, distortion of truth [*Wahrheitsverdrehung*], and slanders upon art that have been pounded into people's heads through years cannot be effaced from those heads so easily" (January 24, 1940).[12] Andreas-Friedrich's diary should be understood, therefore, as a reaction to the Nazis and as a part of the postwar effort for a national "re-education." But in order to re-educate her readers, she must constitute her account as congruent with reality.

Authenticity

The reliability of a historical account can be verified to a certain degree by cross-examining it with other sources. The credibility of an account is based on its connection to the examined phenomenon, thus determining whether or not it is authentic. But the matter becomes more complex when the account includes issues of personal experience, because in respect to such experience the authenticity of an autobiography cannot be verified according to evidence external to the narrative. Rather, authenticity is created in an "autobiographical pact"[13] in which the reader accepts the claims of the author regarding the truthfulness of his or her story (in whatever way "truth" is expressed). In order to support their claims to truthfulness, writers employ "authenticating devices." These are strategies of persuasion that include photographs, supporting literature, a preface by a known person, or various statements that usually appear in a book's foreword.[14]

An important "authenticating device" Andreas-Friedrich is very much aware of lies in the presumed nature of the genre itself. The assumption shared by many contemporaries was that a diary is essentially different from novels and even memoirs in its innate authenticity, which was seen as stemming from two factors. First, a diarist appears to be writing for him- or herself rather than for an audience. This may associate the diary with the private rather than the public sphere and may allow it to be seen as a form of resistance to authority or as an "apolitical" account. Second, a diarist is writing during the events or under their direct impact, and without knowing at the moment of writing what happened "at the end." These characteristics make the diary seem like a reflection of the past rather than a retroactive apology.

We can see these perceived advantages in the 1946 publication of the diary of Ulrich von Hassell, a German diplomat who was executed by the Nazis. In the foreword, the publisher informs the reader that von Hassell's diary was written in a hurry and was not meant to appear in print. Yet he argues that it is important as a human document exactly because of its "defenseless immediacy (*wehrlose Unmittelbarkeit*)": "We are not dealing with the work of a survivor, who has the possibility of describing things from his current standpoint and in accordance with today's situation."[15] According to this logic, diaries are authentic due to their imperfect and unedited character. Andreas-Friedrich follows the same pattern in her foreword when she writes:

> I have deliberately refrained from any subsequent emendations. Of course many rumors current in those days have since been explained, many inaccurately transmitted facts corrected through press and radio. But this very uncertainty about what actually happened was so characteristic of the time that it would be a distortion to make changes now.[16]

Andreas-Friedrich was very aware of the importance of establishing authenticity.[17] As in the foreword of von Hassell's diary, she describes hers as providing the reader with an immediate access to the atmosphere and experience of the past by nature of its "distorted truth." She thus emphasizes two aspects of "truth" in her diary. The first portrays actual occurrences and is supposed to inform the reader about the activities of her resistance group. The second is an experiential truth, which concentrates not on providing historical "facts" but on conveying the lack of reliable information and the struggle over truth as central characteristics of living in Nazi Germany. In doing so she constitutes a clear division between what she defines as the past (the diary entries) and the present (the foreword), in spite of the fact that only a few months separate the last entry of the diary from the foreword.

Immediacy

We have seen so far how diverse issues of truth and authenticity are combined in establishing an account of the Nazi past that would be both credible and would appeal to readers. The assumption is that in order to tell about the past one should have an immediate contact with it. In the postwar years an author's authenticity was, and to a certain extent still is, measured according to two general types of immediacy. The first is based on the text being written during the frame one defines as "the past." Although there are doubts whether Andreas-Friedrich's book is a diary or a memoir written in the form of a diary,[18] her own statement defines its authenticity as being based on this first kind of immediacy. The second type refers to witnesses who may tell their stories decades after the event while still maintaining that their report is authentic. This is what Allan Megill calls "authenticity in the existential sense, deriving its force from the alleged fact that it emerges directly and immediately from the subject's encounter with the world."[19] Although the two types often coexist, diaries are generally assumed to be themselves traces of past experiences, while memoirs are based on viewing witnesses as embodied "traces" of their own past.[20]

Immediacy is generally seen not only as a criterion for measuring the truthfulness of one's account, but also as a way of communicating the experience of the past to readers. However, the wish to convey this experience may have different motives and take different forms. It seems that Peter Doebel's interest in his father's diaries arose not only because they allowed him to personally confront his father and the memory of the Nazi past, but also because the diaries present to him a lost and fascinating world. For Andreas-Friedrich, on the other hand, the past she defines as gone is still exerting its influence on Germany not only as memory but also in all aspects of life. Her claim to be describing the immediacy of experience is a part of her attempt to shape Germany's future. As such, her diary should be seen as according with autobiographical and literary accounts published around the same time that introduced an alternative to the Nazi falsification of truth by using different understandings of "immediate realism."[21]

Memory

Those who ascribe a greater immediacy to diaries than to memoirs ground their assertion, among other reasons, on the fragility of memory. Memory is then viewed as a highly subjective, unreliable, and "distorted" portrayal of the past, guided by the specific needs of the memoirist in the present. Such judgments argue in favor of diaries as presenting an "unmediated" proximity to the past. However, all personal accounts of experience are always mediated through language, genre, and available cultural forms. Furthermore, diarists often write down their experiences not at the exact moment of occurrence, but a few hours, days, and even weeks later. In any case, the act of writing a diary entails the same "distorting" elements one may assign to memories, which are exactly what diaries are: articulations of *past* experiences.

To view diaries as written memories is not to see them as identical to memoirs. The context of writing, and, in particular, writers' assumptions regarding genre and the distinction between past and present, are important components in shaping a narrative. However, "even if it is accepted that memory bears some relation, however attenuated, to an experienced past, it is simply not possible to argue that certain modes of personal memory give more direct access to that past than others."[22]

The promise of immediacy turns out to be an illusion. Yet to say this is not to deny that the promise serves a purpose. Andreas-Friedrich's book was printed in several editions, most recently in the year 2000, and has been cited in German and non-German publications as a source important in casting light on the anti-Nazi humanitarian resistance. Furthermore, other writers used her diary in arguing that not all Germans in Hitler's Germany were Nazis, thus accepting the diary's basic claims. For example, the historian Hans Rothfels found the book to be most useful in his attempt to counter accusations of a German collective guilt, in spite of some doubts he had about the factual truth of her account. Writing about the diary in his 1948 "appraisal" of the German resistance, he thus suggested that "This report about the resistance Group 'Uncle Emil,' though couched in fictional terms, has all the ring of truth."[23]

Endnotes

1 Doebel 2005, 1.
2 Doebel 2005, 1.
3 Andreas-Friedrich 1947b.
4 Andreas-Friedrich 1947a.
5 Andreas-Friedrich 1947b.
6 Andreas-Friedrich 1947a, xiv; Andreas-Friedrich 1947b, 8. All quotes are taken from the American edition of the diary except where it diverges from the German edition.
7 Andreas-Friedrich 1947a, xiii; Andreas-Friedrich 1947b, 7.
8 Pascal 1960.
9 Gerstenberger 2000.
10 This strict separation between fictional and real is artificial, because any act of autobiographical writing uses literary models, and even a fantasy novel may seem to tell something about its author (Zur Nieden 1993). The emphasis here is therefore on the assumptions that guide each genre of writing and its relation to reality.
11 For example, in a speech in 1934 that was printed in several European languages and supposed to demonstrate that the National Socialist Germany contributes to a European peace: "Auch in Bezug auf das jüdische Problem haben wir die Wahrheit nicht zu scheuen. Wir möchten aber wünschen und hoffen, daß der ehrliche Kampf um die Wahrheit nicht von vornherein vergiftet wird durch Greuelmärchen und manchmal fast grotesk anmutende Emigrantenlügen, die einer objektiven Prüfung nicht im mindesten standzuhalten vermögen." Goebbels 1934, 6.
12 Andreas-Friedrich 1947a, 54; Andreas-Friedrich 1947b, 71.
13 Lejeune 1989.
14 See Heinemann 1986, 117ff. The American edition of Andreas-Friedrich's book includes such an introductory note written by the American reporter Joel Sayre, whose purpose is to familiarize readers in the US with the book by characterizing the author and her friends as German democrats.
15 Von Hassell 1946, 5. Emphasis in original.
16 Andreas-Friedrich 1947a, xiv; Andreas-Friedrich 1947b, 8.
17 In her diary she notes that the word itself has become instrumental in the struggle over truth in the Nazi period. In the entry from September 28, 1938, we find the following statement: "'*Authentic*' is the catchword of our day, or rather one of the innumerable catchwords. A profession of honesty as against atrocity stories and whispering campaigns [*Greuelmärchen und Flüsterpropaganda*]." See Andreas-Friedrich 1947a, 5; Andreas-Friedrich 1947b, 15.
18 Peitsch 1990, 300.
19 Megill 1998, 47.

20 Young 1988, 24.
21 Scherpe 1982; Peitsch 1990, 87–100; Brockmann 2004, 191–197.
22 Radstone 2005, 136.
23 Rothfels 1948, 33.

References

Andreas-Friedrich, Ruth (1947a), *Berlin Underground 1938–1945*. Translated by Barrows Mussey, New York, Henry Holt and Company.

Andreas-Friedrich, Ruth (1947b), *Der Schattenmann: Tagebuchaufzeichnungen 1938–1945*. Berlin, Suhrkamp Verlag.

Brockmann, Stephen (2004), *German Literary Culture at the Zero Hour*. Rochester, NY, Camden House.

Doebel, Günter (2005) (ed.), *"So etwas wie Weltuntergang". Kriegstagebücher eines Polizeioffiziers 1939–1945*. Unter Mitarbeit von Thomas Lindner, Mainz, C.P. Verlag.

Gerstenberger, Katharina (2000), *Truth to Tell: German Women's Autobiographies and Turn-of-the-Century Culture*. Ann Arbor, The University of Michigan Press.

Goebbels, Josef (1934), *Das nationalsozialistische Deutschland als Faktor des europäischen Friedens. Rede des Reichsministers Dr. Goebbels vor der Intellektuellen-Union in Warschau, 13. Juni 1934*. Berlin, M. Müller & Sohn.

Heinemann, Marlene E. (1986), *Gender and Destiny: Women Writers and the Holocaust*. New York and London, Greenwood Press.

Lejeune, Philippe (1989), *On Autobiography*. Edited by Paul John Eakin. Translated by Katherine Leary. Minneapolis, University of Minnesota Press.

Megill, Allan (1998), History, Memory, Identity. *History of the Human Sciences*, Vol. 11 Issue 3, 37–62.

Pascal, Roy (1960), *Design and Truth in Autobiography*. Cambridge, Massachusetts, Harvard University Press.

Peitsch, Helmut (1990), *"Deutschlands Gedächtnis an seine dunkelste Zeit": Zur Funktion der Autobiographik in den Westzonen Deutschlands und den Westsektoren von Berlin 1945 bis 1949*. Berlin, Edition Sigma.

Radstone, Susannah (2005), Reconceiving Binaries: The Limits of Memory. *History Workshop Journal* 59, 134–150.

Rothfels, Hans (1948), *The German Opposition to Hitler: An Appraisal.* Hinsdale, Illinois, Henry Regnery Company.

Scherpe, Klaus R. (1982), Erzwungener Alltag: Wahrgenommene und gedachte Wirklichkeit in der Reportageliteratur der Nachkriegszeit. In Hermand, Jost, Peitsch, Helmut, and Scherpe, Klaus R. (eds.), *Nachkriegsliteratur in Westdeutschland 1945–49: Schreibweisen, Gattungen, Institutionen.* Berlin, Argument-Verlag, 35–102.

Von Hassell, Ulrich (1946), *Vom anderen Deutschland: Aus den nachgelassenen Tagebüchern 1938–1944.* Zürich und Freiburg i. Br., Atlantis Verlag.

Young, James E. (1988), *Writing and Rewriting the Holocaust: Narrative and the Consequences of Interpretation.* Bloomington and Indianapolis, Indiana University Press.

Zur Nieden, Susanne (1993), *Alltag im Ausnahmezustand: Frauentagebücher im zerstörten Deutschland 1943 bis 1945.* Berlin, Orlana Frauenverlag.

Arja Rosenholm

Reflections on a Meeting: Elena Rzhevskaia Meets Marshal Zhukov

Elena Moiseevna Rzhevskaia, born in 1919, is a Soviet Russian author of a large body of prose consisting of short stories, novels and autobiographical memoirs of the Great Patriotic War. The particular book making her famous is her autobiographical memory *Berlin May 1945* published first in the West in 1964, and after that in the Soviet Union in 1965.[1] As the subtitle, "Notes of an Interpreter from the Front" indicates, it was the wartime account of a 22 year old Moscow student at the Literary Institute who volunteers for the front as a translator. For Rzhevskaia, the war ended in Berlin. At the very end of the Second World War, the young military interpreter was part of the secret group of Soviet intelligence officers who found the burnt remains of Hitler and Goebbels in the Hitler-Bunker. Rzhevskaia was entrusted to carry the proof of Hitler's death – in her coat pocket were Adolf Hitler's jawbones – to Moscow where much of the evidence recovered from the bunker has remained buried out of reach of public knowledge in the archives for decades.[2] On Stalin's order the findings and evidence were kept in secret files, and the few witnesses – according to Rzhevskaia there were three army participants[3] – were sworn to silence for years. Officially, Hitler's body had not been found, and rumours of his appearance in Argentina and in Franco's battles, only evoked a sense of irritation amongst the Soviet people.[4] Rzhevskaia began writing about Hitler's demise as early as in 1945 but published her eyewitness accounts only after Stalin's death. The full version of the findings was published in Russian in 1989, in her autobiographical fiction *A Distant Rumble* (*Dalekii gul'*) where she confesses:

> Only with time did I finally manage to overcome all the obstacles and make public this 'secret of the century'. By some twist of fate, I played

> a part in not allowing Hitler to achieve his final goal of disappearing and turning into a myth [...]. I managed to prevent Stalin's murky and dark thought – his desire to hide from the world that we had found Hitler's corpse.[5]

This final plot of World War II belonged for many years to the least known episodes, shrouded in mystery outside of the official historiography of war and its final hours, but inevitably, in Rzhevskaia's personal life story. The history of veiling and the muted reminiscences of a woman at war have become "[...] a trope of a military woman's post-war invisibility", as Irina Novikova has rightly stated of Rzhevskaia's career.[6] As also confirmed by several scholars and writers, such as Svetlana Aleksievich, Beate Fieseler and Ol'ga Nikonova, the experiences of Soviet women in war, both in the army and on the home front, have been little investigated through women's representations.[7] Elena Rzhevskaia seems, meanwhile, to have reached a more honourable place in the history of Russian "war prose", to which her interviews testify her inclusion in the male dominated community of the Soviet-Russian writers of the Great Patriotic War, and the latest publications of her prose in two volumes from 2001. However, the reception of her work is witness to the powerlessness of the critics to explain Rzhevskaia's prolonged invisibility and her apparent untimely appearance in the history of Soviet war literature. She was criticized as being both anachronistic with her "belated" work, and at the same time marginalized for coming out prematurely with topics which were too courageous, such as life in occupied areas, Soviet soldiers as war prisoners, love and every day life during the war.[8] The author, seen as a "nobody from off the street",[9] has been subjected to what the mainstream critics avoid reflecting on, that is that war is a gendering practice, and accordingly "marks"[10] the memories of war. Women's reminiscences, in general, have only partly been included in the historical sources organizing the national memory of the Great Patriotic War. Rzhevskaia herself in the interview with Tatiana Bek in 1996, underlines that:" [...] there is no clear female gaze on the Great Patriotic War in our literature".[11] The absence of women's literary reminiscences corresponds with the lack of their public communicative processes.

If, following Maurice Halbwachs'[12] concept of memory, the individual memory forms itself by participating in communicative processes which keep the memory alive and establish it in social communication, then accordingly, without a significant social collective to construct one's memory, there follows oblivion, demonstrated, as in the case here, by the unwritten history of Soviet women's war memories. In the following, I will focus on an aspect of negotiation of how a woman author, such as Rzhevskaia writing of war while moving between different "places of memory"[13] – those invested with individual reminiscences and those of collective memory saturated with political structures and mobilizing loyalties – manages to inscribe her individual memory into the collective canon. The question simultaneously arising from this, is whose collective memory can she lean on in order to (re)construct her individual memory and thus to implicate her voice in a wider history, a voice having suffered from silence and secrets for decades.

Some answers are given by the case story, a "scetch" (*ocherk*), called "*On that Day in Late Autumn. A Story about the Meeting with Marshal Zhukov*".[14] It is an autobiographical testimony of an unexpected meeting in autumn 1965 between a "rank and file" front line translator, as Rzhevskaia sees herself, and the great Marshal Zhukov. Rzhevskaia is invited by Zhukov to his *dacha* to discuss what really happened in Berlin in May 1945. She admits that she was "shocked" when learning that the great Marshal, the Chief Commander of the victorious Red Army and liberator of Berlin, the icon of the Victory Parade in Moscow 1945, was kept uninformed by Stalin of the facts concerning the discovery of Hitler's remains. The key question of the meeting was how *he* should write about what happened in Berlin in his future memoirs without losing his authority, that instead of him, the great marshal, there was this ordinary female war translator who knew, and had kept the secret all these years, and had also written about the discovery in *her* memoirs already published in the West.

What both the story and the reception of this meeting show is the ambiguity of Rzhevskaia's cultural position given to her by the establishment and constructed by her self. The ambiguity consists of an oscillation between the loneliness the writer was left in holding the "secret of the century"[15] and the urgency to be free of the traumatic burden of the suppressed memories she knew were *not* included in the collective memory of the Soviet people:

> If I speak of myself, when I had a task – to bring into public knowledge the 'secret of the century' – that we did find Hitler's dead body [...] to keep silent. It was oppressive, but these facts became state secrets and its announcement could bring you a prison sentence of from seven to fifteen years. It is very long. So I just had to stay silent, and watch history being distorted, and to speak about the secret only with my closest comrades.[16]

While reflecting upon her literary career, the writer herself seems to appreciate the autobiographical text as a special one by referring to its almost cathartic significance.[17] The meeting reveals the writer's most inner need to free herself from the traumatic silence, her desire to share the secret with someone close. However, what happens, in a way, is that while becoming integrated with the collective memory, the woman writer also writes her own exclusion in the sense that by the text making her well known, it is as a voice for a great man. Of all her wide range of literary work, short stories and memoirs focusing on women's experiences in war, this is the story the critics have been interested in the most. It was submitted under heavy censorship disputes, was not published right away in 1965 but only in 1986 in the journal *Znamia*, followed by a film based on the story shown on Russian TV on the 8th and 9th May in 1995, and material from the story was used, or *mis*used, according to Rzhevskaia, by A. Solzhenitsyn for his story on Zhukov *Na kraiakh* published in 1995 with no reference to Rzhevskaia.[18]

Since both Rzhevskaia and Zhukov wrote their memoirs,[19] there is a certain amount of competition between them. For Rzhevskaia, the meeting becomes of value by the fact that her own memory has an authoritative witness. It turns out that only after Zhukov, as a witness, refers to Rzhevskaia in *his* own memoirs "[...] on how the search for Hitler's remains was conducted, has been extensively written about by Rzhevskaia in her book [...]",[20] does *her* individual memory become constructed as collective. Zhukov's testimony turns into a testament, a will left to the symbolic daughter by the father whose Name is guarantor for the truthfulness of her memory. The female memoirist needs a witness in order to tell her story in many ways and it is not her normal world which could offer her a space to "work through"[21] the past pains; in the present world with her family and elderly mother, under the surface of peaceful times, the past continued to possess the subject with its repetitions and returns. As again, *On that Day in Late Autumn*, the life of the memoirist is unpredictably disrupted. The story begins with the mother calling to her daughter that there is "some military voice" (285) on the telephone. The indifference of the mother's attitude arises from her position as a civilian, quite different from the daughter whose experience of the war cannot be shared with her. But neither will the narrator find an equal partner in dialogue with Zhukov who embodies the paternal world of hierarchy: "If I write that this was unknown to me, then people will not believe you" (293), says Zhukov, asserting his authority over that of the "rank and file" woman-translator. The autobiographical 'I' confesses that "[...] I was not sensitive enough, I did not fully master the situation" (295). The double disintegration suggests the narrator's lonely place.

The female memoirist is displaced; her quotidian space and time are broken: she is invited to Zhukov's *dacha*, which is not only the central space of memory but a chronotope[22] with a special character; it is a space like a "heterotopia", which, according to Foucault, "[...] is capable of juxtaposing in a single real place several spaces, several sites that are in themselves incompatible".[23] In this sense Zhukov's *dacha* is a "heterotopia of deviation"; it brings together individuals whose "[...] behaviour is deviant in relation to the required mean or norm [...]",[24] as Zhukov and Rzhevskaia in their search for the "truth". Their counter-memory is directed against the blurred historical memory which has marked the public knowledge of the events of the war with riddles and gaps. They are in a sense "kill-joys" – Zhukov is marked as *persona non grata*; literary critics had already called Rzhevskaia's writings on her "ordinary war" as "boring".[25] They are both fixated on their past loss, on their own truths and the unquestionable trust they had in their most sacred authority, Stalin. They cannot, therefore, be happy with the traces of the victory only.

The development of the memory plot is organized by a symbolic topography. It offers key sites of memory which, according to Pierre Nora,[26] are invested with particular emotive and symbolic significance in the construction of individual and national identities. As a literary-artistic chronotope, the *dacha* is the basic organizing category of the plot development, and a special space: as a "heterotopia" it resists oppositions and hierarchical dualisms which organize the normal Soviet society: it is both a public place with its official status and setting, and a "hired" residence for Zhukov's private family life, a space intertwining past and present. The building acts as a container of "secrets", but due to its heterotopic openness, the secrets can be brought up to the surface and made communicable. If we adopt here the architectural image of the "crypt", coined by Abraham and Török[27] in transgenerational trauma studies, we see the connection between trauma and place resonating with the 'crypt' within the memoirists' psyche, too: as with the haunted house, also the mind is a container of the unpresentable, unnarratable. The traumatic memory connected with Hitler's phantom-corpse has held the memoirists in its possession:[28] Now, in the belated repetition of the witnessing process of the two truth-seeking combatants meeting in an encapsulated community, the past can be returned in the form of a story: the meeting with Zhukov, embodying this very past, gives her the chance to retell her story, and interpret the history. The memoirist enters a self-reflective process of recalling; she looks in the mirror, while imitating the Marshal's daughter playing with the mirror: "And I, too, saw myself reflected in the mirror." (288).

After having taken off her coat, the narrator enters the world of the past: "Here everything was colossal [...] Here entering the rooms of the past – the time, everything was from those faraway days when we won the war" (289), of the era of Stalin in its "colossal" setting being carried over into the 1960s. Over the years, the counter memory had to remain silenced and encapsulated in the 'crypt' of hidden reminiscences, living only in an individual and private space where the memory was blocked from public communication. The individual counter memory was forced into a dilemma between the collective rituals of victory and the private need to mourn over the victims. The autobiographical dilemma, therefore, resonates with the national fate.

The dilemma of having too many memories, as is the case with Rzhevskaia, generates what can be recognized as traumatic memory. It is the unbearable burden of incommunicable memories which the narrator experiences as being so painful, so incomprehensive, that she had to shut them out of her every day civilian life. The memory nevertheless lived on as split from the civil consciousness, and when the time was to come to encounter the "secret", the incomprehensible part was not easily recalled or narrated. That something unpredictable is rising up to the surface from the "crypt" of memory grows obvious when the narrator approaches Zhukov's *dacha*. She says:

> An odd thing happened to me. When we came close to the gate, a big button came off my coat. I bent down to pick it up, fumbled and when I straightened up, I saw in front of the house on the asphalt street, Zhukov – Daddy, said Masha (287).

She stands before her idol, and to his words that they have not met on the front, she reacts,

> [...], that from me to him the destination was great, and I dropped the coat button into my pocket. If I had been standing before him in my uniform without a button, I would have left the encounter with him feeling defeated. (288).

The button and its loss from the coat symbolizes a break in the identity; if the narrator had tried to "button up" her memories with the civilian coat of her mind, the loosening of the button now discovers the fragility of the quotidian identity after having put aside the soldier's uniform for her civilian dress. The loosened button translocates the subject into the time of war where she now seems to stand in front of the high authority, expecting to be criticized because the missing button has caused her uniform to look disorderly. As the narrator now has trouble in recognizing – even accepting – the Marshal in *his* civilian clothes, so are the borders of identity being drawn along the line between war and peace just as fragile.

The button scene is an isolated fragment, without narrative coherence. However, the image activates dynamic and spontaneous reminiscences of the I-recalling, and in its fragmentary character, it is an element which condenses the atmosphere of the narrative and gives the I-narrator its psychological depth. The symbolic image points out how memories long suppressed and now touched upon, unexpectedly, are brought back into the presence, to be reflected upon and assimilated into one's normal life.

The loosened button becomes a semiotic code for a traumatic memory carried along as an embodied memory but hard to put into words. The unexpected disorder resonates with the system of episodic memory.[29] Whether historically truthful or not, the episodic memory is the bedrock of the lived identity with an unchangeable history. And, it is the episodic individual memory that carries on the narrative. The narrator explains:

> It can seem that I write in too much detail, that on great personalities one has to write only of significant things. However, on Zhukov, the army leader and on his events and strategic plans, all the very significant events have been written, and not only once, by competent writers. Personally, I like to tell about the meeting with him in all its details, without which there is no living image of a person. (290)

Here we have the narrator's aesthetic strategy as explicated, as also her strategy of "writing herself" into the literary history, while bearing her own "lived" history. The author clearly plays with the expectations connected with the genre of testimony, that there are others who are more "competent" in writing on great persons like Marshal Zhukov. However, by subversive inversion, playing on "modesty", she defends her right to narrate from a place which shows respect for detail, the close and the ordinary. The testimony refuses abstractions, disrupts chronology and unsettles coherency, giving fragments of the conversation with the specific aim of following the inner disrupted experiences. Instead of panoramic distance, the episodic memory provides the collective history with ornamental details, such as furniture, dress and food, what they eat and drink, first coffee then tea. The aim is not only to recall the past but *how* to recall it: without any details, any "concrete vehicles"[30] arising from individual memory also the collective memory will turn into what she criticizes as "official and lifeless".[31] Here she prevents the "living memory"[32] from becoming petrified into a construction of archives which would replace or substitute for the dynamic process of individual memory.[33] By all this she means *her* memory of Zhukov whom she now bears through *her* language. Zhukov becomes *her* creation, and through *her* incomparable Zhukov, the female author becomes part of the great history to experience her closeness to the very symbols of power. The female author carries, or rather bears the language itself, the "vehicle"

Rzhevskaia had learnt to use as interpreter, chronicler and memoirist. Rzhevskaia's memoirs are full of life: the episodic memory resonates with a strong connection to "*byt*", or "earthiness",[34] as one critic calls Rzhevskaia's prose style. It deprivileges "great" history by confronting it with its own incidentals, side effects, episodes and fragments.

The conversation revives minds and bodies from their "amortized" (305) state. The splashing water – "lively, unexpected voices" (291) – which the narrator to her own surprise suddenly registers behind the wall, symbolizes the stream of emotions emerging from the episodic memory running through and by the words. The figures become enlivened, they are not abstractions of any high ideas or national icons any more but "living persons", as we already heard the narrator saying, and thus also vulnerable to irritating desires. The "goal" of the meeting (291) is achieved in the moment Rzhevskaia learns of Zhukov's confession at feeling devastatingly deceived by Stalin's not telling him about the discovery of Hitler's body: "He [Zhukov, AR.] would have liked to think that Stalin didn't know either" (297), states the narrator. Both discussants will go through their painful memory, but now the hierarchy is reversed – the "rank and file" woman translator becomes the one who knows more than her highly honoured idol as she becomes his trustworthy witness. Rzhevskaia lets us feel how deeply disappointed Zhukov is in Stalin, his assumed confidante and friend, with whom he dined frequently, and who had rewarded Zhukov by having him represent him in the Victory parade, yet still didn't trust him with such a secret: "How can it be that I didn't know about this?" (292), asks Zhukov and cannot stop repeating "[w]hat for?" [...] "What for?" (292). They both experience a trauma: he for not having known, and she for knowing more than the others.

The discussion comes to an end – the discussants leave the room with its ghost of the past, of the memories of war and disappointment, the civilian coats are put on, they go out into the garden to "breathe fresh air" (306). They speak of nature, of families and children, and, here in the garden, as the "happy" parcel of the heterotopia,[35] the narrator's focus again turns self-reflective. If the narrator, by entering the enclosed space, did see in the mirror a person who was still quite unsure, feeling obedient like a daughter before the great Father-figure of the Soviet Army, the subject now leaving the enclosed space of the *dacha* has found new resources in herself and grown into an adult woman who even dares to use irony in her speech (305). The memories of war had offered both veterans an equal position, both defended their own right to be recalled. Rzhevskaia had not given up her position to Zhukov's authority but had insisted on her truth of Hitler's fate. She had defended her position, as she reflects (294), as an autonomous author and witness against Zhukov's blackmail attempt to change her truth for his (293). The dialogue between equals is now over. After being for a moment an "honorary man" as a collaborator in power, the narrator is dismissed to the civilian world to be given back her gender as wife and mother the moment Zhukov asks about her family (305). Thus her gender seems to outweigh her value as author, since Zhukov does not mention her work, but only that of the male authors such as Simonov, Smirnov and Kremlev, whose work Zhukov appreciated (305). Rzhevskaia is reminded of her otherness in the civilian life as a woman writing of the war among the large majority of male authors.

The story's value is ambivalent: the woman narrator tells the story of a meeting which serves as an ethical, juridical and therapeutic liberation from her traumatic silence, but she does need an official person like Zhukov for her story to be narrated. Only after Zhukov has told in *his* memoirs what Rzhveskaia has experienced, does *her* story become included in the collective national memory (294). For a moment the "rank and file" female war translator achieved a primary rank in culture where her private memoirs from the war were not so much in demand, the official memory being ignorant of the abilities and significance of women's writing on war. She, however, takes up a place of her own as a female memoirist of the Great Patriotic War: while, on the one hand, Zhukov is needed as a guarantee for the woman's story, that she was indeed among those who found Hitler's body, and on the other hand, the female memoirist takes up the role as a witness of memory for Zhukov. Six days after the meeting Zhukov has a heart attack, and the narrator sees herself as being perhaps the last person outside his closest circle to see him in good health and forward looking (306). Rzhevskaia becomes the witness bearing the memory of the great Marshal. She is devoted to sanctioning the "outlaw" figure – a position not unlike many Soviet Russian women memoirists who took up the role of the "literary widows"[36] in Stalin's time.

Zhukov becomes an essential part of *her* history, he is her reconstruction of the past to refute all the other stories that, for her, distorted Zhukov's true image.

The narrative shows how both, individual and collective-national memories merge into each other: as a witness of Zhukov's memory Rzhevskaia, the ordinary war translator will guarantee him a memory for future generations, and by doing so she will rise into a primary rank. All the injustice experienced by both Zhukov and Rzhevskaia – irritating enigmas, riddles and unsolved secrets of the history – all that should find its recognition and solution after a clarifying narrative on what really happened in the Great Patriotic War. What the woman narrator learns from Zhukov, of his loneliness at being left excluded from knowledge of the historical events, is a salve for her own loneliness and deceit caused by Stalin's information policy.

In the end Rzhevskaia's history is narrated, and we know what happened in Berlin. But there is, however, something that still holds the narrator back. At the end of the story, the narrator is taken home by Zhukov's chauffeur, and as she steps out of the car, the chauffeur states: "This is an old ZIS.[37] Stalin was also driven in this car". (306).

These are the last words of the narrative. How should we read them? The symbols and the proud tone of the chauffeur indicate that the riddles of the history are difficult to overcome. Is it still that the painful past can be critically encountered only in an encapsulated heterotopia, while outside in the "normal" world the old myths continue haunting, unchanged? Rzhevskaia seems to ask herself, and the reader, whether her and Zhukov's dissenting voices can ever become shared with those of the majority. It is possible that she is also indicating that, in the same way that the national memory has been colonized, so she, too, has been driven in Stalin's and Zhukov's big black ZIS, and attracted to power symbolized here by their car, the vehicle of demoralizing authority and the source of the traumatic memory. The question will remain: how did she, as one of the few besides Stalin to know the Truth, feel and see herself? Notwithstanding Rzhevskaia's repeated ambition to replay the past in order to free herself from its paralysing influence, with this ending here she actually confesses that memory cannot be available as definitive knowledge. Rather it consists of contradictory and juxtaposing fragments of repressed history which can return over and over again in flashbacks and unpredictable associations to haunt people's minds – and still long after the war in Soviet society through the phantom figure of Stalin.

Endnotes

1 Rzhevskaia 2001c, 309–436.
2 Rzhevskaya, "Bearing Witness to the Truth" in http://www.perevod.it//elkost/elena_rzhevskaya/books/books.html and Rzhevskaia 2001a, 267–271 and 2001b, 296.
3 Rzheskaia 2001b, 269.
4 Rzhevskaia 2001b, 296.
5 Rzhevskaia 2001a, 270. Rzhevskaia writes of her dilemma: "The declaration signed by Stalin, Churchill and Roosevelt stated that the allies promised to find the Nazi leaders 'even at the ends of the earth, and bring them before the court of humanity'. But the main leader was right there in Berlin, not far from the Allies' Control Council. There he was, all ready to be presented. All that had to be done was get together the Soviet and German witnesses and carry out the identification, issue a joint statement and close the whole matter. But when the forensic medical team carried out their autopsy of Hitler in Buch on May 8, the Moscow press came out with information that he was still hiding somewhere. It seemed that nothing was about to change. Time would pass and it would be too late to get to the real truth. The witnesses would disperse or die and the testimonies of those still alive would become less convincing as the years went by. We thought then that if not now then at least in some undefined future this silence would in the end be broken. It just seemed impossible that this should not happen. And that meant we needed to establish the facts, facts that would remain just as solid and indisputable at a later point in time." In http://www.perevod.it//elkost/elena_rzhevskaya/books/books.html.
6 Novikova 2000, 158.
7 Fieseler 2002, 11–30; Aleksievich 1985; Nikonova 2005, 186–196.
8 See Kopeliovich 1995 nr. 50, 332 ff.
9 Rzhevskaia 1996, 216.
10 Joseph 2003, 64.
11 Rzhevskaia 1996, 206.
12 Halbwachs 1966 and Halbwachs 1992.
13 Nora's terms are *lieux d'histoire and lieux de mémoire*. Nora 1998.
14 Rzhevskaia 2001b, 283–306. All the quotations are from this text. Page numbers are given in brackets.
15 Rzhevskaia 2001b, 296.
16 Rzhevskaia 1996, 216.
17 E.g. Rzhevskaia 1996, 217ff.
18 Solzhenitsyn 1995, 28–50.
19 Zhukov's memoirs: the first edition "Vospominaniia i razmyshleniia" was published under Brezhnev's reign on condition that criticism of Stalin was removed and Zhukov

has to add an (invented episode of his visit to Leonid Brezhnev with the purpose of having consultations on military strategy).

20 Rzhevskaia 1996, 219.

21 LaCapra 2001.

22 Bakhtin 1978, 494, 521.

23 Foucault 1984.

24 Ibid.

25 Rzhevskaia recalls in her interview for *Voprosy literatury* from the year 1996, 214 how stories she had given for publishing just after the war were returned to her from the publisher with the comment that the stories were too "sad". "You write on the ordinary war [*byt*, AR.] which is hardly worth describing. People are sick of the war".

26 Nora 1998.

27 Abraham and Törok 1994.

28 "To be traumatized is precisely to be possessed by an image or event". Caruth 1995, 4–5.

29 Assmann 2006, 183–184.

30 The Russian word is "material'nye predmety", Kopeliovich 1995, 353.

31 "ofitsial'no i bezbytno", Kopeliovich 1995, 353–354.

32 "zhivaia pamiat'" in Rzhevskaia http://www.ijp.ru/show/pr.php?=02000100259.

33 See Whitehead 2004, 51.

34 The Russian word is "prizemlennost'", Kopeliovich 1995, 353.

35 See Foucault 1984.

36 Holmgren 1994, 136.

37 ZIS = "Factory in the name of Stalin".

References

Abraham, Nicolas and Torök, Maria (1994), *The Shell and the Kernel*. Vol. I. Chicago, University of Chicago Press.

Aleksievich, Svetlana (1985), *U voiny ne zhenskoe litso*. Minsk.

Assmann, Aleida (2006), *Einführung in die Kulturwissenshaft*. Berlin, Erich Schmidt Verlag.

Bakhtin, Mikhail (1978), The Forms of Time and Chronotopos in the Novel. From the Greek Novel to Modern Fiction. *PTL. A Journal for Descriptive Poetics and Theory of Literature*, Vol. 3, 493–528.

Caruth, Cathy (1995),Trauma and Experience. Introduction. In Caruth, Cathy (ed.), *Trauma: Explorations in Memory*. Baltimore, MD and London, Johns Hopkins University Press, 3–12.

Fieseler, Beate (2002), Der Krieg der Frauen: Die ungeschriebene Geschichte. In Jahn, Peter (ed.), *Masha + Nina + Katjuscha. Frauen in der Roten Armee 1941–1945*. Berlin, Museum Berlin Karlshorst Ch. Links Verlag, 11–30.

Foucault, Michel (1984), *Of Other Spaces* (1967) *Heterotopias*. www.foucault.info/documents/heteroTopia.

Halbwachs, Maurice (1966), *Das Gedächtnis und seine sozialen Bedingungen*. Berlin-Neuwied.

Halbwachs, Maurice (1992), *On Collective Memory*. Chicago and London, University of Chicago Press.

Holmgren, Beth (1994), For the Good od the Cause: Russian Women's Autobiography in the Twentieth Century. In Clyman, Toby W. and Greene, Diana, *Women Writers in Russian Literature*. Westport Conn., Greenwood Press, 129–147.

Joseph, Tiffany (2003), "Non-Combatant's Shell Shock": Trauma and Gender in F. Scott Fitzgerald's *Tender is the Night*. *National Women's Studies Association Journal*, Vol. 15 Issue 3, 64–81.

Kopeliovich, Mikhail (1995), Paradoksy pisatel'skoi sud'by. Shtrikhi k portretu Eleny Rzhevskoi na fone sovetskoi voennoi prozy. *Kontinent*, Nr. 85, 1995, 332–358.

LaCapra, Dominic (2001), *Writing History, Writing Trauma*. Baltimore, MD and London, Johns Hopkins University Press.

Nikonova, Olga (2005), Das grosse Schweigen. Frauen in Krieg. Kluften der Erinnerung. Russland und Deutschland 60 Jahre nach dem Krieg. Osteuropa. *Neprikosnovennyi zapas*, Volume 55 Issue 4–6, 186–196.

Nora, Pierre (1998), *Realms of Memory: Rethinking the French Past*. New York, Columbia University Press.

Novikova, Irina (2000), A War in her Own Translation: Elena Rzhevskaya's Distant Rumble. In Liljeström, Marianne, Rosenholm, Arja and Savkina, Irina (eds.), *Models of Self. Russian Women's Autobiographical Texts*. Helsinki, Kikimora, 155–170.

Rzhevskaia, Elena (2001a), Dalekii gul'. In Rzhevskaia, Elena, *Vechernii razgovor. Izbrannoe. Povesti, rasskazy, zapiski*. St. Peterburg, Inapress, 221–282.

Rzhevskaia, Elena (2001b), V tot den', pozdnei osen'iu. (Rasskaz o vstreche s marshalom Zhukovym). In Rzhevskaia, Elena, *Vechernii razgovor. Izbrannoe. Povesti, rasskazy, zapiski*. St. Peterburg, Inapress, 283–306.

Rzhevskaia, Elena (2001c), Berlin, mai 1945. In Rzhevskaia, Elena, *Vechernii razgovor. Izbrannoe. Povesti, rasskazy, zapiski*. St. Peterburg, Inapress, 309–436.

Rzhevskaia, Elena (1996), U vojny – litso vojny. Besedu vela T. Bek. *Voprosy literatury*, Mart-Aprel', 182–221.

Rzhevskaia, Elena. Drugie vremena – drugie problemy. Internet-zhurnal molodykh pisatelei Rossii "Prolog". http://www.ijp.ru/show/pr.php?failn=02000100259 (10.11.2004).

Rzhevskaya Elena, Bearing Witness to the Truth in http://www.perevod.it/elkost/elena_rzhevskaya/books/books.html (29.11.2006).

Solzhenitsyn, Aleksandr (1995), Na kraiah. *Novyi mir*, No 5, 28–50.

Whitehead, Anne (2004), *Trauma Fiction*. Edinburgh, Edinburgh University Press.

Christine Engel

Aleksei A. German's Estranging View of the Great Patriotic War[1]

Films about the Second World War are extremely popular in Russia today. This may seem surprising at first glance, since more than 60 years have gone by since the war ended. But if one looks more closely, one immediately sees that the victory of the Soviet Union over Nazi Germany is still seen as the most important event of the 20th century, and that this victory is the only remaining symbolic frame for the Russian collective identity.[2] The film endowment of the Russian Ministry of Culture willingly supports all projects on this theme, including those that are not overtly patriotic or heroic. Such films may be in the minority, but this makes them all the more worth mentioning. The best examples are two films from young directors, not only because they set a new accent within the genre by following the narrative of that "Germans are people too", but also because they both pursue high standards of cinematographic realization. One of these is *Polumgla* (2005) by Artëm Antonov. I have already written about this film elsewhere.[3] The other is *Poslednii poezd* (2004; The Last Train) by Aleksei A. German, whose composition and referential structure I will be analyzing in the following.

Aleksei Alekseevich German (*1976) is the son of the well-known director Aleksei Iur'evich German. His debut *Poslednii poezd* (2004) presented a film that drew a great deal of popular attention. This black-and-white film, which has received numerous prizes and awards (see the filmography at the end of the article) treats the subject of war from a perspective that seems unusual for a Russian audience. The film's two protagonists are two Germans, a doctor and a military postman. They arrive at a train station in Belorus' in the winter of 1944, and the camera shows the last days of their lives. The film does not press these figures into the usual friend-enemy paradigm, nor does it discuss the question of guilt or innocence usually so central to the genre. Instead, the film's decisive argument grows out of the idea that war has neither a dramaturgy nor a plot, and that any "bird's eye view" or overview is little more than an illusion.

Themes and Composition

The action of *Poslednii poezd* largely centers on the figure of the surgeon Paul Fischbach, a heavyset, clumsy man over 50 (see image 1) who is now supposed to report for duty at a military hospital on the Eastern front. But in the moment of his arrival, the German front collapses under the thrust of an unexpected Russian counterattack, and the military hospital is evacuated, leaving Fischbach behind with an exhausted medic and a heavily wounded soldier. When Fischbach sets out through the snowy forests and steppes in search of his scattered unit, he loses all sense of orientation. He then chances upon the military postman Kreuzer, who is also wandering aimlessly. On their way together, they witness attacks, blind murder, marauding, and arson. The film never quite clarifies the identity of the attackers, and there is no direct reason for all this murdering. Partisans and a scattered group of German emerge from the forest schematically, as do fleeing villagers. Their only closer encounter is with a group of Russian civilians, a man and three women who, in a state

Image 1:
Fischbach in the train compartment (min. 1.54)

of total exhaustion, have taken refuge in a half-collapsed hut. Although they recognize Fischbach and Kreuzer as Germans and consequently see them as a danger, the man decides not to kill them. But the film's last sequence shows Fischbach and Kreuzer what seems to be a hopeless situation: the group of Russian civilians themselves becomes a victim of an attack, and again, the attacker is uncertain. There are indications that Russian partisans have killed their own people: the man has been hanged, the women shot, and the building set on fire. Kreuzer tries to help, but his efforts are in vain and he breaks down with exhaustion and dies in the snow. Sitting on an empty suitcase, Fischbach holds the hand of a dying, vomiting girl, who looks directly into the camera with a piercing gaze before the camera pans up into the cloudy grey sky (see image 2). The closing titles make it clear that Fischbach also died without ever being found (see the sequence protocol in the appendix).

The schematic depiction of the partisans and Germans, who come out of nowhere from the foggy woods makes it difficult for both protagonists and audience to tell friend from foe (see image 3). The film shifts this dividing line, re-drawing it not between Germans and Russians, but between those in the grip of the general carnage, and those who do not become murderers even in situations of existential despair and danger. This neutralizes the standard stereotypes of "us" and "them" typical to Russian war movies.[4] It is also significant that the word "enemy" is never even mentioned once throughout the film's dialogues. Instead, the war

Image 2
Fischbach and the dead girl (min. 74.55)

appears as an event that pulls everyone in and washes them away, or as Kreuzer formulates it: "Is there any justice in us being driven forward, driven, driven, and driven?" (min. 51). The film underlines this fateful connection to occurrences that leave no space for purposeful, planned actions that might alter the course of events: all the movie's characters have a terrible cough; they wheeze and choke and either die of cold and hunger or are killed. To emphasize their common situation and, more importantly, to show that war has neither a dramaturgy nor a plot, as Fischbach puts it (min. 71), none of the figures in the film occupy any commanding position. Russians only appear as partisans, fleeing civilians, and, in the opening sequence, as prisoners of war, while the Germans appear as soldiers passing by alone or in small groups, and as the wounded or the staff in the field hospital. This makes the film's cast of characters very different from that of other war movies, in which there is always at least one officer, and, if one goes back to the iconography of the Brezhnev era, often includes the general staff as well as Stalin's "guiding hand". *Poslednii poezd*, on the contrary, never mentions the names of Hitler or Stalin at all.

The film's choice of two heroes – both of them almost civilians and unarmed – subverts and rejects any military pathos from the outset. Such pathos is very typical for most recent films on the Great Patriotic War; a good example is the film *Zvezda* (The Star, Dir.: Nikolai Lebedev, 2002) with its troop of virile young military scouts.[5] In *Poslednii poezd*,

Image 3:
Attack in the woods (min. 61.05)

Fischbach's corpulence and clumsiness as well as his middle age makes it impossible to imagine him as military hero. Instead, he embodies a comfortable bureaucratic type who has been catapulted from an orderly life, albeit without the joys of a family, into the fog of war, where life has no value anymore. This is diametrically opposed to his profession as a helper and a healer, and the film expresses this in that Fischbach cannot actually help the wounded or the sick: he stands by helplessly as Russians and Germans die, and cannot save anyone or anything. We discover that Fischbach had become a doctor precisely because he had been traumatized in the First World War as an eighteen year old conscript. The growing helplessness and subjection to the circumstance is indicated through the loss of clothing; (like Kreuzer) Fischbach loses everything that might have protected him in the beginning. He loses his suitcase, his gloves, his hat, and even his glasses.

Written by A.A. German, the screenplay was initially conceived for a short film, and was only developed into a full feature film of 82 minutes in the course of production.[6] Nevertheless, its composition is very convincing and clear. The film consists of two parts of equal length (32' and 34') with four sections and clearly marked as a middle (for more detailed information see sequence protocol in the appendix):

1.1 Fischbach's arrival at the railway station (4')

1.2 Car ride to the field hospital (9')

1.3 In the field hospital (12')

1.4 Fischbach and Kreuzer meet (7')
Impact of artillery shells (as a marked middle) (3')

2.1 Russian civilians in a log cabin (10')

2.2 Fischbach and Kreuzer in the forest (dialogue) (8')

2.3 Ambush in the woods (4')

2.4 Burned cabin with bodies (12')

Perspective and Visual Language

The film's visual language is marked by the idiosyncratic signature of the camera man Oleg Lukichev; it is full of long shots, hidden cuts, and close-ups. Most importantly, the close-ups, which make up a majority of all angles, visualize the film's central statement, namely that there can be no overview of war. The use of black and white gives the film a documentary note that refers to the time of the action and the film material common to newsreels. The most remarkable thing about this film, however, is that the camera follows the two Germans throughout. The camera shows us what the respective figure can see, not only taking the direction of his gaze, but imitating his height as well, be it kneeling, standing, or lying down. So, typically, the film's perspective imitates the movement of the human eye on the one hand, and also creates the impression of a hidden camera. This also gives the unspeakable atrocities in the film a certain dramaturgical development. For example, in the scene where Fischbach and Kreuzer come to the razed hut and see the hanged man, one first sees the hanged man's feet, and only then does the (camera) eye rise slowly, confronting the audience with the whole horrible scene. Moreover, this kind of camera perspective frames the limited visibility of the characters as they move through man-high grass through swamps and steppe, past bare tree trunks (see image 4). This presents a convincing visualization of hopelessness and forsakenness.

Image 4:
Fischbach and Kreuzer (min. 65.39)

German draws his cinematographic language from well-known directors like Akira Kurosava, Aleksandr Sokurov, or Andrei Tarkovskii, but most importantly, he cites the films of his father. The most noticeable inter-iconic references are to his films *Proverka na dorogakh* (1971, premiered 1986; Check-up on the Road/Checkpoint) and *Khrustalev mashinu* (1998; Khrustalev, My Car!), both of which were also shot in black and white and are marked by a subjective camera and a lively interest for the details of everyday life. This proximity to his father's handwriting prompted some reviewers to dismiss the film as "derivative".[7] Yet as Pëtr Vail' notes, there is a clear difference in their intentions: if the son highlights the ontological problem of "how one can live", his father places the ethical question of "how one should live" in the foreground.[8] Unlike *Proverka na dorogakh*, *Poslednii poezd* does not rest upon the development of a plot, but concentrates on observing figures that are confronted with their own dying and the dying of others.

Aside from the camera, the film is also keyed to the perspective of its characters in terms of language, with the Germans speaking German throughout the film. This confronts the Russian audience with a foreign language that only becomes comprehensible by reading subtitles. The use of spoken Russian is limited to a sequence of around ten minutes (min. 38–48). For a Russian audience, the estrangement effect is very strong, since the "Fritzes" in movies about the Great Patriotic War usually speak Russian.

In using spoken German, it may seem that *Poslednii poezd* is part of a larger tendency in recent war movies. German can also be heard in the TV series *Shtrafbat* (The Penal Battallion. Dir.: Nikolai Dostal', 2004), or in the films *Svoi* (Our Guys; Dir.: Dmitri Meskhiev, 2004) and *Zvezda*. However, in these films, spoken German usually has the function of marking the enemy as such, stigmatizing him as a totally different person who "is not one of us" in the usual dichotomic value scheme of friend and enemy.[9] Yet another use of a foreign language spoken can be found in Aleksandr Rogozhkin's *Kukushka* (2002) and Artëm Antonov's *Polumgla* (2005), both of which work toward a common basis of communication that primarily utilizes body language and everyday knowledge. Antonov goes as far as to have German actors play the German roles.[10] A.A. German, in contrast, distances himself from both Russians and Germans and moves to the neutral position of an observer. The main roles in *Poslednii poezd* are played by Russian actors and spoken by professional German speakers. A.A. German takes a rather unusual approach in casting his main characters. Fischbach is played by the theater historian Pavel Romanov, with whom A.A. German studied for a year, while Kreuzer is played by Petr Merkur'ev, who is well-known as both a musicologist and an actor. The role of the medic Ralph is played by Aleksei Devotchenko, who usually acts on stage.

Spatial Composition

In the descriptions of perspective and cinematography above, it has already become clear that A.A. German and his team have given a great deal of attention not only to technical visuals, but to the film's semiotics as well. The film consciously subverts the commonplace idea of a front, thought as a line along which a military confrontation takes place in an orderly fashion. Instead, it mediates a territory in which there is no visibility, no overview, and no direct way to reach a goal, since there is no path to be seen. The fog, the bare trees, and the high grass of the swamp force a circular movement through unchanging territory. This use of space robs the main characters of their orientation, both literally and figuratively speaking (see image 5). This loss of orientation also affects the spectator,

Image 5:
Kreuzer in high steppe grass (min. 28.55)

who is no longer able to tell friend from foe, since all minor characters are no more than outlines in the fog. Precisely this circumstance helps to unsettle common habits of viewing that have been schooled by the established conventions of war movies as they emerged in the 1970s, as a "grand style" of battle panoramas and victorious attacks.

On the symbolic level, the use of space in this film points toward a journey into the unconscious, that is, into the depths of the psyche. As in *Stalker* (1979) by Andrei Tarkovskii, this territory is marked as a zone in itself that operates according to its own unusual and unknown rules. In both films, the transition into this zone is clearly marked: in Tarkovskii's film, the three men ride in on a rail trolley, and at this point, the film turns from black and white to color, accompanied by nature sounds and chirping birds. In *Poslednii poezd*, the journey leads from a place that still operates according to rules – even if these are the rules of war – into the unpredictable space of the forest. The transition is marked by the Adagio from J.S. Bach's Harpsichord Concerto No. 3, whose quiet tones are accompanied by the howling of the wind (min. 10). On the visual level, this is the moment at which the car with Fischbach veers from the road and drives on through deserted, snow-covered terrain, as two other vehicles continue down the road that has almost been snowed under completely. This transition is marked additionally through a close-up of high grass and two dried out deciduous trees, counter-cut with a shot of the car's headlights in the fog (see image 6). By driving into the forest, Fischbach

Image 6:
Car turning off the road (min. 13.54)

enters a zone in which civilization has been suspended, and all restraints on affect have been lifted, a zone of slow dying as a transition from life to death. Unlike Stalker, where the three men do not actually make the last step and return to the squalor of their previous surroundings, *Poslednii poezd* does not let its characters leave this zone alive.

Dialogue

In general, the film does not have much dialogue. On a verbal level, it presents long stretches of speech fragments that do not cohere into any intelligible conversation, once again expressing the film's central statement, namely that there is no narrative in war. The speech fragments uttered by the four Russian civilians in the hut – a man and three women – are only mumbled and hard to understand in terms of acoustics (min. 38–40). In contrast to this general laconicity, there are two sequences in which Fischbach and Kreuzer hold relatively long monologues (min. 31–35, min. 50–57). What emerges here with a great clarity is the counterfactual function of the verbal level: the monologues express hope for an imminent arrival, and for a turn in the war, and, most importantly, that everything will be all right somehow in the end. One can also hear such hope in the fragmented conversations of the Russian civilians in the hut. The theme of false (or falsified) hope is underscored through the musical theme of the triumphal march from Verdi's opera Aida, which Fischbach whistles with a medic and an orderly at the field hospital (min. 20, min. 25).

In terms of dialogue, the film also develops another central theme, that of the intelligent person who finds himself in a situation in which he recognizes his position but is helpless to do anything about it. The film's figures have no chance of realizing their desires, nor can they control their actions or intervene in the course of events. Moreover, the war does not provide a stage for any kind of self-representation. Life as a stage, as a social, communicative event, loses all meaning and is limited to an exclusively creaturely dimension. This thematic complex can be heard in references to performances on stage. One of the Russian women in the hut is a musician, and in one of his monologues, Kreuzer tells us that he has always dreamed of playing the role of Hamlet, but always only got minor parts (min. 33).

The ambivalence between a coming-to-terms with the situation and the hope that some external power might intervene is also transposed onto a metaphysical level, which the film renders on dialogic and visual levels. For example, Fishbach says that he sometimes feels like someone is watching for above and smiling (min. 55). Another hope also contrasts with the characters' reduction to a very basic, creaturely level of existence, namely one that connects death to a notion usually found in Buddhism, that the next life might be that of an animal, be it a dog or a bird. This context adds semantic relevance to the images of horses (min. 15) or to a remark made by one of the Russian women, who says that she was a horse in one of her dreams (min. 40). In the last scene, which ends with the camera falling toward the grey, overcast sky, the film takes on the viewpoint of a heterodiegetic narrator who does not belong to the world of the story's characters. Moreover, the soundtrack expresses a quiet hope in the civilizing power of humanity through art with a reprise of the Harpsichord Concerto's Adagio, which now rises above the howling wind and accompanies the credits. On the level of dialogue, this idea finds its expression through the reference to Shakespeare (min. 33) as well as a Pushkin quote (min. 43).

In expressing the conviction that art could save humanity, A.A. German draws a connection to the ethos of Andrei Tarkovskii, one that the latter expressed with the greatest clarity in his film *Andrei Rublev* (1969) as well as his writings. Both directors have something else in common: both believe that films encapsulate time, and that film is the only medium capable of capturing temporality and its specificity in any adequate way. In this sense, A.A. German's characteristic love for the details of everyday life gains the additional meaning of saving the details of the everyday from oblivion. This intent also finds its expression ex negativo in the closing titles, which tells us that Fischbach's body was never found and that his memory did not even live on in old photo albums (see sequence protocol in the appendix).

Conclusion

Despite – or because of – his youth, A.A. German has succeeded in showing the Second World War from a very different perspective than in most recent Russian films on this theme. The film subverts the widespread tendency in Russia to tend to the memories under the aspect of victory, thus strengthening the only remaining symbolic brace of collective identity. In this sense, it is all the more surprising that a film like Poslednii poezd was able to receive the support of the Russian Ministry of Culture, even though it goes against all the canons and established discursive lines. It is also strange that this film did not provoke an outrage among critics or the audience, though it was occasionally reproved for its exaggerated naturalism.[11]

With his film, German has shown that it is possible to place new accents in the Russian film discourses on the Second World War. His main achievement is that he stands out against any romantization of violence whatsoever. This differentiates his work from those films that depict war as a game with its own rules, such as Aleksei Balabanov's film on the war in Chechnia *Voina* (War, 2002).[12] A.A. German even succeeds in mediating a humanity that is not connected with the customary Russian messianism in anyway. This also shows that A.A. German refuses to resort to other stereotypical narratives in treating this theme. This makes him very different from other directors such as Artëm Antonov whose film *Polumgla* is in search of new ways in which to depict war, but refers back to the traditional values of the Russian countryside and its space. What seems most surprising about *Poslednii poezd*, however, is its fundamental rejection of the patriotic pathos that is so typical for all other movies of this genre, inspiring a "holy wrath" against the enemy in one way or another.

Endnotes

1 Translated by David Riff.
2 Cf. Gudkov 2005, 61.
3 Cf. Engel 2008.
4 Cf. Zubarina 2003.

5 See Engel 2007.
6 Cf. Solnceva 2004.
7 Cf. e.g. Zubavina 2003.
8 Cf. Poverkh barer'ov 2003.
9 Cf. Liderman, 13.
10 See Engel 2008 for a more detailed analysis.
11 Cf. Medvedeva 2006.
12 Cf. Engel 2003.

References

Engel Christine (2003), Kulturelles Gedächtnis, neue Diskurse. Zwei russische Filme über die Kriege in Tschetschenien. *Osteuropa*, Vol. 53, 604–617.

Engel, Christine (2008), 60 Jahre danach: Neue Sichtweisen auf den Großen Vaterländischen Krieg im Film "Polumgla". In Fieseler, Beate and Ganzenmüller, Jörg (eds.), *Kriegsbilder. Mediale Darstellungen des Großen Vaterländischen Krieges der Sowjetunion, 1941–2005.* Essen (in print).

Engel, Christine (2007), Ein ewiger Stern im patriotischen Diskurs: "Zvezda" 1947–2002. In Deutschmann, Peter (ed.), *Kritik und Phrase. Festschrift für Wolfgang Eismann.* Wien, 143–170.

Gudkov, Lev (2005), Die Fesseln des Sieges. Russlands Identität aus der Erinnerung an den Krieg. *Osteuropa*, Vol. 55, Issue 4–6, 56–72.

Liderman, Julia (2008), *Kurs na patriotzm i otvet rossiiskogo kinematografa v 2000-e gody. Novye sjuzhety, novye budzhety, novye fil'my o voine* (in print).

Medvedeva, N. (2006), Poslednii poezd. http://novkovcheg.ru/printer_48.html (22.6.2006).

Poverkh barer'ov (2003), "Poslednii poezd". Fil'm Alekseia Germana-mladshego. Avtor programmy Dmitrii Volchek. http://www.svoboda.org/programs/OTB/2003/OBT.103103.asp (31.10.2003).

Solnceva, Alena (2004), German. Nastoiashchii, no 'malen'kii'. *Vremia novostei*, Nr. 19, 5.2.2004. http://www.vremya.ru/print/90809.html (4.4.2008).

Zubavina, Irina (2003), Shinel' otca. Poslednii poezd. Iskusstvo Kino, Vol. 17, http://www.kinoart.ru/magazine/12-2003/repwertoire1203/zubavina03_123/. (4.4.2008).

Poslednii poezd filmography:

Russia, 2004

Kinostudiia PiĖF
Duration: 82 min.
Languages: Russian, German (with Russian subtitles)
Directed by Aleksei Alekseevich German
Screenplay: Aleksei Alekseevich German
Camera: Oleg Lukichev
Starring Pavel Romanov, Petr Merkur'ev
Co-starring: Aleksei Devotchenko, Irina Rakshina, Aleksandr Tiurin

Prizes at film festivals in Venice, Saloniki, Wiesbaden, Rotterdam, Minsk, Kiev, Moscow, Anapa, Ul'janovsk, St. Petersburg

Appendix: Sequence protocol of Poslednii poezd (82 min.)

Time	Visuals	Audio and dialogue
	Opening titles (white text on black background, titles in red)	
(1.1)	**Fischbach's arrival at the railway station**	
1.20	A train is standing in a railway station; a glance into a compartment through the window (frame): a fat man with glasses (= Fischbach) sits chewing and drinking tea from a Russian tea glass; a freight train reflects in the window as it pulls into the station; Fischbach gets out with two suitcases and a bag	Drawn out train-whistle. Fischbach coughs a little. Sound of a train pulling in. Trainwhistle.
2.40	Fischbach (F) is standing on the snowy tracks; he picks up his luggage and sets off past two German soldiers, past three railway workers, Russian prisoners of war	Soldier: "You can look at fire, water, and your paycheck forever."
4.13	F. slowly passes the German freight train, a few German soldiers overtake him.	
4.31	A soldier on the freight train asks for a light.	Soldier: "Do you have a light?" F.: "No, I don't smoke."
4.43	A guard tower is in the shot; three children pass by; F. passes smoking sentries at the barrier; they are bundled up to protect themselves from the cold.	German voice (Off): "And then we'll go to Germany and we'll live there and be happy, but we won't take you with us."
5.17	A black limousine is waiting for F.; the driver (a soldier) puts his luggage in the back; a smoking, bundled-up soldier is in the foreground.	The driver apologizes for his lateness; a guard dog barks. Driver: "The sky is cloudy, a blizzard is on the way."
(1.2)	**Car ride to the field hospital**	
6.21	F. and the driver drive off. A horse drawn cart crosses the road.	Driver: "Doctor, you've come at the wrong time. Everything is quiet, no one is shooting, everyone is waiting for the Russian retreat."

6.59	In the car, F. is on the backseat; the camera follows his gaze, which rests on the back of the driver's head and shoulders. His face remains expressionless as he listens.	Driver: A monologue about doctors and childhood ailments.
8.26	The car stops and the driver gets out; he asks the soldiers sitting by the roadside for a cigarette; they smoke.	
9.24	The big black limousine and a military motorcycle get in line behind the horse drawn cart; the barrier bar goes up and all three vehicle start; the road is clearly visible.	
10.10	Both other vehicles drive down the street to the right, but the car with F. drives straight on. Close-up of F. without glasses, a thin beard on his upper lip and chin.	
10.34	Fog, grass, two bare deciduous trees; car from the front with headlight; a totally deserted area; the car drives over uneven terrain off-screen to the right.	Adagio from the Harpsichord Concerto No. 3 by J.S. Bach, accompanied by the howling of the wind.
11.26	A close-up of F. who is peering from the window; a snow-covered area, a tank overtakes the car; more German tanks stand around like skeletons.	
13.13	The car passes soldiers who hardly stand out against the snowy landscape in their overexposed uniforms; two trucks pass the group; close-up of F.; tanks and group of trees through rear window.	The wind whistles.
13.49	High steppe grass, wind bent. The car's headlight emerge from the fog; snow is blown away by the window; the car drives off-screen to the right; pure milky fog.	The sound of the car's motor.
(1.3)	**In the field hospital**	

14.24	Car (seen from the back) arrives at a bridge with wrought iron railings, a gate opens, a mansion in the background; a truck with wounded drives off, a bundled-up soldier carries a folded wheelchair.	Soldier: "Doctor, you should turn back, we're all being evacuated." F.: "No, no thanks." Voice from off camera: "Come on, come on, move your asses!"
15.26	F. gets out and the luggage is unloaded. F. goes to the entrance: a truck with a plane blocks our view.	F. "Excuse me, where can I find the commanding officer?" Soldier: "Over there, in the war." Voice from off camera: "Hurry, hurry, you have to move faster!"
15.50	In the building: big empty room with two horses; F. crosses it and goes to the next room.	
16.31	F. enters the ward with two rows of beds next to the walls. A thin man is sitting leaning over in a wheelchair, the field surgeon Ralph (R), seen from behind. A wounded man is carried by on a stretcher.	Fragmented dialogue between F. and Ralph (R) on the hopeless situation at the front.
18.31	A heavily wounded patient is lying in bed. R. is smoking; R. from the front.	R.: "He's beyond help, let him be."
19.56	An orderly is also in the room; R. and the orderly look out of the window onto the foggy park (view from outside). Soldiers are clearing up munitions (their orders: put everything into the pit and add some water); R. and orderly from outside the window (frame). Trucks and motorcycles drive off.	Conversation between orderly and R. on the hopeless situation.
20.50	R. and orderly.	R. (coughs), orderly whistles triumphal march (from off screen).
21.58	R. and F. sit by the heavily wounded patient's bed (his face is totally burned). R. is smoking. F. eats an apple, cutting it with his pocket knife.	Ralph coughs, F. and R. have a conversation about women's superstitions about childbirth.

23.25	R. and F. sit by the bed.	R.: "Fischbach, do you know how to shoot?" (Coughs, smokes). F.: "Yes, actually, tried it a couple of times 25 years ago in France, but I never hit anyone thank god."
24.24	F. leaves the ward with his bag.	R.: "Can you check to see if the car has come? In the backyard. You can find the door at the end of the corridor." F.: "These boots don't fit."
24.46	R. from the front, lies down on the bed next to the heavily wounded man; both are shown in a medium framing shot.	Explosion
25.07	F. at the back entrance; view through the gate arch; smoke; F. in glasses, scarf, and military cap seen from the front.	Explosion; F. coughs; more explosions.
25.48	R. comes, both close up.	R. and F. whistle the triumphal march F.: "They say that fat people are comfortable. But I'm wild and crazy." (laughs affably)
26.21	R. goes crazy, physically attacks F., pulls his cap from his head and throws him into the snow. F. gets up, finds his glasses with difficulty, breathes heavily, and holds on to his heart.	R.: "Get out of here!" R.: "Go find yourself a cushy spot at headquarters. Nobody's coming for us. We're going to die here."
27.21	R. in the ward. He dismisses the orderly and sits down in a wheelchair. The orderly brings a footbath and a rifle. A lingering shot of R. and the wounded man.	R.: "You can go. Klaus and I are staying." He coughs and whistles the melody again.
(1.4)	**Fischbach and Kreuzer meet**	
28.38	Man with a military field cap (military postman) fights his way through snow and man-high steppe grass. He has no gloves, no bag, no weapon. Sinks in and gets up again. Camera from back, from front, from the side, slightly above, below.	Rustling wind

31.03	Kreuzer (K) meets F.; F. is sitting rigid in the snow.	K.: "Doctor! Get up! My name is Kreuzer. I'm the postman."
31.35	The two stamp off through birch trees, K. is on camera.	K.: "We saw one another on the train. You got off in Poland at one stop and almost missed the train."
32.38	Shot of F. without glasses and with a cap, scarf, and bag.	F. talks to himself and says he wishes he were a stone in water.
33.08	F. and K. from the back, stamping through a clearing with clipped trees	K. keeps coughing; F.: "My wife is waiting for me in Dresden." K.: "We're never going to get out of here." F.: "We'll get out, I have money." K.: "Oh forget about your money."
33.37	F. and K. in the forest from a variety of angles	K. holds a monologue about his experiences as an actor
34.31	F. and K. in the forest from a variety of angles	F.: "I don't understand where the front is. We're surrounded by partisans. But we're not really soldiers." K. coughs and coughs. F.: "If the partisans catch us, please kill me, I'm begging you." K.: "How am I supposed to kill you, with my bare hands? If they get us, we'll suffer."
35.25	Shot of K. alone	K.: "Doctor, don't stop, it won't be far now."
(Mid)	**Impact of artillery shells (as a marked middle)**	
35.30	A shell lands.	Explosion

35.38	K. falls to the ground with his hands in his pockets. Another shell lands, earth and mud fly. Blood drips from K.'s nose, he crawls over the ground, past a bog hole. The camera follows him closely. Shot of F.'s legs. He drops his bag to the ground. Still lying on the ground, K. pulls a cigarette from his jacket, lights it, gives it to F. who takes it and smokes. F. sits down next to K.	K.: "They were aiming at you, they probably thought you were a tank."
38.11	Another shell lands, spraying earth and mud into the sky.	
(2.1)	**Russian civilians in a log cabin**	
38.25	Forest clearing. A young woman with an ear cap of fur coughs and goes to a small log cabin. She hugs herself with her arms to keep from the cold. She enters the cabin through a rag curtain. A second woman in a dark fur cap is waiting inside. A third woman in a bright knit wool hat and a chubby man come into view.	Bits of dialogue in Russian about dreams. Coughing.
39.53	The man in the cabin sweats with exhaustion. Coughs.	Bits of dialogue in Russian about the confused situation.
41.24	Sick girl (app. 15 years old) with a fever in bed. Coughs. The other women are taking care of her.	Bits of dialogue in Russian about illnesses.
42.40	The wind whistles. The woman in the light wool hat looks out of the glassless window of the barn. In the barn, visibility is poor. The woman peers through the window; the chubby man comes running, stumbles in front of the house, coughs, pulls his gun, shoots. There is screaming.	Bits of dialogue in Russian.
42.46	The two women in the dark fur hats on the bench in front of the cabin.	One of the Russian women talks about her dreams.

43.39	Russian woman in light wool hat inside by the window; she is restless.	Bits of dialogue in Russian.
44.31	Man comes running, trips, loses his hat. Cocks the gun, there is a shot. Close-up of the pistol and the man's abdomen.	Man (in Russian): "Get out of here! Go! Go! Get out of here." One of the women screams terrified (off camera).
45.05	K. is standing in front of the man. He gets on his knees. Two women are heading for F. in the background.	Man: "Freeze! I said stand still!" K.: "I can't hear you. I can't hear anything. I'm the postman." They both cough
45.31	The woman in the white wool cap (W) takes F.'s bag and opens it; the woman with the dark fur cap is beating F. with a stick, hitting the nape of his neck and his upper back.	Coughing. Woman (W) (in Russian): "Calm down."
45.55	Man wipes the sweat from his forehead.	Man: "Get out of here." (Coughs)
46.08	Woman with fur hat vomits; woman in the wool cap takes the gun; the man takes it back again.	W: "For some reason, I don't feel sorry for them. They're killing us, you know." Man: "My hands are totally frozen." W: "What can I...?" Man: "So what (…?) should I tell them?" W: "Take this, don't forget." Screaming. W: "This is stupid somehow, and now my feet are wet."
47.05	Shot of F. and K.	K.: "Fischbach, what are they saying? I can't understand a single word. I don't want them to kill us. I can't go on."
47.26	The man coughs and clumsily loads his gun.	K. (to the man): "I can't go on. Can't you shoot us already? Why don't you shoot us, you asshole. Go to hell!"

47.59	F. and K. are walking away. A thick fog is falling.	
48.19	Tree trucks. Wind. The man and the women go back into the hut.	
(2.2)	**Fischbach and Kreuzer in the forest (dialogue)**	
49.12	Bare birches, fog, tree trucks; K. is lying on his back in the dirty snow (a close up of his face from above), his head uncovered.	K. (in a quiet voice, breaking off, coughing): "That was terrible, terrible, I was standing there and thought the lights would go out and that everything would disappear into darkness. Everything goes black and there's no more me. (Coughs). Like in a dream. And if we die here, no one will ever know. They'll find our bones in a hundred years, and then they'll throw them away. It's so strange that everything will still be here except for me. This tree will still be here. Doctor, we haven't done anything bad to anyone? So why? Is it fair for the waves to drive us, drive us, drive us on?" (coughs)
51.10	F. is lying in the dirty snow on his back (a close-up of his face from above), his head uncovered. F. eats snow. K. is lying on his back (a close-up of his face from above, from the side, then from the front).	F.: "No, Kreuzer, we won't die, there will be another life, maybe we'll become birds or dogs, only God knows." K.: "Are you a Buddhist?" F. tells about his terrible experiences in the First World War.

53.20	K. on his back (close up of face, from above, from the side). F. on his back (close up of face from above). Camera pans from F. to K. and back (from above).	K. and F. about his fear and the impossibility of retreat. F.: "Sometimes I think that somebody is watching us from above and smiling. Strange, isn't it?"
57.32	F. and K. are still lying in the snow. K. is exhausted and falls asleep. F. takes a few steps and sees a kneeling soldier unwinding something.	F.: "Are you sleeping, Kreuzer? Everything will be alright. I can't sleep."
(2.3)	**Ambush in the woods**	
58.43	Kneeling German soldier, coughs (camera at knee level). Behind him, one sees two more (from leg to hip), then a stretcher with a wounded man, and two bearers (obviously a squad from the field hospital. A Russian in a fur hat drinks from a tea kettle, and doesn't see the three of them. There is a shot, not fired by the Germans, and the Russian is hit. Blood flows from his mouth.	Quiet bits of conversation in German. A shot. More explosions. Mortar shells.
59.40	The German drop the stretcher and shoot. They also get shot at, and one of the Germans falls to the ground. From the right, four partisans come on screen, shooting one of the German point blank. There are bodies on the ground. 5 or 6 more partisans come on screen as outlines. You can't see them clearly. They kill and take what they need from the dead. Fog.	The moaning of the wounded.

60.59	Sharp focus, clear visibility. Partisans carry away the body of the Russian. A group of civilians comes onscreen from the right: women with (milk) cans, bundles, backpacks, accompanied by two more partisans.	
61.42	More Russian civilians pass by with carts (from right to left)	Folk melody (Russian soldier's song), whistled (off camera)
61.53	Everyone is gone. Three German bodies are lying in the snow, surrounded by man-high tree trunks.	
62.14	Another group of civilians on carts, sleds, and on foot pass by, leading a goat. The camera is at waist level, cutting off their faces. A partisan takes the gun off one of the dead German soldiers.	The whistling continues.
62.35	Another dead German body (close up). Fog closes in.	
63.43	A figure comes onscreen from the right. It is K., he walks up to the body, it's probably Ralph (though this is not clear). K. drags him over to F. F.'s big backside in the camera.	K.: "I'm bringing him." F.: "He's already dead, Kreuzer." K.: "Doctor, you haven't even looked at him. You can't do that." F.: "Kreuzer, the bullet hit him in the chest."

64.27	F. cumbersomely walks from corpse to corpse, feeling their throats for a pulse. K. also goes from corpse to corpse.	F.: "They're barbarians, really barbarians." F.: "You've looked at this one here three times already, he's dead. I treated him a year ago once. In Germany." F.: "Let's go, Kreuzer, before they come back. It's enough, save somebody later. We can't help anyone here. Come on, we have to go back. Leave me alone. We're stuck. We have to go back, there are partisans over there. We won't get out. I never had trouble with my heart, but now my heart hurts. We drove and drove and drove and now, we've reached our destination."
65.21	K. and F. (framing shot), near a man-high tree trunk. More tree trunks.	F.: "I'll never see my wife again. She's left me for some engineer, some little engineer. She was twenty years younger than me. I lied to you like a little kid. I don't have anyone anymore. I don't even have children." K. keeps coughing, louder than F.
66.18	Camera pan to the clearing in the distance (from above); fogbanks close in.	
(2.4)	**Burned cabin with bodies**	
66.26	F. and K. slowly walk alongside the burned, collapsed cabin.	A woodpecker knocks.
67.25	F. comes across a female corpse. It is the woman with the dark fur cap. She's lying on her back. Her face is burned.	
67.40	The camera follows F.'s point of view: smoldering wood. The camera pans to the next dead body.	

68.32	F. slowly leaves the remains of the cabin behind.	A woodpecker knocks.
68.41	K. and F. look up a tree. The feet of a hanged man (the chubby Russian man from before) come onscreen. The camera glides upward along his body.	K.: "That's how it is." F.: "Russians kill Germans and Germans kill Russians."
69.26	F. takes a few steps back to the hut and sees something. K. picks up a plank, the sick Russian girl from before is lying underneath, heavily wounded. Close-up of the girl's face, vomit spews from her mouth.	F.: "Leave it, Kreuzer, it's unpleasant and looks horrible. Let's go on, it's enough. This will take a bad end."
69.55	K. picks up the girl. F. bends down to her.	K.: "Doctor, she's alive!" F.: "You really have a good soul. I've often heard that postmen are good people. I never believed it." F.: "Bring me something so that I can sit down."
70.49	K. brings an empty suitcase.	K.: "Sit down, Doctor."
71.06	F. tries to calm the girl down by speaking to her; sits down. K. comes from the smoldering ruins with an umbrella and a cigarette; he hands F. the umbrella. K. covers the girl with his coat.	F. "Everything is so senseless. There is no dramaturgy, and there is no plot." F: "Go, Kreuzer, get a little air, you can't help here anyway."
72.09	F. talks quietly and soothingly to the girl who is still vomiting.	K.: "Doctor, everything will be alright." F.: "I think I may have even lost some weight. I've always dreamed of that. But now that I'm getting thinner I wish I were fat again."
72.33	K. takes a few steps away from the hut, wobbles, leans against a bare tree trunk, squats, falls down with folded arms and doesn't get up. He is dead.	

73.04	Close up from above: K.'s dead face. Deep wrinkles on his forehead. Fogbanks.	
73.16	Cut: hanged man.	
73.19	Cut: F. sits there with closed eyes. The shredded umbrella is open. He is breathing heavily. The camera slowly moves down along his body. He is holding the girl's hand. The girl is dying and turns her dying face to the camera.	The girl groans.
74.35	F. is still sitting there. The girl is dead. The ruins are smouldering.	A woodpecker knocks and the wind whistles.
75.20	The camera pans to the bare forest in the background and falls up into the grey sky.	Quiet music, harpsichord concerto by Bach (as before), at first over the wind and then louder and louder (without wind).
75.54	Closing titles in Russian: "Nothing is known of Paul Fischbach's last days. His body was never found. In the trying times that followed, he was forgotten by everyone he knew and by everyone who knew him. His name was erased from human memory. Since he had no children and no close relatives after the divorce from his wife, it might have happened that some friends' grandchildren asked about this clumsy heavyset man when they saw his photo in the albums, and they too shrug their shoulders and laugh. Time passed and swallowed all those old albums as well."	
76.17	Credits	

Suzanne Ament

Lyric and Legacy, Melody and Memory: World War II Songs and the Shaping of Memory and Identity

The participants in World War II created a body of songs from 1941 to 1945 that is remembered as "songs of the war years." The body of song created was huge; hundreds of songs appeared as brand new creations or as spin-offs of older songs. Numerous songs survived the rigors of popular approval, sensors' marks, and the fluctuating politics during and after the war to become a coherent, recognizable set of songs, accepted by state and population alike, as a legacy from the war years.

During and after the war, these songs shaped the perception of the war and the psychological response to it, and fostered a sense of identity for individuals and groups who heard the music. Multiple layers must be considered in order to define and comprehend why these songs had such a long-lasting effect on society.

This paper examines the various elements that shaped and defined this legacy for the past 65 years. Some elements involve the songs themselves; the content resonated with the listener and often evoked a mood in the collective citizenry. The lyrics are critical for conveying messages about the war. The melody too has an impact, a physiological one that might trigger emotional and physical reactions. Also, the factors of time and distance from the war shape what people respond to or seek out in the songs.

The make-up of the audience is not homogenous. There are several generations: those who saw the war, their children, and a second post-war generation. These generations still have their own "language," different from the other generations, by which they interpret and react to the war. Each generation, "[...] can refer to individuals' recognitions that they share a common identity because they have all been marked – psychologically, emotionally, sometimes bodily by a specific and temporally bounded common experience."[1] Or in some cases, they were not touched by that experience.

Each generation may have a different interpretation of the songs, their reasons for listening, and their emotional closeness to the songs. Those born after the war heard the songs from their older relatives, in pioneer camps, at school, in films and on the radio. Their memories were not linked with hardships of war or sacrifice but rather with the experiences at summer camp, home, or school. Perhaps, as Nina Tumarkin intimates in her discussion of the cult of the war, many young people were bored with or even actively resented these state rituals of the past generations, but, at least in the case of song, there were many other non-governmental avenues which exposed them to the genre.

The younger generation obviously places these songs in an historical context; it is not "their" music, but nevertheless the music conveys more than old fogies doddering in past memories. People of all ages know these songs, and most could actively sing some of them.

Another element that shaped the culture and interpretation of songs over time is the control that the party and state held over the perspectives released to the general public. Depending on the era, the productivity of artists, the availability of recordings, and the level of emphasis placed on the war, the population would perceive and retain "relics" from the war differently.

Nina Tumarkin describes this shifting process aptly in her work on the cult of World War II. Significantly though, she does not discuss at any length the cult in musical terms. I contend that music, and especially song, had a fairly "sacred" place in this cult and thus remained more or less untouched. Perhaps this is because of the portable and personal nature of songs. Even if the state tried to ban these songs, this was impossible as long as the people could remember and sing. If the state couldn't sensor the individuals who informally sang them, then it also could not change the words.

While the body of song remained more or less intact from the war years, the state did indeed, according to anecdotal evidence, shape the public availability and prominence of songs. Record collections were sold; pioneers learned war songs in their summer camps and military training; and war films contained songs. Radio programs were aired to seek the texts and histories of the lesser-known songs created during the war. For the wartime generation, the state renewed and revived old memories, and for the younger generations, it educated and familiarized them with the war songs.

The functions for songs – mobilizing, healing, reflecting, and commemorating – were negotiated during the war between the party and the people via the state arts organizations and individual preferences. The State's initial push that songs should "inspire hatred," elicit "revenge, and inspire the troops to battle," was met with soldiers' responses that they were already fighting the enemy constantly and needed something different from songs. They needed hope to return home to loved ones, and to have a rest from the horrors of war they faced ceaselessly.

By war's end, songs played a special role. Most of the songs carried themes of caring, longing for home, and missing comrades and friends. Most did not celebrate Stalin, the military prowess, or even victory. And if they did, there was always a hint of melancholy for the loss that accompanied the victory.

During the war, people negotiated the kinds of songs that they needed and the songs in turn shaped the people's view of the war and of themselves. Units that were awarded their own song sang it proudly as a symbol of recognition for bravery and sacrifice in the face of the enemy.

The lyrics greatly determined the function of a song for its audience. Whatever the reality was, song texts often imparted a sense of hope. For example, in *Let's Have a Smoke* and in *Where are my War-time Buddies?* both written near the end of the war, the narrator is remembering the war from a safe place in the future. Lyrics speak of folding up the greatcoats and later unpacking them in remembrance.

The message is that the listener, too, has survived beyond the war to look back. There were assurances that home hearth and loved ones awaited, or, in the case of *Vasia Vaselek*, that even if the first girl didn't wait, someone else would come along. A few songs emphasized taking vengeance upon returning – notably *Five Bullets* and *The Fateful Rock*. These messages of hope, victory and a future life gave the displaced, the injured, and those separated from loved ones the possibility of reunification, and a bright outlook replete with children, a home and, most of all, peace. These messages appealed to a core human value – to be needed, remembered, and wanted.

Another element of the lyric was its authenticity in discussing serious themes like death and loss. *In the Forest at the Front* describes a soldier pondering the possibility that he might die the next day. Songs like *Evening on the Quay, Song about the Dnipr,* and *Farewell, Rugged Cliffs,* all realistically attest to losing cities and homes to the enemy. Once victory did come and survivors returned home, those who had loved these songs could see them as symbols of victory and regaining what had been lost. Ultimately, the lyrics represent that each person who fought and suffered was valuable precisely because he or she fought and survived. Thus, these songs that people claimed as their own during the war also became symbols of victory in the collective sense after the war. The legacy of these songs is that they represent the success of each individual who came through the crucible.

Lyrics are important because they carry the cognitive message of the song; they are poetic or romantic. Yet songs inherently contain melody as well. Some songs were created from existing melodies, which gave a sense of familiarity to the listener, who only had to change the words in order to learn the new song. Using existing melodies also allowed people to create their own versions, even if they were not musically inclined. The best examples of this are the numerous versions of the lyrics for the melody of *Katiusha.* Whoever had their own versions of this song would be reminded of it by the mainstream version and feel tied to that melody because of their personal memories.

If melodies were created during the war, then later, the veteran would flash back to the time they heard that song and the memories and feelings accompanying it. Since songs generally represented positive moments in the war experience, memories would be positive. The veteran might take to whistling or singing it, or might use it at a special occasion; hence, preserving the song for themselves and conveying it to the next generation.

Performers and audience alike noted that the occasions when war songs were played had positive connotations. Soldiers welcomed artists to the front with flowers, gifts, and notes of appreciation. The artists felt useful and appreciated and wanted to sing and look their best for the soldiers. Several memoirs recounted how hearing the music prompted men to reflect, go into their own worlds, and even cry. Sometimes audiences would request a song to be repeated several times.

These elements may not totally explain the strength of the legacy. Recent research summarized thoroughly by Daniel Schneck and Dorita Berger depicts the link that music has to the physiology of the human body. Music therapy was established as an intervention for trauma victims of World War II. The idea is that music and its elements – rhythm, melody, tempo, etc. – have direct and measurable effects on human biological systems. If a system is threatened beyond its normal state, then physiologically it goes through certain biological changes, which if prolonged, may endanger the life of the system. This can be reversed, they say, "Functionally adaptive responses are triggered by the body's yielding to continuous forcing functions, a process called physiological entrainment."[2]

Music is the tool that brings about this "entrainment." The different elements of music have direct effect on a number of systems and in a variety of ways. Studies have shown that music can affect all biological systems of the body. It can act in a variety of ways: to excite, inhibit, sedate, stimulate, and ameliorate.

According to Schneck and Berger, "music and the body share a unique symbiotic relationship independent of cognition."[3] So even unconsciously, the soldier, the singer, or the patient, when hearing music, is going through a therapeutic process. Music, "[...] directly stimulates the body's own self-healing and or adaptive mechanisms [...]."[4] Thus the soldier hearing the war song even after the war is calmed, his body removed from the anxious state for even a short time, achieving entrainment.

"When something happens more than once, the body gets used to it and a 'conditioned reflex network' is created. The nervous system remembers both how and how often it responded to a certain stimulus."[5] So, when the soldiers requested songs other than the marches and exhortations to kill the Germans, they may not have been reacting simply to the cognition that this was something they were already doing and did not need a reminder. The physiological effects of marches and driving melodies drove biological systems, already under stress and entering the fear spiral, even closer to the state of endangerment. These soldiers unconsciously sensed that these songs were neither healthful, nor helpful.

In the same way, when an artistic brigade performed, the music acted upon its listeners through its many elements. The soldiers returning from battle were stressed, in pain, or exhausted. The music acted upon them, since it was lyrical, relaxed, and sometimes light-hearted, by reversing the stressed or fearful state. People consciously cried or enjoyed themselves, but were probably unaware their body systems were working towards health, immunity, or balance. Once the war was over, and the body with its "memory" reheard these songs, the body reacted by bringing about those same physiological changes that would affect the person positively and create a sense of "better," thereby reinforcing the connection with the song.

Two caveats come to mind when considering this element of song legacy. First, Schneck and Berger note that different people have different reactions to the elements of music: "The body of any given individual may have a way of recognizing in music his or her unique electromagnetic pattern – a musical DNA print, if you will, [...] a 'C major' or an 'A minor' personality."[6] This layer of unpredictability might render it impossible to accurately interpret what is happening in an individual. But it might well explain the different points of view concerning music and its function. The man in Gorky Park on Victory Day 1991 who asserted without hesitation, "There was no music during the war; things were too bad for that," might be a person who had a harder time resonating with the music. Perhaps he was too traumatized to be affected positively by it, so he believed there was no music.[7]

At the other end of the spectrum, Eva Bobrova and her daughter Lena believed that they survived the Leningrad blockade because of Irma Iaunzem's music.

> It seemed like everything was over ... no strength to go on living... and suddenly there came an unusual shuffling sound from the radio and then a song began ... The voice that sang was unbelievably touching, nice, and dear. 'Mama, that is life! ... We must live.' So my dearest Irma Petrovna, you with your song returned us to life.[8]

Most people would fall between these two extremes, recognizing that there was music, and feeling like it had some sort of positive effect.

The second difficulty also stems from unpredictability. Whereas the music therapist, or the physician, can administer "doses" of the elements of music and measure the responses, the historian can never recreate the exact sound. Did the ensemble have a soprano singer, use rhythm instruments, and was it on key? There is no control for estimating the real effect the music had.

Schneck and Berger freely admit that much work is necessary to fully understand this connection between music, the body, and the mind. However, it is plausible that in trying to understand the factors that led to the preservation of songs after the war, at least for the generation that lived through the war, this phenomenon must be considered.

After the war, the images of it were presented in different ways at different times. Tumarkin's book recounts these changes and attempts to understand the various movements, opinions, and symbols that arose. Generally, song is absent from this account. One case in particular stands out. Although the banner that was flown over the *Reichstag* was preserved and became "the Holy of Holies," symbolizing the complete defeat of the Fascists, there is no mention of one of the best-known and loved Soviet singers who appeared on those steps, under that flag, to glorify victory. Lidia Ruslanova, already a military favorite traveled to Berlin, where she performed Russian folk songs at the victory. Perhaps she is absent from the later remembrances of the war because she fell victim to one of Stalin's post-war purges of those close to General Zhukov. She was arrested in 1947 and spent 5 years in Vladimir prison for anti-Soviet propaganda, ironic given the theme of her concert in Berlin. The only protest she could make against her arrest was to stop singing, even though she had given everything she had in the war effort.[9] Despite her later rehabilitation, and her resumption of performances, she is not exulted as one of the figures in the new style of war commemoration.

The absence could also be intentional. The songs of the war years best symbolized something that the cult did not want to resurrect. The historian Mikhail Gefter had some letters from the front he felt would never be published. "The letters were too personal and too lyrical. Our readers are supposed to learn that our young men fought for the motherland, for Stalin, rather than for themselves or for each other or for genuine freedom."[10]

The nation had indeed carried out a heroic act in bringing victory, but so had the many individuals who carried out the work. Lela Gefter (former navy nurse in the war) said, "I know that the regime here has for years exploited the war to militarize the youth and so on, but nonetheless, for our generation the memory of the war is a holy memory,"[11] A writer and war survivor, Viacheslav Kondratiev, noted in his article "Paradox of Nostalgia for the Front" in *Literaturnaia Gazeta*, "there was one strange thing about the war. We felt freer than we had during peacetime. This freedom came from the sense that one was truly responsible for one's country."[12]

Amir Weiner notes something similar, "The millions of peasants turned soldiers who fought and won the war after the defeats of 1941–42 returned to their towns and villages with a heightened sense of their own capabilities and of the magnitude of their achievements."[13]

If this were true for the majority of the population, then the songs would be a symbol of personal success, a sign of freedom, and the potential for achieving something beyond and despite the state that tried to control them. A Russian-Jewish émigré reinforced this with her view that she hated the USSR, but upon hearing the song *The Sacred War*, she came close to tears and got nostalgic over the people's ability to have defeated the Germans.[14]

No one ever denies the horrors of war; in fact, many have declared they hoped it would never happen again. Yet, they also stated that there was something different and special about that time. Some saw it as people caring for one another; others as freedom or people taking responsibility. The songs became a symbol of that feeling. The songs carried a message of hope, brought respite to hard and frightening work, and built unity between front and home. The music provided a ladder by which people could climb out of the terror of war, and create a vision for the future. The songs commemorated and celebrated the individual as being the basis for success of the collective.

So why did Tumarkin assert that the cult was over by 1995, at the fiftieth anniversary of the victory?

> Most of the people who had come to Victory Park did not seem to experience any feelings about the war; they simply came to stroll, to look, to drink, and in general to enjoy themselves. Even when a singer

> sang one of those most moving of wartime songs, I didn't see anyone wiping away a tear.[15]

Perhaps they felt by that point that they now had responsibility; freedom had been granted them after the collapse of the USSR. Likely those who truly remembered physically, emotionally, and mentally were absent.

In some ways, the legacy years are over – the death of the last survivor will take that first-hand experience away. Yet, in other ways, the legacy continues. These songs approved by state and population alike, a body of song-literature definable and preserved, shall remain a symbol of something rarely seen in Soviet history – something that truly unified party, state, and individual. Since the songs represent the sense of individual freedom and responsibility, then if that is threatened again (as it may be in Putin's Russia), then perhaps the songs will be resurrected as symbols of the value of individuals and their true cooperation in the face of oppression.

As Wolfe notes, the cult of the war is being shaped yet again by Putin. Busts of Stalin are reappearing; Stalin's speeches have been cited; and Lenin remains in Red Square. "This suggests that Putin considers his most pressing task not to consolidate the market and democracy in Russia, but to project a sense of collective identity and purpose that would encompass and not refuse the Soviet past."[16] In this context, the songs might be recalled in their status as symbol of Soviet victory. Ironically, once again, the songs could end up representing both the state and the people; on the one hand establishing legitimacy for a regime trying to strengthen its control, on the other, symbolizing the hope for freedom and the role of the individual.

Endnotes

1 Wolfe 2006, 253.
2 Schneck and Berger 2006, 20.
3 Ibid., 24.
4 Ibid., 26.
5 Ibid., 104–105.
6 Ibid., 125.
7 Personal interview with an unnamed veteran, author's archive, May 9, 1991.

8 Lobarev and Panfilov 1994, 393–394.
9 Zhitie 1990.
10 Tumarkin 1994, 36.
11 Ibid., 147.
12 Ibid., 204.
13 Wolfe 2006, 263.
14 Interview with Elizaveta Efimova, author's archive, August 13, 1989.
15 Tumarkin 1994, 221.
16 Wolfe 2006, 278.

References

Ament, Suzanne (2006), Reflecting Individual and Collective Identities: Songs of World War II. In Goscilo, Helena and Lanoux, Andrea (eds.), *Gender and National Identity in Twentieth-Century Russian Culture*. DeKalb, Northern Illinois University Press, 115–130.

Ament, Suzanne (1996), Ph.D. dissertation: *Sing to Victory: The Role of Popular Song in the Soviet Union during World War II*. Bloomington, IN, Indiana University Department of History.

Lobarev, Grigorii P. and Panfilov, M.M. (1994), *Ob ogniakh-pozharishchakh. Pesni voiny i pobedy /comp.* Moscow, Respublika.

Schneck, Daniel J. and Berger, Dorita S. (2006), *The Music Effect: Music Physiology and Clinical Applications*. Philadelphia, Jessica Kingsley Publishers.

Tumarkin, Nina (1994), *The Living and the Dead: the Rise and Fall of the Cult of World War II in Russia*. New York, Basic Books.

Wolfe, Thomas C. (2006), Past As present, Myth, or History?: Discourses of Time in the Great Fatherland War. In Lebow, Richard Ned, Kansteiner, Wulf and Fogu, Claudio (eds.), *The Politics of Memory in Post War Europe*. Durham, N.C., Duke University Press, 249–283.

Zhitie, Odnoi Pesenitsi (1990), *Govorit I Pokazyvaet Moskva*, October. Issue 42 and 43.

Serguei Alex. Oushakine

"Despite It All, We've Won": Chechen War and Military Songs*

For more than a decade, the war in Chechnya has remained on the margin of the public's attention in Russia. No influential public mobilization – be it pro-war or anti-war – has been triggered in the course of the Chechen war. Episodic attempts of politicians and public intellectuals to raise larger issues about the state's military policy or the public's indifference to it did little to bring people together. With few exceptions, there were no major public protests or political campaigns against the war. Neither the grim fate of thousands of refugees from Chechnya, nor tragic reports about victims of suicide bombings and hostage-taking outside the region could mobilize the public. The military draft provoked no mass revolt on the part of potential conscripts. Deaths of soldiers seem to concern no one outside the circle of relatives and close friends. No federal organization that could defend rights and interests of the Chechen war veterans and their relatives has emerged either. Instead, relations between the state and the war context were usually triangulated by private, individual efforts, while the war itself was symbolically relegated to the remote geographic province. It appeared that the war became an integral and imperceptible part of the post-Soviet informational landscape. Inevitable and yet hardly noticeable at the same time, the Chechen war has been transformed into yet another grim fixture of a post-communist habitus, along with corruption, mafia, poverty, and general lawlessness.

NTV, an independent Russian TV-channel, which provoked the anger of the Yeltsin government for its anti-war reporting from Chechnya during 1994–1996, succinctly summarized the general attitude on December 11, 2004 in a televised event designed to commemorate the

* The essay is based on materials that I collected in Barnaul (Altai, Russia) during my fieldwork in 2001–2003 and shorter visits in 2004 and 2005.

tenth anniversary of the outset of the war. As the ceremony's presenter framed it in the opening line: "The war has not vanished into history yet, but authorities (*vlast'*) and society have already forgotten about it".[1] This public amnesia is striking, given the post-Soviet context of the war. Unlike secretive military involvements of the Soviet army in East Asia, Africa, or Latin America in the last half of the twentieth century, the Chechen war is not a minor-scale operation that could be kept confidential.[2] By the spring of 2006, there were at least one million soldiers and officers who took part in the "combat activity (*boevye deistviia*) in the North Caucasus region".[3] While rarely represented in the mainstream media, oral and written stories of their war experience do circulate among the civilians, undermining the government's desire to fully control the war coverage.

It is not so much a lack or distortion of information about the war that produces the public amnesia. Sources of this indifference lie elsewhere. What was crucial in public perception of the Chechen war was its deep political ambiguity, and the overwhelming distrust that this ambiguity caused. Throughout the 1990s, the Russian government rapidly changed its policies towards Chechnya and radically shifted its support and alliances, producing a deep-rooted feeling of suspicion about the underlying goals of the war. The initial "war for independence" was quickly transformed into a large-scale *razborka* (sorting out), into a war "between gangs in Moscow and those in Grozny".[4] Contradictory accounts of war casualties that circulate in the Russian mass media increased this uncertainty further. Permanent public disputes over numbers of the dead do not just demonstrate different ways of counting bodies. They inevitably re-confirm a public distrust for any official information regarding the war. Discarding official and alternative sources of information as mere propaganda, people more and more often resorted to personal narratives, rumors, contradictory testimonies, and popular culture (cinema, song, memoirs) in order to make sense of the war. Suspicion often took the form of stories about oil interests that some Moscow politicians have in the Caucasus; about Russian officers who sold arms and soldiers to Chechen rebels; about massive misappropriation of funding allocated by the federal government for military and civic programs in Chechnya, and so forth. Bordering on the edge of military folklore, these stories were as multiple as they were unsurprising. Focused on conspiracy and exchange, they draw attention to clashing systems of ethical and political coordinates that were activated by post-Soviet changes.

Our Own Apocalypse

Throughout the 1990s, Russia's cultural industry demonstrated the same distancing attitude to the war in Chechnya. Concerned with this situation, the July 2000 issue of *Iskusstvo kino* (The Art of Cinema), an influential Russian journal of film theory and criticism, asked film- and TV-directors working on the topic of the Chechen war to explain the lack of "an adequate" representation of the regional wars of 1980–1990s (Afghanistan, Chechnya, Tadjikistan, Georgia, Moldova) in Russian cinema. Comparing the omnipresence of Vietnam in the American film, the journal pointed to the fact that in Russia there were "literally four or five films" that dealt with recent wars.[5]

Responses fluctuated between two poles. On the one hand, the lack of attention to recent wars was interpreted as a clear sign of denial. As Sergei Govorukhin, a Russian film-director, framed it, "We should not just talk, we should scream about things happening in Chechnya. Instead we put on the appearance that nothing serious is happening. ... It is regrettable that society doesn't want to know the truth about this dirty campaign".[6] On the other hand, the same situation was associated with difficulties of the process of symbolization itself. As Sulambek Mamilov, a film-director born in the Chechen-Ingush Republic, observed:

> The point in question is neither a lack of civic temperament on the part of film-directors, nor their infantilism ... rather it is a state of shock that they are experiencing. The horror reported on TV, the blood, the suffering, the refugees are so shocking that it takes time to restore your capability of comprehending this tragedy, and to take a stance regarding it.[7]

The stance was taken eventually. However, the two most notable and commercially successful films of 2002–2005 outlined a direction that was very different from the one expected by the participants of the round table. *War* (*Voina*, dir. Alexei Balabanov, 2002), a film about Russian soldiers and British journalists taken hostages by the Chechen fighters, presented the war in the Caucasus as a deadly clash of culturally and religiously different mentalities. Framed as a Russian soldier's story about the Chechen war, the film traces the soldier's survival in the midst of total betrayal. It is a tale of an abandoned average Russian Ivan who defends his life with all available legal and illegal means. Often labeled as chauvinistic, bluntly anti-Chechen, and anti-Western, *War* was one of the most popular films of the year.[8]

Feodor Bondarchuk's *Company 9* (*Deviataia rota*, 2005) was another major attempt to revisit Russia's painful military history. Based on a real story, the film was an epic tear-jerker about a group of Soviet soldiers who defended a crucial position in the mountains in the very end of the Afghan war. Simply forgotten by their commanders in the midst of the massive withdrawal from Afghanistan, these soldiers died in a fight, unnecessary and unappreciated. The biggest Russian blockbuster since 1991, *Company 9* reinforced the general tendency to portray war as a matter of personal endurance and sacrifice.[9] "We have won our own war," emphasized the general message the epilogue of the film, "We were simply forgotten. Yet we have won it."

Fascinated by the film's artistic quality – "the sublime and cruel" at the same time – the media almost unanimously supported a new trend to depict the "war-as-it-is," leaving disturbing political questions aside.[10] Still, the anxiety about the universal captivating effect produced by the film made itself known, even if inadvertently. One of the journalists, comparing *Company 9* with its American counterparts, noticed: "This film has been already called our own *Apocalypse Now*. It seems, however, that it will be our *Apocalypse Yesterday, Now, and Forever*".[11]

The metaphors of "our own war" and "our own Apocalypse" are helpful in understanding both the symbolic absence of Chechen (and Afghan) war memory and a quick attempt to gloss political issues over with images of individual or collective survival. Taken as a separate, isolated phenomenon, the failure to symbolize the war experience implies that other forms of post-Soviet life have already been integrated, appropriately classified, and represented. In this isolationist approach, the status of "war memory" is usually reduced to "holes" and "gaps" in an otherwise smooth narrative. Yet, "our own Apocalypse" strongly suggests that there is no smooth post-Soviet narrative to speak of. I think it was precisely this fragmentation of established forms of signification and exchange that forced people to focus on waging their own "local wars." The "forgotten" Chechen war, in this context can be seen as a symptom that helps us understand better contemporary Russian culture, state, and society.

Recycling Contours of Victor

In the second half of the 1990s, the re-cycling, re-making, and reincarnating of Soviet cultural symbols emerged as one of the major tendencies of post-Soviet cultural industry. Usually, cultural observers cite as one of the most successful and influential post-Soviet cultural projects of this type a somewhat nostalgic show *Starye pesni o glavnom* (Old songs about the most important). First broadcast right after midnight on Dec. 31, 1996, the show brought together major Russian pop-stars to perform golden hits of the Stalinist period in highly stylized costumes and settings borrowed from famous Soviet films. The show enjoyed an incredible commercial success and popular recognition. For four years, it was the major attraction of the New Year's Eve. Despite its incredible popularity, the project was officially closed in 1999. Yet the tendency survived. In 2001, the Russian pop-singer Oleg Gazmanov, known for his strong patriotic sentiments and close connection with the political leadership of Moscow, started a similar, though more politically oriented, project called *The Songs of Victory* (*Pesni pobedy*). Again, contemporary Russian stars were called upon to revitalized songs of the Soviet past. In 2001, in an interview Gazmanov explains the motivation behind the project:

> There were two important moments for us. First, we wanted to make these songs sound totally contemporary, as if they are born again. Second, I wanted this project to be totally positive; this is why I picked not just any song that was performed during the war, but the songs of the victorious generation. This is why the word *Victory* is so prominent

> in the title of the project. These are not just war songs, but an artistic testimony (*svidetelstvo*) of the great victory.[12]

Not surprisingly, the project was supported by the same TV-company that produced and sponsored the *Old Songs About the Most Important*. The *Songs of Victory* has become an annual event, attracting every year more stars and more people. Perhaps, its biggest success was achieved on May 9, 2005, during the celebration of the 60th anniversary of the Victory day. As many newspapers reported, more than 1 ml. spectators attended the *Songs of Victory* staged in Park Pobedy in Moscow.[13]

Gazmanov, certainly, was not alone in his attempt to utilize, as he put it, the "energy (*energetika*) of these songs in order to remind the young generation the history of the Victory".[14] Stimulated by festivities organized around the 50th anniversary of Victory Day, the military and patriotic *chanson*, as it is often called in Russia, experienced an obvious upsurge. War ballads, marches, lyrical romances are regularly played on radio and TV channels. New cover-versions are frequently recorded not only by major pop-stars but also by famous classical singers. This commercial cultural industry relies on some sort of a grass-root support, too. In many cities throughout the country, there are annual festivals of war songs, as well as competitions for the best performance of these songs organized among students. The tendency seems to be so strong that some cultural critics in Russia, alarmed by this cultural development, have already defined this process as a attempt to "*militarize*" the musical genre.[15]

Clearly, there is a big difference between performing songs about hiking trips and summer camps (so typical for the culture of the Russian bards), and songs about loss and suffering epitomized by the war *chanson*. It is not the aesthetic *enjoyment* that the war song genre activates in their performers. The war song genre reveals a paradox. Worn-out clichés and strikingly repetitive poetic configurations are evoked precisely in those dramatic moments when we are supposed to be especially genuine in our remembrance of loss and victims. Yet, there is no spontaneous expression of feeling here. Nor is there any abrupt recollection of the past. Instead, there is a literal recourse to the available repertoire of expressive gestures, forms of narration, and types of symbolization.

I suggest a two-part explanation to this phenomenon. Following an old anthropological tradition, I argue, that the popularity of the genre might have little to do with the actual content of these songs, important as it might be. Rather, I want to draw attention to the performative aspect of this genre. Songs – as well as music in general – are indeed actions. They are performances in which people take part. From this point of view, songs, as any ritual, can be seen as a pattern of actions in which shared values – i.e., "shared concepts of relations" – are affirmed, explored, and celebrated".[16]

It is crucial to realize that the unifying ground here is not so much ideological as aesthetic. The commonality of relations and values is produced/performed/established through the reproduction of the form – in this case, through the reproduction of the internal relationship of sounds. This completed sonic structure – the overall combination of rhythm and melody – is replicated – or at least projected – onto the social level, as would be with any ritual. The *actual* social order (people and institutions) and the *imaginary* social order (reflected in songs) coincide, – if only temporarily – in the community of performing people.

To frame it yet another way: the repeatable form of the song provides a symbolic structure – a melodic and rhythmical contour that could be paralleled by the corresponding structures of expressions and behavior.[17] The musical contour suggests a formal receptacle that helps to organize experience, emotions, and memory. Ready-made, formulaic, ritualistic structures (songs) function as an interface, as a mediator that brings the individual experience and its meaningful expression together. Feelings acquire here their own narrative structure, without, however, being fully determined by it.

The production and re-production of these formulaic "contours" have their own transformative effect. As many scholars of the ritual have pointed out, the usual gap between available categories and daily practices, the gap between experience and expression, often results in people's attempts to re-establish control through "symbolic reformulations" and concerted ritual actions.[18] Articulation and ritualized performance of songs are used as a way of joining and confirming *in public* previously non-connected or even non-existent forms and systems of meaning.

I suggest that the current deployment of the war songs provides a particular form of *affective link* framed as the patriotism of despair: The personal attachment to country and the personal feeling of individual or group belonging are created through a repetitive, ritualized articulation and recognition of loss. The establishing of shared values is reached through the incessant circulation of metonyms of individual and/or collective traumatic experience. Emotional recollections of loss and symbolic reconstructions of suffering bring together history, nation, and the individual.

"Despite It All, We've Won!"

One of the crucial aspects of postsocialist condition is a spectacular collapse of the general cultural context (symbolic order), within which actions and identities used to make sense. What I want to stress here is the formal aspect of this collapse: the downfall of socialist ideology in the 1990s cannot be limited to the disintegration of a particular value system. It also rendered meaningless the existing rituals of recognition. Social status, social achievements, and social biography suddenly became ostensibly devoid of familiar prescriptive clues.

The ambiguous status of the Chechen war, coupled with the state's persistent attempts to keep the war within a closely regulated symbolic context, added to the post-Soviet uncertainty yet another layer. As a result, in the absence of normative frameworks or routinized practices for making the Chechen war personally and socially meaningful, both people and institutions tended to resort to the strikingly mechanical application of Soviet-style symbols.

At times, the symbolic impact of such prosthetic reliance on Soviet signs could be chilling. For instance, a young Altai serviceman, severely wounded during the first Chechen war, described how in 1996, upon his return from Chechnya, the city's government issued an identification document to prove his entitlement to such benefits as free local transportation and reduced rent. The unclear legal status of the Chechen war, its participants, and victims, however, resulted in a category impasse: the ID listed the soldier as an "invalid (*invalid*) of the Great Patriotic

War (*Velikaia Otechestvennaia voina*), with a second-degree disability." While being literally out of synch with reality, from the economic point of view, this identity, granted by the state, equated the soldier with other generations of veterans entitled to welfare benefits. Inevitably, this accent on the formal and the procedural created a tension. As the veteran observes, "some people give me a crazy look, when I show this ID. Once in a while, [someone] will sneer: "So, how exactly did you manage to take part in [the Great Patriotic War]?"[19]

The story brings to light the uneasy nature of recognition. Being the subject's "fundamental need," recognition by others has a crucial "supplementary dimension" – reciprocity, as Jacques Lacan liked to point out.[20] Reciprocity is not the same as mutuality here; rather it is a commitment to the same discourse; it is a commitment to the same set of imaginary positions from which one's particular location and one's particular experience could be "seen," described, and thus acknowledged.[21] Within this context, public indifference to the fate of Chechen war veterans (and to the signs of their presence) reveals a lack of a common vocabulary of public symbolism.

It is against the background of the incomplete symbolic exchange between the veterans and the state, as well as between the veterans and society, that ex-combatants created a new socio-symbolic context by reclaiming the legacy of Russia's previous wars and re-appropriating them for their own public rituals. Songs provided veterans with a literary framework in which the narrative continuity with the past became possible. As a result, the link between the Great Patriotic War and the Chechen war that seemed so strikingly out of place in the mid 1990s became the rhetorical norm ten years later. Images of suffering soldiers of the Second World War were conflated with descriptions of veterans' experience of the Chechen war.

By appealing to the legacy of the Second World War, the current generation of veterans invoked memories of loss, experienced in 1941–1945 almost by every family in Russia. Crucially, it was not the type or the purpose of a particular war that became acknowledged in this newly created ritual of recognition. Nor was it a victorious end that was celebrated. Rather, patriotic values were evoked as a particular state of emotions, as a repetition of a familiar configuration of painful events.

The commemoration of the tenth anniversary of the beginning on the Chechen war organized by *NTV*, that I mentioned earlier, is a good example of this enactive remembering practiced by veterans in public. The event was broadcast on December 11, 2004, exactly ten years from the day when Boris Yeltsin signed a decree that called to restore the "constitutional legality" in the Chechen Republic. Staged in a big concert hall filled with veterans and their families, the event drew attention to the "forgotten war," to the sad plight of hostages, soldiers, and their relatives. Personalized stories of officers and civilians, and various award ceremonies were interspersed with performances of professional and amateur singers. Newly written songs about the war in Chechnya were supplemented by the active recycling of songs about the Great Patriotic War. In the very end of the event, the two anchors of the ceremony tried to connect all historical dots in a linear narrative. Addressing the audience, one of the presenters summed up the general message: "There are no victories in civil wars, – yet all of you – those who are here today, and those who are not with us anymore – all of you, have won your own victory. Selflessly and loyally, you served your Fatherland (*Otechestvo*); at the time when the Fatherland is not going through its best period." The second host of the event followed the theme and praised the soldiers in the room, emphasizing the fact that they had done everything they could to ensure that "our country would regain its previous dignity and grandeur" (*dostoinstvo i velichie*). The presenter concluded by personalizing the historical link between different generations:

> Veterans of the Great Patriotic War are looking at you. Because only to you they could entrust the country that they have saved from Fascism, along with the banner of the Victory, which they carried throughout the Great Patriotic War from Ukraine to Germany. The banner that was raised on the top of the Imperial Chancellery in Berlin on May 2, 1945.

The banner was carried in, accompanied by a guard of honor. Then followed a short video-clip, spelling out historical parallels that might have been left unnoticed otherwise. Black and white images of Soviet cities and Berlin, destroyed during the Second World War, were seamlessly blended with images of the devastated Chechnya. The footage of the Russian flag raised in Chechnya was carefully preceded and echoed by archival shots of a Soviet flag, waiving above the Reichstag in Berlin.

The effect of the video-narrative was amplified by the soundtrack, the song "Despite it all, we've won" (*I vse-taki my pobedili*) from a late Soviet film about a veteran of the Great Patriotic war:

А было вначале, солгать не могу,	Things weren't easy at the start; I won't lie about it.
Буксиры молчали на том берегу.	Towboats sat silent on that shore,
На том берегу, на том берегу	On the shore, On the shore
На том берегу, где мы были...	Where we were, too...
А мы покидали свои города,	We were abandoning our hometowns
И в них оставалась душа навсегда...	Leaving our souls to stay there forever...
И всё-таки, и все-таки,	Despite it all, Despite it all
И всё-таки мы победили!	Despite it all we have won.
Ушанки чернели на алом снегу,	The scarlet snow was blackened by lost hats
И губы немели на том берегу.	And lips became numb on the shore.
На том берегу, на том берегу,	On the shore, where we stayed
На том берегу, где мы были...	Where we stayed back then.
За каждой спиною был свой Сталинград	There was a Stalingrad behind every back
И в мерзлых траншеях - ни шагу назад	There was no retreat from frozen trenches.
И всё-таки, и все-таки,	Despite it all, Despite it all
И всё-таки мы победили!	Despite it all we have won.
И выцвела соль у солдатских рубах.	The salt of sweat discolored soldiers' shirts
Та соль возвращенья, как мед на губах	That salt of return is like honey for us.
На том берегу, на том берегу,	On the shore, on the shore
На том берегу, где мы были...	Where we stayed back then...
И сколько бы нас не осталось в живых,	Regardless of how many of us are still alive/
Жив голос погибших друзей боевых!	The voice of our dead buddies is here.
И всё-таки, и все-таки,	Despite it all, Despite it all
И всё-таки мы победили!	Despite it all we have won.
И все таки мы победили	*Despite It All, We've Won*
сл. Г. Поженян, муз. П. Тодоровский	Lyrics by Grigori Pozhenian, Music: Piotr Todorovski

Originally written in the early 1980s, this song about the Great Patriotic War provided initially a striking contrast to the state-supported representations of the war. *Despite it all* lacked both – the paralyzing melancholy, so typical for the Soviet war songs, and the ostentatious self-glorification that dominated the official (epic) version of the war during the Brezhnev period. Released during perestroika, the song suggested a different way of remembering the war: it downplayed the overall scale of the war, and focused instead on telling details. Providing neither striking metaphors, nor memorable images, it portrayed the war as an incoherent ensemble of everyday fragments of the war life; as a disjointed collection of metonyms of loss; as a "confused story of confusion".[22]

It had no patriotic motivation that some songs written during the war had. Nor did it exploit the usual theme of family ties, which was supposed to inspire the soldiers. Suggesting no clear and complete narrative, the song presented the victory as a broken-up story of the individual perseverance, as a result of personal ability not to give up, regardless of what was happening around. Anchored in multiple, yet disjointed elements (towboats, hats, lips, shirts), the war experience was, at the same time, disconnected from larger aspects of the war.

This *close-up vision* of the war, this historically specific focus on the detail that was supposed to represent the whole, made possible two crucial post-Soviet tendencies in memorizing the current war experience. First, the original stylistic *fragmentation* that was pioneered in late Soviet war songs emerges as one of the *main narrative* devices through which the late-Soviet and post-Soviet wars are experienced and represented today.

Secondly, the avoidance of *any* overarching symbolic frameworks in this type of songs, a deliberate escape from any ideological theme that could offer a unified vision of the war, was resulted in the post-Soviet period in a peculiar form of military *ahistorism*. Specific cultural and ideological components of different wars were marginalized. What became crucial instead was an ability to trace the resemblance of fragments of different wars. It was an ability to link together structurally similar details that were supposed to substitute for the whole.

In its post-Soviet incarnation, in the course of the commemorating event, *Despite it all* was suddenly imbued with a different significance. Not only did the song reduce the war experience to the personalized ability not to give up, but also it endowed the post-Soviet disaster in Chechnya with some historical dignity of the victory in the Second World War. As a performative event, the song not so much reminded the participants about the shared values, shared experience, and shared relations, but enacted this commonality in a totally new context. The participatory nature of the song, taken together with its rigid (*complete*) semantic and rhythmical structure, turned it into a socio-symbolic tool that re-ordered historical experience; that is, to say, into a tool that established a new socio-symbolic frame within which disjointed elements of social memory could be connected with (or disconnected from) each other.

The fragmented perception of the Great Patriotic war offered in the song provided a frame of comparison, but also a method of writing a new military history. In a similar way, newly written songs about the Chechen war bracket off overall context in order to highlight meaningful details. However, this metonymic remembering is now accompanied by a historically specific "will to connect" that links together similar fragments of incommensurable wars. Stringing different wars in a seamless timeline, current songs re-contextualize military experiences both in the past and in the present. Performative and narrative at the same time, songs emerged not only as an "instrument" used by yet another generation of veterans to inform their audience about a forgotten or marginalized war.[23] Also, and more importantly, military songs were presented as an invitation to join the act of narration. The social and sociological importance of this genre is hard to overestimate. Suffice it to mention that *Bratstvo*, the first organization of the Chechen war veterans in Barnaul, emerged precisely as an outcome of a festival of soldiers' songs.[24]

I finish with two examples that highlight the transformative function of songs in a particularly striking way. In the first, the poetics of loss helps to create a new temporal and spatial reality, by restructuring recent and remote history. In the second example, the song emerges not just as a communicative gesture but, more importantly, as a participatory event through which veterans' experience is acknowledged, recognized, and confirmed.

The song *Everything is Cool* (*Vse putem*, by Roman Bulgachev) is a part of the fourth volume of the CD series *Black Tulip*. The CD is dedicated to "those who have fought and who still fight, carrying out the Motherland's orders." Using the accompaniment mostly as background, Andrei Vasil'ev, a singer with a husky baritone, narrates (rather than sings) the story in which the same situation is repeated in three different geographical places at three different periods of time:

Пронеслась свинцовая метель,
кончились военные года
Из далеких западных земель к дому возвращались поезда.
Майский воздух голову кружил.
Часто вечерами при луне, собирались, кто остался жив,
Поминали тех, которых нет.

Все сидели за общим столом, В непривычной такой тишине,
И, казалось, все будет путем, в нашей послевоенной стране.

Время колесо свое кружит, Время отделят боль от ран
Но негаданно вписалось в жизнь слово непривычное Афган.
А уйдя из городов чужих, на душе оставив горький след
Часто собирались те, кто жив, поминали тех, которых нет.

Все сидели за общим столом, в непривычной такой тишине.
И казалось все будет путем, в нашей послевоенной стране.
Пацаны рождаются на свет,
чтобы не глядеть на мир с колен,/Как ты встретил 21 век
на чеченской выжженной земле?

В сапоги солдатские обут, гимнастерка белая в пыли.
Сын солдата, взявшего Кабул,
внук солдата, взявшего Берлин.
Все сидели за общим столом,
в непривычной такой тишине....
И казалось все будет путем в нашей послевоенной стране,
всем казалось, что будет путем....

Leaden snowstorms were finally over
And the time of war was ended, too.
Trains were running home from the West
Spring in May excited every head.
Often, in a local neighborhood/ Brightened by the evening moon,
Veterans commemorated those/ Who failed to return.

Sitting at the table outside/ Slightly muted by a lack of noise
"It's over," everybody thought/ And everything will be cool

In our post-war country.
Time is spinning quickly all its wheels/
Time is setting pain and wounds apart.
The unusual word "Afghan" Settles in our lives.

Carrying bitter scars in their souls/Foreign cities left behind,
Veterans commemorated those/ Who failed to return.
Sitting at the table outside/Slightly muted by a lack of noise
"It's over," everybody thought / And everything will be cool.
In our post-war country.

Guys have not been born to look/ At the world from their knees.
Dressed in a dusty T-shirt/ Wearing soldier's boots,
The son of the soldier/ Who took Kabul
The grandson of the soldier/ Who took Berlin
How did you celebrate the New Century/
In the burnt-out Chechen land?
Sitting at the table outside/Slightly muted by a lack of noise
"It's over," everybody thought / And everything will be cool
In our post-war country. Everything seemed so cool.

(*R. Bulgachev, Everything is Cool. 2003*)

In his discussion of the main difference between writing poetry and writing history, Reinhart Koselleck, a German historian, pointed to the long-standing tradition of juxtaposing the synchronicity of events in poetry and diachronic sequencing of events in history. Unlike a historian, who is concerned with the time-bound relationships and constellations of things, the poet "is able to cluster incidents as closely as he wishes".[25] This logic of poetic clustering is, certainly, fully employed in the song, demonstrating how the "postwar" is never realized, how "a lack of noise" is always interrupted. The joining of different episodes, the constructing of alternative chronotopes (Grozny–Kabul–Berlin, West-East-Caucasus) produces a generational continuity. To be more precise, this joining of generations transforms the horizontal unity of brothers-in-arms into a vertical unity of ancestors. The symbolic re-zoning of events and generations turns military brotherhood into a paradigmatic unit, into a pillar that supports a newly written history. The double symbolic effect of this clustering not only allows for the domesticating of wars, for making them into a part of everyday life ("at the table, outside"). More importantly, it locates them on the same plane; continuity-as-repetition brackets off crucial differences and emphasizes the formal resemblance, the shared biographical "contour" ("Son of the soldier who took Kabul/ Grandson of the soldier who took Berlin").

Emotionally invested, these songs about the brotherhood of men, who have been able to sustain the continuity of their military profession, do reach people who have not been necessarily affected by the Chechen war. In December 2002 in Barnaul I attended a concert of a vocal group, Slaviane (Slavs). The group is a frequent participant in events organized by the Altai Committee of Soldiers' Mothers and veterans of local wars; it also had a tour in Chechnya, giving concerts for policemen and military deployed there. The group is quite popular in the region, and its latest CD has an endorsement from the regional bishop.

Slaviane's show had a title: "Songs of Russian Squadrons" (*pesni russkogo voinstva*). The six soloists, young men in their early twenties, all dressed in black, were accompanied by a full-fledged orchestra of "folk Russian instruments," as the playbill explained it. Among a diverse arrangement of war songs from different periods of Russia's history, one was about officers of recent wars written by Oleg Gazmanov, the singer behind the project the *Songs of Victory.*

During its performance, there was a clear emotional rapport between the singers and the audience. Following a strong affective impulse, people started rising from their seats when Slaviane began the chorus line: "Officers, officers your hearts are a target/ For Russia and freedom without the end/ Officers, Russians (*rossiiane*), let freedom shine/And make our hearts beat in unison".[26] It was hard not to follow this collective emotional impulse; it was almost impossible to distance it, or ignore it. By the middle of the song, there were 400 or so people in a hall standing, and silently looking – in unison – at the stage.

It is precisely this binding social power of publicly performed rituals that veterans appealed to in their attempts to get their "message" to different groups. Providing "quotable" symbolic formulas, songs frame discursive intonation and channel emotions. They reshape – however temporarily and locally – practices of perception, and often result in signs of respect for the military. Limited in their effect by time and space, songs, nonetheless, offset established social hierarchies by pointing to possibilities that have not been realized, or by negating those that have already been implemented.

These emerging public rituals were the very first successful attempts to break the silence and amnesia associated with the Chechen war. The breakthrough came with a price: new symbolic frameworks tend to be excessively sentimental; they are twisted in their chronology; they are dubious in their comparisons; and they are overstretched in their implications. The choice of their symbols is restricted. And moving from one war to another (from Berlin to Chechnya), they flatten and militarize history. This primacy of military identity often results in attempts to rewrite the nation's history either as a chain of accidental military successes ("*despite it all*"), or as a succession of personal and societal traumas. Such a dominance of a traumatic narrative for emplotting the post-war life, I suggested, might be seen as a sign of a general state of the post-Soviet symbolic order: solidarity emerges in the process of sharing losses, and communities are built around practices of incorporating past suffering in the present. Despite it all, this version of patriotism of despair seems to be winning over a large audience. Or, at least, it has been able to mobilize an expected emotional response from the audience that had used to "forget" about the war in Chechnya.

Endnotes

1 Chechnia 2004.
2 Rossiia i SSSR v voinakh XX veka 2001.
3 Moshkin and Savchenko 2006.
4 Rigi 2007, 38.
5 *Iskusstvo kino* 2000.
6 Govorukhin 2000, 7.
7 Mamilov 2000, 11.
8 Zvereva 2002; *Iskusstvo kino* 2002.
9 Kishkovsky 2005.
10 Dolin 2005.
11 Shumiatskaia 2005; italic in the original.
12 *Proekt Pesni Pobedy* 2001.
13 Keshokova 2005, 5.
14 See DVD *Pesni Pobedy*, Music-trade, 2006.
15 Schuplov 2001; see also Shaburova 2005.
16 Small 2001, 346–7.
17 see Kivy 1989, 77.
18 see e.g. Vygotsky and Luria 1994, 109–111; Comaroff 1985, 120.
19 *My zhdali vas, synov'ia...* 1999, 31.
20 Lacan 1991, 247.
21 Lacan 1997, 51.
22 Hynes 1997, 153.
23 Mosse 1990, 20.
24 Shaul'skaia 1999, 95–6.
25 Lessing as quoted in Koselleck 2004, 205.
26 Gazmanov n.d.

References

Chechnia (2004), Chechnia: 11 dekabria 1994 – ... *NTV.* Broadcast on Dec.11, 2004., 60 min.

Comaroff, Jean (1985), *Body of Power and Spirit of Resistance. The Culture and History of a South African People.* Chicago, Chicago University Press.

Dolin, Anton (2005), Voina – Mat' rodna. *Gazeta*, September 28, 24.

Govorukhin, Sergei (2000), Obshestvo ne khochet znat' pravdu. *Iskusstvo kino*, 7, 7–10.

Hynes, Samuel (1997), *The Soldiers' Tale: Bearing Witness to Modern War.* New York, Allen Lane.

Iskusstvo kino (2000), Na toi voine, neznamenitoi... No. 7, 5.

Iskusstvo kino (2002), Proshchai, oruzhie? No. 11, 5–21.

Keshokova Alina (2005), Priamaia liniia. Pobednyi klich Gazmanova. *Moskovskii komsomolets*, No. 97, May 05.

Kishkovsky, Sophia (2005), From a Bitter War Deafeat Comes Russia's Latest Blockbuster Action Movie. *The New York Times*, Oct. 29, 2005, B. 9.

Kivy, Peter (1989), *Sound Sentiment.* Philadelphia, Temple University Press, 1989.

Koselleck, Reinhart (2004), *Future Past: On the Semantics of Historical Time.* Trans. Keith Tribe. New York, Columbia University Press.

Lacan, Jacques (1991), *The Seminars of Jacques Lacan. Book I. Freud's Papers on Technique 1953–1954.* Trans. John Forrester. New York, W. W. Norton & Company.

Lacan, Jacques (1997), *The Psychoses. 1955–1956. The Seminars of Jacques Lacan. Book III.* Ed. by Jacques-Alan Miller. London, W. W. Norton & Company.

Mamilov, Sulambek (2000), Filmy o Chechne ne nuzhny gosudarstvu. *Iskusstvo kino*, No. 7, 11–12.

Moshkin, Mikhail and Savchenko, Gennadii (2006), Veterany raznogo sorta. *Gazeta*, Issue 81, May 17.

Mosse, George L. (1990), *Fallen Soldiers: Reshaping the Memory of the World Wars.* New York, Oxford University Press.

My zhdali vas, synov'ia... (1999). Barnaul, Izdatel'stvo Altaiskaia Pravda.

Proekt Pesni pobedy (2001), May 9, http://eskadron.narod.ru/news/09.05.2001.htm

Rigi, Jakob (2007), The War in Chechnya: The Chaotic Mode of Domination, Violence, and Bare Life in the Post-Soviet Context. *Critique of Anthropology*, Vol. 27 Issue 1, 37–62.

Rossia i SSSR v voinakh XX veka: Statisticheskoe issledovanie (2001), Moscow, OLMA-Press.

Schuplov, Aleksandr (2001), Idet mobilizatsiia pesni. *Nezavisimaya gazeta*, January 20.

Shaburova Olga (2005), Voina, soldat i pesnia: natsional'no-patrioticheskii diskurs v konstruirovanii rossiiskoi maskulinnosti. *Gendernye issledovaniia*, 13, 85–100.

Shaul'skaya Marina (1999), I togda sozdalos' "Bratstvo". In *My zhdali vas, synov'ia....* Barnaul, Izdatel'stvo Altaiskaia Pravda, 95–6.

Shumiatskaia, Olga (2005), Apokalipsis vchera, segodnia, vsegda. *Moskovskie novosti*, September 30, 28.

Small Christopher. Why doesn't the whole world love chamber music? *American Music*, Fall 2001, 346–7.

Vygotsky, Lev and Luria, Alexander (1934), Tool and Symbol in Child Development. In van der Veer, Rene and Valsiner, Jaan (eds.), *The Vygotsky Reader*. Oxford, Blackwell 1994, 99–174.

Zvereva, Galina (2002), "Rabota dlia muzhchin"? Chechenskaia voina v massovom kino Rossii. *Neprikosnovennyi zapas*, Vol.26.

Helena Goscilo

History and Metahistory in Soviet World War II Posters

Dulce et decorum est pro patria mori.
Horace

A really successful war, a psychologically Good War, requires not merely the extirpation of a cruel enemy abroad. It requires as a corollary the apotheosis of the pure at heart at home.
Paul Fussell, "Writing in Wartime: The Uses of Innocence"

Graphic Anticipation

Deservedly acclaimed as masterpieces of graphic art,[1] Soviet World War II posters impress by their strategic evocation of endemic traditions; their eloquent visual/verbal rhetoric; and their adaptability to developments on the battlefront. Indeed, one can trace various stages of the war through the thematic evolution of the genre, which adjusted its emphases according to perceived propaganda needs, embraced multiple styles, and assimilated the conventions of such mini-genres as *lubok*, caricature, and the postcard.[2] An analysis of the posters, if organized according to chronology and focus, offers both a historical record of the war's progress, and insight into the psychological mechanisms on which artists relied for their iconography, tapping into the populace's profound allegiances, fears, pride, and self-identity.

Even before WWII, the post-Revolutionary strategy of proselytizing the state's vigilance and impregnability mandated that Soviet graphic artists consolidate people's faith in the invincibility of the Red Army through reassuring images that bolstered confidence in the regime.[3] Accordingly, everyday posters exalted Soviet soldiers' patriotic courage and skills, promoting the nation's vaunted strength and glory. As during World War I and the Civil War, artists mined a long-established national iconography sedimented in collective memory so as to project the unassailable power embodied in the nation's medieval epic heroes [*bogatyri*], such as Il'ia Muromets, Alesha Popovich, and Dobrynia Nikitich, entrusted with the sacrosanct duty of protecting the borders of Rus' from foreign invasion.[4] A typical example of pictorial rhetoric rooted in historical precedent is Viktor Govorkov's *Slavna bogatyriami zemlia nasha* [Our Land Is Famous for its Bogatyrs] (1941), produced several months before Hitler's invasion of the USSR (Fig. 1). Through elementary but clever visual parallelism, Govorkov analogizes the contemporary Soviet soldier, outfitted with modern equipment, and his fabled ancient predecessor, the *bogatyr'*. The homology between the contours of their headgear as well as their raised arms emphasizes continuity and tradition, on the one hand, while the repetition of the circular shape (binoculars and gun opening) in the foregrounded image references the new technology (its roundness roughly duplicating the *bogatyr'*'s mace) of alertness and deterrence, on the other. Dual in its temporal markers (though unified through iteration of lines), the iconography is both historical and prophetic, for it relies simultaneously on memory of past triumphs and confidence in modern gear to trumpet the Soviet army's readiness to safeguard the nation's future from any and all foes.

Mapping the War

On 23 June 1941, a day after Germany declared war on the USSR, posters plastered on the walls of Soviet houses pinpointed Nazis as the foe, and replaced vigilance with righteous violence. One of the first such works, the Kukryniksy's *Besposhchadno razgromim i unichtozhim vraga!* [We'll Smash and Annihilate the Enemy without Mercy] (23 June 1941), in semi-caricature depicts a soldier's bayonet aimed at the dehumanized, atavistic Hitler's head, which, symbolically, has torn through the Molotov-Ribbentrop Non-Aggression Pact of August 1939, rendered meaningless through violation (Fig. 2). A more naturalistic visual by Feodosii Bochkov at approximately the same time likewise proleptically enunciates Soviet victory over the enemy, portraying the synecdochic Soviet soldier from the aggrandizing perspective of what graphically equals a cinematic low-angle shot (Fig. 3). As in pre-war posters and in the majority of later images, the dominant color here, apart from the basic black, grey, and white, is the red that symbolized the Bolsheviks and, in the context of war and its inevitable injuries and fatalities, blood.[5] Thus it both inspired patriotic confidence and galvanized bellicose passions.

A deluge of explicitly anti-Nazi graphics followed in the next four years, by artists ranging from the three renowned Viktors – Deni(sov), Ivanov, and Koretskii – to Dmitrii Moor and less prolific talents, such as Boris Mukhin and Nikolai Zhukov. As the war escalated, the changing themes of the posters registered its key phases – and concomitantly the nation's shifting priorities. In that sense, the posters function as a chronicle and a collective visual memorial to the USSR's subjective experience of the war, its emotional pendulum swinging between the two extremes of desire/hope and fear. One week into the German invasion, with 150,000 Soviet soldiers either dead or wounded,[6] posters' initial sweeping promises of victory began to alternate with exhortations to replenish the diminished military ranks (Fig. 4). Though assurances of victory and calls to enlist, redouble all effort, and conquer the enemy persisted throughout the war, more specific motifs spotlighted specific moments in the conflict.

The 872-day siege of Leningrad, launched on 8 September 1941,[7] initiated the subgenre of city-specific posters (Fig. 5). When the Germans advanced into Moscow two months later (25 November), the overriding message became the imperative to defend the nation's ancient capital. After the Germans were routed, the tone changed to one of triumph (Fig. 6). The case of Stalingrad, stormed on 16 September 1942, generated another series, one that did not substantially distinguish that city's fate from others', though the ferocious fighting there reportedly reduced the life expectancy of a Soviet private soldier during the prolonged battle to an average of 24 hours[8] (Fig. 7). Two million people perished in that confrontation, including one million Soviet soldiers and 500,000 civilians.[9] Only by finally resorting to the tactic of "the fighting retreat"[10] did the Soviets force the surrender of the main German army on 31 January 1943. This bloody butchery marked Germany's first major defeat,[11] to be followed by others as the tides of war turned: in May 1943 German troops in the Crimea capitulated to the Soviet army, and continued to do so in central areas and cities of the USSR.

By mid-1944, with the German armies' enormous losses in Belorussia, predictions of Nazi defeat sprang not from morale-boosting rhetoric, but from empirical circumstances, and constituted a popular theme in the posters circulated that year.[12] Regaining terrain in its determined march westward, the Soviet army on 23 October 1944 invaded Germany, and launched a casualty-heavy but ultimately successful offensive against Berlin in mid-April 1945. While Soviet soldiers hoisted the red flag over the Berlin *Reichstag* and graphics depicted a symbolically enormous hammer-and-sickle banner flying over the Kremlin (Fig. 8), Germany signed its official surrender in General Zhukov's headquarters on May 8–May 9 according to Moscow time, and thereafter celebrated on that date as *Den' Pobedy* (Day of Victory) (Fig. 9). Unsurprisingly, in posters during early 1945 and immediately after 9 May, exultation replaced exhortation. The words *slava* and *geroi*, radiant images, and triumphant scenarios now overran posters: for example, those of prisoners liberated by the conquering Soviets (Fig. 10) and of spruced, jubilant, repatriated soldiers welcomed home by families and comrades (Fig. 11).

In tracking the war's course, posters relied on sundry techniques to mobilize and encourage the population through the four years of carnage and devastation: photomontage, caricature, witty comic-like "stories" of reversals, images accompanied by verbal promises, assertions, threats, predictions, appeals, and short "poems" – above all by Samuil Marshak, many of whose slogan-verses rivaled in popularity Konstantin Simonov's home-front-directed poem *Zhdi menia* [Wait for Me], also the title of Aleksandr Stolper's 1943 film, scripted by Simonov. Whereas some artists opted for a single strong image calculated to have an immediate visceral impact, others purveyed narratives or, more rarely, depended on wit – such as Dmitrii Moor's 1941 scatological jab at the caricatured Nazi leadership, denigrated as *na G* [Ending in G – for the word *govno* – shit] (Fig. 12). In the clever interplay between the verbal and the visual, the four Cyrillic G's not only conceptually evoke feces but collectively compose the symmetrical swastika.

Roughly speaking, WWII posters comprised the following six thematic categories: (1) the enemy, usually conceived as a beast, a degenerate, or a sniveling coward; (2) Russian soldiers as steadfastly valorous heroes; (3) daring partisans; (4) home-front workers in industry or agriculture, indefatigably toiling to supply the Soviet troops with food and arms (Fig. 13); (5) vigilant citizens from all walks of life intent on flushing out spies and guarding secrets from the enemy (Fig. 14); and (6) women and children, either violated by the Germans (Fig. 15) or pleading for rescue, and later, expressing gratitude to their countrymen-saviors. To hearten those at home, posters shunned images of male vulnerability, rarely featuring Soviet soldiers killed or wounded. A rare exception is Koretskii's *druzhba narodov* [friendship of nations] poster, in which, tellingly, the injured or slain Soviet has Asiatic features – clearly, not a "pure" Russian (Fig. 16).

Four aspects of World War II Soviet posters deserve special attention for their deployment of psychological devices to quicken patriotism, stimulate hatred and resistance, and reinforce traditional, emotion-laden values: (1) the anathematization of the enemy as a base animal; (2) a stunning diversity of roles in female iconography; (3) a historical perspective for framing the Soviet soldier, and (4) self-citations within posters. The reminder of my analysis is confined to the last two categories, since they rely on memory.

Historical Precedent

Many posters exalting the Soviet forces invoked historical precedents[13] – a stratagem especially favored by Viktor Ivanov and inspired by Stalin's words at a military parade on 7 November 1941: *Pust' vdokhnovliaet nas v etoi voine muzhestvennyi obraz nashikh velikikh predkov.* [May the courageous/manly image of our great ancestors inspire us in this war].[14] Comparisons between soldiers at the front and a broad spectrum of earlier exemplary military heroes, which mined the past for uplifting parallels, presumed the population's recollection of its national history. Universally admired figures analogized with current Soviet fighters were the unconquerable *bogatyri* of medieval times (Figs. 17, 18), on at least one occasion enrichingly mediated by a citation from Viktor Vasnetsov's famous painting of 1898 (Fig. 19). Aleksandr Nevskii was a particularly apposite predecessor, inasmuch as during the thirteenth century the sanctified prince-defender from Novgorod vanquished the Teutonic Knights – and gained a new life in Russian culture through Sergei Eisenstein's film, released just a few years before the invasion of the USSR (1938) (Fig. 20). No Soviet citizen could fail to recognize the significance of Dmitrii Donskoi, the duke of Muscovy who routed the Tatars at the battle of Kulikovo in 1380 – a milestone in Russian history verbally resuscitated in Blok's famous poem of 1908, *Na pole Kulikovom* [On Kulikovo Field], and its hero visually memorialized in the Novgorord Millenium Monument unveiled in 1862 (Fig. 21). Kuz'ma Minin and Dmitrii Pozharskii, familiar to all Russians through Ivan Matros's monument in Red Square, likewise resonated in popular remembrance of the duo's expulsion of the Poles from Russia with the all-volunteer army they organized during the Time of Troubles (1612) (Figs. 22, 23). However remote temporally, these paragons of patriotism and military prowess functioned as inspiring paradigms for emulation: Earlier Russian victories implied the triumphant outcome of WWII in a politicized mini-lesson in the lustrous phases of the nation's history.

More recent historical ideals included the indomitable eighteenth-century Marshal Suvorov (Fig. 24), revered not only for his routing of Poles, Turks, and the French, but also for his personal bravery, superior leadership, and skill in elaborating combat techniques that served as the basis of Russian military maneuvers into the twentieth century. His valor and pristine record (he never lost a battle) doubtless are what prompted the Soviet government to create the Order of Suvorov in 1942, thereby officially certifying his status and achievements as a model for contemporary fighters. At the same time, posters revived Russia's long-standing self-perception as Europe's self-immolating rescuer from Napoleon's imperial aggression. They evoked both the wily Mikhail Kutuzov (Fig. 25), the star of Borodino in 1812, and the disgraced Napoleon – the latter poster spelling out the continuity between a proud past and the harrowing present (Fig. 26).

Some graphic artists strived to intensity the effect of historical reminders through composite portraits, such as the Kukryniksy's tripling of renowned heroes from three different eras – Nevskii, Suvorov, and the anecdote-popular Civil War hero, Chapaev, with verses yet again by Samuil Marshak (Fig. 27). That device crested in a peculiar work by

Petr Aliakrinskii, whose atypical, old-style, densely packed 1942 design resembled a mini-overview of all military highlights and outstanding heroic personalities from Russian history (Fig. 28). Intended to kindle national pride, these images operated on the uncomplicated principle, "We've done it before; we can do it again." And Moor's *Ty chem pomog frontu?* [How Did You Help the Front?], of course, appropriated and revised his Civil War recruitment poster, *Ty zapisalsia dobrovol'tsem?* [Have You Enlisted as a Volunteer?] (Fig. 4)

Citations

Once the Soviets launched their offensive, several posters intensified their message and historicized their contents through visual intertexts. Since, from the outset of the war, posters appeared in TASS windows,[15] on walls, and in newspapers, artists correctly assumed the populace's familiarity with their war graphics. If in the first year of battle the predictions of Soviet victory had scant empirical basis, by late 1942 the seemingly superhuman resistance in Stalingrad bred realistic hope for Soviets' survival. And by 1944 the Germans' retreat and the merciless pursuit by the Soviet and Allied armies provided solid grounds for anticipating the Nazis' defeat. Nikolai Zhukov's 1942 poster *Bei nasmert'!* [Shoot to Kill!] functioned as an instant and active response to the appeal of Viktor Koretskii's image, printed earlier in the newspaper *Pravda* (5 August 1942),[16] of a woman and child confronted by a Nazi bayonet, *Voin Krasnoi armii, spasi!* [Warrior of the Red Army, Save Us!] (Fig. 29). To signal the dialogic nature of his visual, Zhukov reproduced Koretskii's poster on the wall behind the foregrounded Red Army soldier doing his utmost to comply with the SOS. This sort of dynamism comfortingly suggested that cries for help would be answered, acted upon.

Recognizability of earlier images similarly informed Golovanov's self-quotation. His 1944 naturalistic depiction of the representative, smiling Soviet soldier at rest in a bucolic landscape bears the promise, *Doidem do Berlina* [We'll Make it to Berlin]. Hanging on the wall of his 1945 poster *Krasnoi armii – slava!* [Glory to the Red Army!], it participates in the later work's assertion of that vow's fulfillment (Fig. 30). The same soldier, decorated and cheerful, stands beside the wall, which bears the triumphant words *Doshli!* [We've Made It!] and *Slava russkomu narodu* [Glory to the Russian People]. The Kukryniksy's 1945 poster likewise recast their earlier 1941 visual, but substituted a map of Berlin for the Non-Aggression Pact, the bayonet stabbing the blood-spattered Führer through his swastika'ed heart (Fig. 31). Calculated to promote faith in optimistic claims and declarations, such dialogic ties also intimated a reliable system of communication among the population, and between the population and the army, validating Stalin's trope of the Soviet Union as a close-knit *bol'shaia sem'ia* [Big Family]. And that trope organizes the Golovanov poster that not only incorporates a document certifying a soldier *Geroi Otechestvennoi Voiny* [Hero of the Fatherland War], but also cites Moor's earlier apostrophizing call to arms, which, as noted earlier, itself references Moor's famous Civil War poster (Fig. 32). Golovanov's substitution of a little daughter for the soldier intensifies the emotional appeal, accentuates the *semeinost'* [familial nature] of the *bol'shaia strana* [big country], and directs us to the *svetloe budushchee* [radiant future]. In short, WWII graphics participated in the comprehensive Soviet practice of constructing the present as an amalgam of the past and the future.

Memory was one of the Soviet Union's mantras and patron saints. The creation of war-related posters continued even after the restoration of peace in the USSR, though the post-war messages either were retrospective or, more frequently, mobilized citizens to rebuild cities devastated by war. Today Russia ensures that its experience in World War II will not sink in Lethe. That task is accomplished in multiple ways: by the museum at Poklonnaia Gora in Moscow; the ubiquitous Monument to the Unknown Soldier; films that reassess the war; books about WWII films, richly illustrated with stills and film posters, such as *Sto fil'mov o voine* [A Hundred Films about War] (2005); postcards and collections of posters that reproduce the best-known WWII graphics; and exhibits and publications organized around *Den' Pobedy* – most recently, the volume titled *Plakaty voiny i pobedy* [War and Victory Posters] (2005), with more than two hundred reproductions. A key force in these endeavors is the publishing house *Kontakt Kul'tura*, which accounts for the postcards, the reproductions, and books mentioned above. Its name unambiguously adverts to its self-appointed goal – to prevent post-World

War II generations from losing contact with the history and culture of their national heritage. In short, to keep memory alive.

Endnotes

1 The lavishly illustrated volume by Paret et al. contains the astounding remark, "The Russian people deserved far better posters than their government produced." Paret 1992, 160.
2 On the role of *lubok* in Russian war posters in the nineteenth and twentieth centuries, see Norris, 2006, passim.
3 Shkliaruk 2005, 5.
4 See Viktor Vasnetsov's *Vitiaz' na rasput'e* (1882) and *Bogatyri* (1898). On the significance of these two images in Russian and Soviet culture, see Helena Goscilo (2008), Viktor Vasnetsov's Bogatyrs: Mythic Heroes and Sacrosanct Borders Go to Market. In Kivelson, Valerie A. and Neuberger, Joan (eds.), *Picturing Russia: Essays on Visual Evidence*. New Haven, Yale University Press.
5 The imperative of speedy production and, later, financial considerations under austere conditions explains artists' reliance on only a few basic colors.
6 Rees.
7 As a result of the city's protracted blockade, hundreds of thousands of Leningraders died of starvation, exposure, and disease. Leningrad was regained by Russians only on 27 January 1944.
8 Rees.
9 Vladimir Petrov's *Stalingradskaia bitva* (1949), with music by Aram Khachaturian, offers a dramatic depiction of the prolonged battle.
10 Stalin's order that troops stand against the enemy at all costs had proved ineffectual, whereas "the fighting retreat" was a successful strategy. Hitler likewise prohibited retreat and refused to abandon any conquered land, even when doing so was advisable.
11 Of the 90,000 German soldiers who surrendered in Stalingrad, only 5,000 returned to Germany alive (Scaruffi 1999).
12 Rees.
13 As Stepen Norris has shown, the appeal to historic heroes and their triumphs, particularly as documented in the genre of *lubok*, flourished in World War I and earlier. See especially Norris 2006, 135–185.
14 Shkliaruk 2005.
15 By analogy with the ROSTA windows of the earlier period, when graphic artists also collaborated with literati. See Shkliaruk 2005, 5–15, to which I am indebted.
16 Shkliaruk 2005, 11.

References

Baburina, N.I. (2000), *Rossiia – 20 vek: Istoriia strany v plakate*. Moscow, Panorama.

Clark, Toby (1997), *Art and Propaganda in the Twentieth Century*. London, The Everyman Art Library/Calmann and King Ltd., especially 103–124.

Norris, Stephen M. (2006), *A War of Images: Russian Popular Prints, Wartime Culture, and National Identity 1812–1945*. DeKalb, Northern Illinois University Press.

Paret, Peter, Irwin-Lewis, Beth, and Paret Paul (1992), *Persuasive Images: Posters of War and Revolution*. Princeton, NJ, Princeton University Press.

Rees, Laurence. Hitler's Invasion of Russia in World War II. http://www.bbc.co.uk/history/world wars/wwtwo/hitler_russia_invasion_print.html. Accessed 27 September 2006.

Scaruffi, Piero (1999), A time-line of World War II. http://www.scaruffi.com/politics/wwii.html. Accessed 27 September 2006.

Shkliaruk, A.F. (2005), Za nashu pobedu! In Snopkov, P.A., Snopkov, A.E. and. Shkliaruk, A.F. (comp.), *Plakaty voiny i pobedy. 1941–1945*. Moscow, Rossiiskaia gosudarstvennaia biblioteka, Kontakt-Kultura, 5–15.

Snopkov, P.A., Snopkov, A.E. and. Shkliaruk, A.F. (2005) (comp.), *Plakaty voiny i pobedy. 1941–1945*. Moscow, Rossiiskaia gosudarstvennaia biblioteka; "Kontakt-Kultura," n.p.

Vashik, Klaus (2005), Metamorfozy zla: nemetsko-russkie obrazy vraga v plakatnoi propagande 30–50-kh godov. Trans. Arkadii Perlov. In L. Gudkov (ed.), *Obraz vraga*. Moscow, OGI, 191–229.

Figure 1

Figure 2

Figure 3

Figure 4

Figure 5

Figure 6

Figure 7

Figure 8

Figure 9

Figure 10

Figure 11

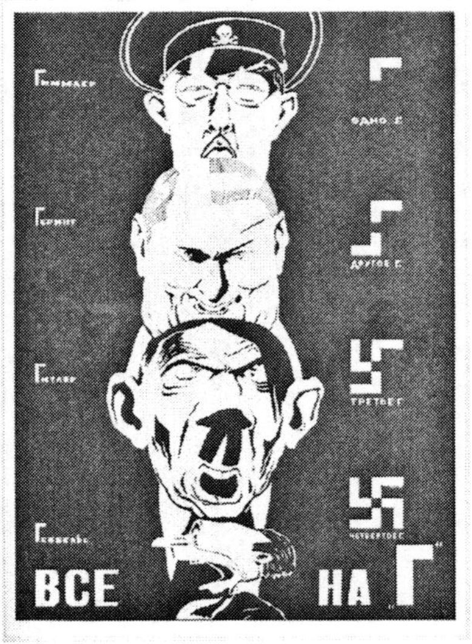

Figure 12

Figure 13

Figure 14

Figure 15

Figure 16

Figure 17

Figure 18

Figure 19

Figure 20

Figure 21

Figure 22

Figure 23

Figure 24

Figure 25

Figure 26

Figure 27

Figure 28

Figure 29

Figure 30

Figure 31

Figure 33

Hierarchies of Memory

Peter Carrier

Political and Ethical Contexts of Collective Memories of the Second World War*

Specialists of "memoriography", the body of scientific literature dealing with memories and their transmission via memorial representations, generally agree that contemporary collective and individual memories of the Second World War are incompatible. Much of this literature identifies a discrepancy between these two levels of remembrance, before going on to suggest ways of reconciling them, or to propose alternative models of remembrance in groups which do not succumb to this dichotomous paradigm. However, it is precisely the speculative nature of suggestions for solutions to an apparently chronic gulf between individual and collective memory which leads "memoriographers" to fall back on ethical and political assumptions. In this essay, I will therefore explore the ethical assumptions underlying three approaches to understanding the impact of memories of the Second World War in contemporary Germany: the political institutional production of memorial narratives; the conversational transmission of memory in family institutions; and the transmission of memory in educational institutions.

Political Institutions

Political debates about the symbolic legacy of the Second World War, which were particularly vociferous during the 1980s and 1990s in response to attempts to rehabilitate a hitherto negative reception of Germany's role in the Second World War, have given rise to a field of

* I would like to thank Alon Confino and Kobi Kabalek for their valuable comments on earlier versions of this essay, and Marjaliisa Hentilä of the Finland Institute in Berlin for generous financial support.

memoriographical study in its own right. Chancellor Helmut Kohl's policy of blurring boundaries between "victims of war", by performing public gestures which symbolically lumped together dead army officers and victims of persecution, has been a recurrent object of such study. The Chancellor's visit to the cemetery at Bitburg in 1985 or the *Neue Wache* national war memorial in Berlin (reinaugurated in 1993) are typical examples of Kohl's symbolic revisionism.

Geschichtspolitik, a term reputed to have been coined by Chancellor Kohl himself, refers to both the practice and the study of politically motivated manipulation of public images of the past. This term is translated either as "politics with history" (that is, the practice of using history to legitimise political decisions) or as "history with politics" (the analysis of the use or misuse of history for political legitimisation). The latter strives to deconstruct "official" narratives (of governments or specific political parties) motivated by political interests, and explores what is variously called "political memory"[1] the "power to ascribe meaning",[2] or typically asks "Who" (that is, what party) does such and such a historical event "*belong* to?".[3]

This approach to memory studies draws on a wealth of metaphorical language in order to underscore the utility of memory for the legitimisation of state authority. A recent study about *Memory and Power in Postwar Europe*, for example, aims to "investigate how memory is personally re*worked*, officially recast and often violently re*instilled*".[4] *Geschichtspolitik* consistently resorts to military metaphors. History is conceived by one author as a weapon in the hands of political warriors, and memory as an intellectual or emotive impulse making the minds of passive rememberers managable: "History – or the *construction* of the past – is clearly an appropriate resource for mobilising people in the political *battle* for influence and power".[5] The very word *Vergangenheitsbewältigung*, commonly used to denote the process of "coming to terms with the past", is likewise rooted in the notion of forcefully overcoming (*bewältigen*) the after-effects of the Second World War and the Holocaust. Thus memory is frequently perceived as the object of "strategies",[6] involving "actors" and "recipients"[7] who "control the perception of reality".[8]

What do these metaphors of violence, force and control tell us about memories of the Second World War in Germany? First, they indicate that the perceived task of the state is to persuade people by appealing to their sense of history. Second, they indicate an assumption, on the part of their authors, that social memory may be willfully "constructed" by representatives of institutions, in particular states, with the help of historians, as if there is one-way top-down communication – from those who actively "shape"[9] messages to those who passively do the remembering!

The core ethical assumption underlying political approaches to collective memory has arisen in anticipation of the disappearance of eyewitnesses of the Second World War, leaving historians and historical representations to take on the task of relaying memories of the event. "The Germans," says the historian Edgar Wolfrum, "are at a watershed of memory, for one simple reason: until now, communicative and collective memory were decisive, for they thrived on the living memories of eyewitnesses. [...] Today, the Germans are standing on the threshold of cultural memory [...]." The author further cites the famous Holocaust Monument in Berlin, inaugurated in May 2005, as proof of this switch from communicative (living) memory to cultural (symbolically transmitted) memory.[10]

The idea that we pass from communicative to cultural memory following the death of the last witnesses is questionable, for the very cultural (rhetorical and visual) symbols we use to preserve impressions of the past are themselves objects of communication. Stories can be passed down from one generation to the next or thrive as half conscious family secrets; they are no less "communicative" as a result. Even in the presence of monuments, and in the absence of witnesses, we interpret signs by means of communication – either with objects (asking ourselves what they mean) or with others (by discussing their meaning with them). Any suggestion that cultural memory supersedes communicative memory is effectively a denial of the ongoing ethical duty of all people (not only professional historians) to interpret the meanings of traces of the past.

Family Institutions

Memoriography dealing with memories transmitted within families in everyday situations could hardly be more methodologically removed from

Geschichtspolitik. For the notion that memory is shaped and transmitted via politically motivated master narratives is precisely what research into conversational narratives of the war transmitted within family units aims to disprove. The most obvious expression of the current public fascination with family memories is the wave of popular confessional testimonial literature in Germany, recent examples of which are Ute Scheub's account of her relationship with her father, *Das falsche Leben. Eine Vatersuche* (A False Life. In Search of My Father, 2006), Katrin Himmler's reckoning with her great uncle Heinrich Himmler in *The Himmler Brothers* (2007) or, in France, Jonathan Littell's prizewinning novel *Les bienveillantes* (The Kindly Ones, 2006), an imagined account of an SS officer's autobiography. Add to these the plethora of websites, and even local self-help groups, inviting people to exchange personal witness accounts and to write their family histories.

The most quoted scientific work on the transmission of memories of the Second World War within families is that of the research group on "Traditions of Historical Consciousness" at the universities of Hannover and Essen. The best-selling study, *Grandpa Wasn't a Nazi*,[11] based on 182 qualitative interviews carried out in the late 1990s with forty families from East and West Germany, demonstrates how three generations perceive the role of their family members in the Second World War on the basis of the first generation's account of what it saw and did, followed by their children's and grandchildren's account of what they had heard about the war period, especially from their relatives. The primary purpose of this study was to expose the rhetorical gymnastics of self-justification performed within the family unit. Grandfathers justify their acts of violence while judging those of others as "crazy".[12] Their children and grandchildren talk about their forebears in vague terms, heroicise them by magnifying small acts of defiance, or by projecting other people's acts of resistance onto their own grandparents. They commonly distinguish between "Germans" (when referring to themselves) and "Nazis" (when referring to others).[13] However, the aim of this research is not simply to show that people perceive themselves as victims (this is the focus of recent debates in Germany over the firebombing of German cities in 1945, and over plans for a Museum for Expellees), but to reveal the logic of their rhetoric: the vague language used to deny unpleasant facts to themselves and to others; and blatant self-delusion. Some of the interviewees cannot accept, morally, what their grandparents did or might have done and thus heroicise them. Even when they know about their grandparents' direct participation in killings, they fail to acknowledge the relation between the private image of their grandparents and the remote and cruel historical events. There thus appears to be a hiatus between private and public knowledge of the Second World War.

By exposing fallacies underpinning family memories, and by presupposing that public knowledge and even historical education has had no influence on private memories, this project has been politically explosive. It even postulates a *proportional* relation between public knowledge and private memory: "The more comprehensive the knowledge about war crimes [is], [...] the stronger is the need to develop stories to reconcile the crimes of 'the Nazis' or 'the Germans' with the moral integrity of parents or grandparents."[14] In other words, the more people know about their family members' involvement in crimes, the more they wish to defend them against the facts. The researchers even establish a *causal* relationship between knowledge of the war and family memory narratives: "[E]ducation that delivers a comprehensive historical knowledge of Nazi crimes paradoxically evokes a need to remove one's relatives from this framework of knowledge."[15]

Research on "Traditions of Historical Consciousness" focuses not on the psychological process of denial, but on rhetorical defence mechanisms. It ascribes the hiatus between knowledge of family history and of collectively remembered historical events, between the smaller and the large crime, to the "loyalty" of grandchildren and children to their forebears, that is, their wish to preserve the "moral integrity" of the family, and to "protect" their elders from knowledge of the facts.[16] This research undoubtedly furthers our understanding of everyday attitudes towards the Second World War and the Holocaust in Germany. It recognises the role of cognitive processes played in the transmission of historical knowledge, acknowledges the role of rhetoric in the conceptualisation of memory, debunks the assumption (upheld by *Geschichtspolitik* specialists, for example) that historical master narratives sent out by states and public institutions are adopted unquestioningly by the public, and counteracts the apologetic trend in public discourse about the Second World War, which stresses the continuing sense of victimisation upheld by many German people on account of the Allied bombing of Germany in 1945.

However, it raises a number of questions which are not answered in publications issuing from the research group. Can we assume seamless loyalty to parents and grandparents, which is a prerequisite for childrens' connivance at their parents' failure to recognise the consequences of their own acts?[17] And do these children and grandchildren really believe in what they say to the interviewers? One cannot rule out the possibility that the loyalty expressed here is inauthentic and performed by family members out of a sense of obligation to their elders, to the interviewers, or to the microphone.

Harald Welzer, who coordinated this research, defends the primacy of the family as a context in which genuine historical consciousness is transmitted by drawing on a Romantic conceptual dichotomy between "official stories" and "felt history",[18] between "cognitive historical knowledge" and "emotional impressions of the past", between a family "album" and a school "lexicon".[19] However, while the focus on family loyalty is intended to expose the role of affect in the transmission of historical memory, one could equally argue that loyalty is also what binds the interviewees to institutional contexts of memory *beyond* the family, which includes the authority of the very research institution for which the interviews were carried out! There is, admittedly, a qualitative difference between the durability of loyalty to one's family and to educational or research institutions, but there are no grounds on which to polarise the issue by arguing that a family demands an emotional bond, while educational institutions demand pure cognition. In reality, both private and public contexts of memory demand cognition and loyalty (even intense loyalty, for limited periods) at the same time.[20]

In short, research on "Traditions of Historical Consciousness" starts with a premise that unfairly disregards contexts of memory outside the family institution and, in particular, explicitly dismisses the pedagogical function of public (state) commemorations and educational institutions. It claims that memory is distinct from knowledge, cannot be *learnt*, and is determined by kinship. Such determinism could hardly be more remote from Halbwachs's notion that memory can be communicated between groups and institutions, and that loyalties to different contexts of memory may coexist.

Educational Institutions

In order to overcome the polarisation of research into memories of the Second World War in Germany between studies about the "politicisation" and the "privatisation" of historical narratives, researchers in the fields of education, historical didactics and public history, as well as in the pedagogical sections of memorial museums, have explored contexts in which private and public narratives interact. Monuments and museums are institutions designed precisely to foster encounters between individuals, associations, journalists, artists, architects, politicians, historians, tourists and school pupils in which active participation is encouraged, and understandings of the past are negotiated. They therefore eschew, in principle, the dominance of any one historical narrative over another. In contrast to approaches which underscore the purely political or private contexts in which collective memory is transmitted, studies of such intermediary contexts of collective memory respond to the need to adapt history teaching to increasingly multilingual and multiethnic pupils in Germany. In order to "prevent disintegration into different disconnected communities of memory", the historian Bernd Faulenbach characteristically proposes the "democratisation of memory, which is pluralistic and participatory but not arbitrary, not centralistic, but decentral [...]".[21]

Recent empirical studies of the effects of historical education on the children of migrants have shown that group loyalties are often ambiguous, split between families and the host society.[22] In a laudable attempt to bridge the gap between state and family memorial narratives, the educational specialists Bernd Fechler and Viola Georgi explore ways in which children of migrants may "borrow" or even appropriate the historical narratives of their host country. Although the "negative historical heritage" of the Second World War in Germany presents an obstacle to immigrants' sense of social inclusion, it nonetheless does not exclude them altogether.[23] By acquiring knowledge of the Second World War and the Holocaust, these pupils are faced with a *choice* between different types of historical belonging. According to Georgi, for example, pupils make these choices according to four key models of self-identification: as "victims" of discrimination in contemporary Germany, who likewise identify with victims of the National Socialist regime; as "bystanders" or "perpetrators" who adopt or "borrow" a sense of guilt; as members of an ethnic group which has no connection to crimes committed during the war; and as members of "humanity", without reference to membership of either historical group.[24] We may conclude from these findings that the communication of memories is complex, and involves individuals in multiple coexisting social contexts. Neither political nor family contexts may therefore be considered in isolation from other institutions in which memories are transmitted.

The Common National Referent

It has become commonplace to state that a certain number of shared historical memories are a prerequisite for a stable society. Yet the very unlikelihood that memories of the Second World War can be genuinely shared ensures that they are objects of dispute. As such, memory is quintessentially an object of ethics. Whether coerced from above (in political institutions) or from below (in family institutions), or negotiated in intermediary institutions, memory binds and divides both individuals and groups alike. The three methodological approaches to the study of social memory outlined above presuppose that memory is communicable, but that communication is confined to limited groups, resulting in a hiatus between official and inofficial, public and private, or family and state memory. However, they propose radically different solutions to this dichotomy. *Geschichtspolitik* presupposes largely passive receivers of politically produced memorial narratives, and confines the ethical dimension of memory to the authority of the state to act as an ethical role model. By contrast, the conversational family approach ascribes authority over memory to a private sphere which is largely impervious to the public sphere, and whose ethical code is governed by insincere perpetrators and the overindulgent attitude of their offspring.[25] Work on educational contexts shows that pupils are partially loyal to the history of their ancestors, but also that the opportunity to voluntarily "borrow" historical memories presents them with the ethical responsibility to choose and sustain parallel narratives.

Each of these three approaches is replete with political and ethical assumptions about the role of memories of the Second World War in contemporary Germany. While *Geschichtspolitik* confines its horizon to state "production" or "casting" of memory, the conversational approach to families largely reduces collective memory to a function of kinship. Only studies on intermediary institutional contexts such as schools can show how members of different memorial groups interact. Yet even here, Fechler and Georgi inquire only into migrant pupils' receptivity to their host country's narratives as a measure of their capacity to become integrated in the host society, and thus ignore the influence of migrant pupils' narratives on this society! All three approaches, focusing on the state production of memories, the reproduction of memory in relation to kinship, and the degree to which children of migrants appropriate standard memorial narratives of their host country, share a common national referent. For their authors, and their memoriographies of the Second World War, not only analyse memorial contexts. Having been nurtured within a common "German" national context since unification in 1990, they now reproduce this context in their wake.

Endnotes

1 Herf 1997, 1.
2 Winckler 2004.
3 Neuss 1996.
4 Müller 2002, 2 (my italics).
5 Wolfrum 2001, 5 (my italics).
6 Bruner 2002.
7 Fröhlich and Heinrich 2004.
8 Wolfrum 2001, 6.
9 Müller 2002, 34.
10 Wolfrum 2001, 144. Müller defends the same idea. See Müller 2002, 13.
11 Welzer et al. 2002 & 2005.
12 Welzer 2005, 6.
13 Welzer et al. 2002, 201; Welzer 2005, 17.
14 Welzer 2005, 8.
15 Ibid., 16.
16 Ibid., 11f.
17 Other studies indicate quite different reactions by children and grandchildren. See Rosenthal 1998.

18 Welzer 2005, 29.
19 Welzer et al. 2002, 9f. For a discussion of the myth of objectivism, see Lakoff and Johnson 1980, 185-94.
20 Halbwachs explains frameworks of memory with the example of a railway carriage compartment, in which one is momentarily thrust for a short period of time into a rather intimate social group in which memories are formed collectively within that group. See Halbwachs 1925, 130f.
21 See Georgi 2006, 364.
22 Fechler et al. 2000.
23 Georgi 2006, 357.
24 Fechler 2000; Georgi 2003, 299–308.
25 See Welzer et al. 2002, 206.

References

Bruner, Lane (2002), *Strategies of Remembrance. The Rhetorical Dimensions of National Identity Construction*. Columbia, University of South Carolina Press.

Elias, Norbert and Scotson, John (1965), *The Established and the Outsiders. A Sociological Enquiry into Community Problems.* 2nd ed. (1994), London, Thousand Oaks, New Delhi, Sage.

Fechler, Bernd, Kößler, Gottfried and Lieberz-Groß, Till (2000) (eds.), *'Erziehung nach Auschwitz' in der multikulturellen Gesellschaft. Pädagogische und soziologische Annäherungen*. Weinheim and Munich, Juventa Verlag.

Fröhlich, Claudia and Heinrich, Horst-Alfred (2004) (eds.), *Geschichtspolitik Wer sind ihre Akteure, wer ihre Rezipienten?* Stuttgart, Franz Steiner Verlag.

Georgi, Viola (2003), *Entliehene Erinnerung. Geschichtsbilder junger Migranten in Deutschland*. Hamburg, HIS Verlag.

Georgi, Viola (2006), Historisch-politische Bildung in der deutschen Migrationsgesellschaft: Zwischen nationaler Gedächtnisbildung und demokratischer Erinnerungsarbeit. *International Textbook Research*, Vol. 28 Issue 4, 355–366.

Halbwachs, Maurice (1925), *Les Cadres sociaux de la mémoire*. Paris, Albin Michel, 1994.

Herf, Jeffrey (1997), *Divided Memory. The Nazi Past in the Two Germanys*. Cambridge, Mass., Harvard University Press.

Lakoff, George and Johnson, Mark (1980), *Metaphors We Live By*. Chicago and London, The University of Chicago Press.

Müller, Jan-Werner (2002), *Memory and Power in Post-war Europe. Studies in the Presence of the Past*. Cambridge, Cambridge University Press.

Neuss, Raimund (1996), Wem gehört der deutsche Widerstand? – Der Streit zum 50. Jahrestag des 20. Juli 1944. *German Life and Letters*, Vol. 49 Issue 1, 102–119.

Rosenthal, Gabriele, (1998) (ed.), *The Holocaust in Three Generations: Families of Victims and Perpetrators of the Nazi Regime*. London and Washington, Cassell.

Welzer, Harald (1998), Erinnern und weitergeben. Überlegungen zur kommunikativen Tradierung von Geschichte. *BIOS*, Vol. 11 Issue 2, 155–175.

Welzer, Harald, Moller, Sabine and Tschuggnall, Karoline (2002), *Opa war kein Nazi. Nationalsozialismus und Holocaust im Familiengedächtnis*. Frankfurt am Main, Fischer.

Welzer, Harald (2005), *Grandpa Wasn't a Nazi: The Holocaust in German Family Remembrance*. Trans. Belinda Cooper, American Jewish Committee.

Winkler, Heinrich. (2004) (ed.), *Griff nach der Deutungsmacht. Zur Geschichte der Geschichtspolitik in Deutschland*. Göttingen, Wallstein Verlag.

Wolfrum, Edgar (2001), *Geschichte als Waffe. Vom Kaiserreich bis zur Wiedervereinigung*. Göttingen, Vandenhoeck and Ruprecht.

Tobias Privitelli

Two Different Wars? World War II as "Second Imperialist War" and "Great Patriotic War" in the Russian-Soviet Tradition

Introduction

Perception of World War II in Russia is still characterized by a strict division of the war into two periods, the first comprising the 22 months after the signing of the Molotov-Ribbentrop Pact, the second the period after June 1941 when the Germans invaded the Soviet Union. Soviet propaganda consequently labeled these periods differently, the first as the *Second Imperialist War* (1939–1941) and the second as the *Great Patriotic War* (1941–1945).

Of course, in Russian collective memory the second period with its desperate fight against the aggressors prevails. For the average Russian, the "real war" began on 22 June 1941, despite the fact that the Soviets had been involved in World War II from 17 September 1939 on when the Red Army invaded Eastern Poland. In the following months, the Soviet Union annexed the Baltic Republics, Bessarabia and certain border areas of Finland.

This article attempts to demonstrate to what extent the official Stalinist interpretation of World War II has conditioned the Russian public discourse on the war in the last 60 years. It investigates the roots and the consequences of the rigorous distinction between "somebody else's quarrel" (1939–41) and Russia's "battle for survival" (1941–45).

1939–41: World War II as *Second Imperialist War*

According to Stalin's instructions, Comintern head Dimitrov drafted a directive on the reasons and prospects of the war on 8 September 1939:

> The current war is an imperialist and unjust war. The bourgeoisie of all the warring states is to be held responsible for it. This war cannot be supported by the working class of any country, not to mention the communist party. This war is not being waged against fascism by the bourgeoisie despite the affirmations of Chamberlain and the leaders of social-democracy. This war is taking place between two groups of capitalist countries for world domination. The international working class can by no means defend fascist Poland which had refused the assistance of the Soviet Union and which oppresses other nationalities.[1]

These formulations unmistakably recalled Lenin's tenet on imperialist wars which held that the internal contradictions of capitalism would inevitably evoke large-scale conflicts between the capitalist powers. Such clashes, however, were said to smooth the way for socialist revolutions; whereas the first imperialist war had brought socialism in one country, the second was expected to revolutionize great parts of Europe.[2]

"Imperialist" was a common expletive in the Marxist-Leninist vocabulary applied in the interwar period mainly, but not exclusively, to the colonial powers Great Britain and France. "Fascist", on the other hand, labeled the aggressively anti-Bolshevik variant of capitalism as established in Italy. In a fascist state, capitalism was said to have thrown of its pseudo-democratic mask and to attack the workers movement directly.[3] Since in the Soviet understanding, an aggressive attitude towards socialism was the essential feature of fascism, the term became a general epithet to defame a broad range of enemies of the Soviet Union including social democrats ("social fascists"). From the 1920s on, Soviet propaganda also applied the term to the authoritarian nationalist regimes in Eastern Europe (e.g. Poland and Bulgaria).

Nonetheless, in the 1920s, Soviet strategists feared the military power of the imperialist states the most; Britain was classified as the most likely aggressor, acting in all probability in alliance with the Soviet Union's western neighbors.[4] Anti-fascism dominated Soviet propaganda as of the early 1930s, as Japan conquered ever more territory on the Asian mainland and Hitler rose to power. While military planning started to concentrate on a joint attack by the fascist states, Moscow's policy of Popular Fronts was supposed to resist the advance of fascism in Europe on the basis of coalitions with non-communists.

The official anti-fascism of the 1930s, however, did not prevent the Politburo from seeking an agreement with Germany. In fact, the Kremlin did not consider fascism to be *principally* worse than imperialism, but simply as a variety of the same capitalist evil. This pragmatism allowed the Soviet Union to sign the Molotov-Ribbentrop Pact on 23 August 1939 and to escape an involvement in the major struggle of the *Second Imperialist War* until June 1941.

But the new political course also required a propaganda offensive to return the attention of the Soviet public towards imperialism. "Fascist Germany" was removed from the list of epithets the propaganda usually used when referring to foreign countries ("Imperialist Britain", "Poland of the Pans"). After the signing of the pact, the propaganda department of the Central Committee started to revise publications written in the spirit of anti-fascism. For instance, in the 1940 re-edition of Voroshilov's collected works, the term "fascism" was either deleted or altered to "imperialism":

> *Prewar edition*: "We also know that the sabers and battle axes of international *fascism* are being sharpened against us."
>
> *1940 edition*: "We also know that the sabers and battle axes of international *imperialism* [emphasis in both phrases by T.P.] are being sharpened against us."[5]

But the public was still accustomed to perceiving fascism as the main threat, and it was difficult to revert to anti-imperialism within a few days. The political direction of the Red Army warned its propagandists that they might be confronted with questions "in the spirit of simplified anti-fascist agitation" when explaining the signing of the Molotov-Ribbentrop Pact to the troops.[6] Therefore, its guidelines emphasized that western aggressivity had caused the war:

> England and France stand for the prolongation of the war and against concluding peace. While Germany seeks a speedy end of the war and peace, the Anglo-French bourgeoisie, acting under the false flag of a struggle for 'democracy', is the aggressor.[7]

At the same time, the – officially neutral – Soviet Union enlarged its territory. On 17 September 1939, the Red Army invaded Eastern Poland in order to liberate the Ukrainian and Byelorussian "blood-brothers" from the "Polish yoke". Inner degeneracy and inviability, not external aggression, were said to have caused the collapse of Poland which, by the way, was still labeled "fascist".[8] Appropriately, the "broadening of the socialist front" in Poland, the Baltic States, Bessarabia and Finland was sold as verifying the truth of Lenin's prophecy that imperialist wars would provoke new revolutions. And propaganda, of course, did not elaborate on the fact that the Bolshevik rule in these territories was not based on local revolutions, but on the force of the Red Army.

1941–45: World War II as *Great Patriotic War*

Things changed fundamentally when Germany invaded the Soviet Union on 22 June 1941. On July 3, in his first radio address after the attack, Stalin coined the term *Great Patriotic War* for the Soviet resistance struggle:

> The war with fascist Germany cannot be considered an ordinary war. It is not only a war between two armies; it is also a great war of the entire Soviet people against a German fascist army. The aim of this people's Patriotic War against the fascist oppressors is not only to avert the danger that is hanging over our country, but also to aid all the European peoples who are groaning under the yoke of German fascism.[9]

Obviously, the Politburo doubted that pure Bolshevik ideology would suffice to mobilize the Soviet citizens for the defense of their fatherland and it drew on Russian national sentiments; the label *Great Patriotic War* recalled the *Patriotic War* fought against Napoleon in 1812. Yet an increasing recourse to pre-revolution history had characterized propaganda already since the mid-1930s on and thus facilitated the establishment of war patriotism.

During the war, patriotic propaganda frequently referred to glorious episodes of the tsarist past. Writer Alexander Fadeyev, for instance, declared in 1943: "In the course of its history, the Russian people defeated all foreign conquerors – Mongolian tribes, German mongrel-knights, Poles, Swedes, Napoleon's Frenchmen, the intervening western powers of the years 1918 to 1920."[10] For Fadeyev, it was the historical destiny of the Russians to lead all Soviet nationalities in their fight against the Axis powers. Resistance required not only a temporary reconciliation with the non-Bolshevik past, but also between the persecutors and the persecuted of the preceding years. Nevertheless, in the naming of the enemy, a political, not a national notion prevailed; the Soviet Union was fighting "fascists", not "Germans".

In his radio address of 3 July 1941, Stalin claimed that the principles of the Soviet peace policy had impelled him to sign a pact with the Nazi regime. With this agreement, the Soviets had gained one and a half years for the strengthening of their defenses. Stalin ascribed the rapid fascist advance to their "sudden and treacherous" attack. Whereas the Wehrmacht was able to apply its warfare experience from the battles of the previous months, the USSR had not even completed its mobilization. With these statements, Stalin predetermined for decades the Soviet discourse on the Molotov-Ribbentrop Pact and the military debacle at the beginning of the war.[11]

The Soviet Cold War Discourse on World War II

To a large extent, Stalin's own book *On the Great Patriotic War of the Soviet Union* framed the guidelines for the Soviet public discourse on World War II up to his death. The notion of the *Great Patriotic War* emphasizing heroic Soviet self-defense rather than a global war against fascism remained in use and prevails even in present-day Russian historiography. Some Russian historians, however, have gone over to applying the term "World War II", if only to underline their unconventional point of view.[12]

The essential message of Soviet Cold War publications on the war was that the USSR had played the decisive role in the defeat of fascism; they accentuated the fact that the Soviets had suffered the heaviest losses and claimed that the operations on the Eastern Front had been of greater importance than those in other theaters.[13]

Sometimes, Soviet historiography directly addressed unfavorable western interpretations of the war period. When in 1948 the US State Department issued a compilation of documents called *Nazi-Soviet Relations 1939–1941*, the Soviets reacted by publishing *The History Forgers*, a brochure that blamed the West for having enabled Hitler's rise by undermining the Soviet policy of collective security and by strengthening the German economy.[14]

But in general Soviet post-war historiography neglected the period of Soviet-German collaboration and did not delve into topics such as the winter war.[15] Propaganda aimed at establishing an uninterrupted tradition of Soviet anti-fascism, linking the earliest period of Bolshevik rule with the continuing fight against fascism in the guise of western capitalism. Whereas the Western allies had accepted the Soviet wish to ignore the secret protocol of the Nazi-Soviet Pact as evidence during the Nuremberg trials, the subsequent decades saw an increasing divergence in the way the former allies assessed the war and especially the Molotov-Ribbentrop period. The theory of totalitarianism with its comparisons of Nazi and communist violence further widened the gap.

Khrushchev's de-Stalinization campaign did not spare Stalin's role during the war; it was suddenly possible to criticize him, for instance, for having ignored the signs of an upcoming German attack. The works of that period addressed such delicate topics as the purges of the High Command, heavy losses and insufficient preparations.[16] But this moderate criticism ended when Brezhnev took over in 1964. Historian Alexander Nekrich was the first to feel the change of course; his 1965 monograph *June 22, 1941* was banned for its critical assessment of Stalin's behavior on the eve of the war.[17] Nekrich's "anti-patriotic" perception of the party and military leadership of 1940–41 did not fit into the official historiography under Brezhnev, which praised Stalin once again as the "architect of victory".[18] Whereas the typical interpretation of the Khrushchev era tended to conclude that the Soviets had won the Great

Patriotic War *despite* Stalin, under Brezhnev, the victory supplied another piece of striking evidence of Stalin's grandeur as a statesman.

Perestroika eventually enabled a pluralistic public debate on World War II and allowed former taboos such as the Katyn massacre to be brought into focus. The positions held in the Russian publications of the late 1980s and 1990s ranged from apologies of Stalinism to Suvorov's icebreaker hypothesis.[19]

On the one hand, the Yeltsin government welcomed the disclosures of historians since they cast a poor light on the oppositional communist party. On the other hand, the new Russian Federation was eager to be considered the successor of the state that had triumphed in the Great Patriotic War. The Yeltsin cabinet, alarmed by miserable opinion polls, saw the 50th anniversary of the victory in May 1995 as an occasion to demonstrate its unambiguous Russian-Soviet patriotism; the *Poklonnaia Gora* memorial park in Moscow and the Zhukov statue near the Kremlin are conspicuous manifestations of this endeavor. Nevertheless, the protest march of the communists on 9 May 1995 is reported to have attracted much more participants than the official celebration.[20]

The Official View of the War in Putin's Russia

Putin's regime re-established a uniform view of the Great Patriotic War which became a crucial element in the new Russian national ideology. Many recent movies and television series on the topic are reminiscent of the Soviet cinema in their praise of heroism, although they often focus on the fates of individuals, rather than on battles. The official human losses still seem to be based on political considerations rather than on historical studies. Whereas Stalin had spoken of 7 million dead, the figure rose to 20 million under Khrushchev. In accordance with Yuri Polyakov's demographic research, the official number in the 1990s was 27 million.[21] In 2005, a booklet distributed by the Russian embassies on the occasion of the 60th anniversary of Soviet victory mentioned 47 million "direct and indirect casualties".[22]

It is revealing how the same booklet describes the Soviet expansion during the Molotov-Ribbentrop period:

> On 17 September 1939, Red Army troops crossed the Polish border to stop the German aggression. Western Ukraine and Western Belarus which belonged to Poland at that time could reunite with the Ukrainian and the Byelorussian Soviet Republics.
>
> In the end of September/beginning of October 1939 the USSR signed treaties of mutual assistance with Latvia, Lithuania and Estonia which prevented the seizure of these republics by German troops at that moment. In August 1940, all three republics were admitted to the USSR. In this period, the head of the Soviet State, Joseph Stalin, could not even guess that Germany would attack the Soviet Union. He even maintained quite close treaty relations with this country which allowed him to fulfill his foreign policy objectives. Thus, as a result of a short war between the USSR and Finland due to a boundary dispute in 1939–1940, the Finno-Soviet border was shifted slightly to the northwest.[23]

This official statement reflects the Stalinist apology and ignores decades of historical research within and outside of Russia. Once again, the Soviet conquests of 1939-1941 are depicted as purely defensive measures in the face of the German threat. In the Molotov-Ribbentrop period itself, however, propaganda rarely invoked the German threat; instead it justified the Soviet westward advance as aimed at liberating the local workers and at preventing an *imperialist* invasion. Evidently, until June 1941, the Politburo regarded it as inconvenient to publicly accuse the German ally of bad intentions. The assessment of Stalin's policy from 1939 to 1941 as a sort of defensive anti-fascism appears to be a *post factum* interpretation.

The recent dispute over the Tallinn monument demonstrates how difficult it is to reconcile the Molotov-Ribbentrop period and the annexation of the Baltic States with the old-new concept of the Great Patriotic War. As in Soviet times, the unambiguously positive self-perception of the Russian state requires the invention of an anti-fascist continuity between the pre-war policy of collective security, the *Second Imperialist War* and the fight against the invaders after 1941. This tradition makes the history of the Soviet Union appear to be an uninterrupted chain of anti-fascist struggles. In the 1930s, the Soviets supported the *anti-fascists* in Spain. In 1939–1940, they liberated the inhabitants of the neighboring countries from their local *fascist* oppressors. In the Great

Patriotic War, the USSR defeated a *fascist* aggressor, whereas during the Cold War it had to combat both *fascist* western propaganda and *fascist* resistance movements in the Sovietized territories.

In the state-controlled media, ignorance and re-interpretation characterize the discourse about the period preceding Hitler's attack. On the other hand, the concept of the *Great Patriotic War* continues to play an essential role in Russian-Soviet identity, not least by providing the most important positive and negative reference points in Russian-Soviet history: the greatest collective triumph as well as the prototype of Russia's "eternal enemy" – the fascist.

Endnotes

1 Dimitroff 2000, 275.
2 Van Ree 2002, 212.
3 McDermott and Agnew 1996, 131, 243–244.
4 Glantz 2004, 32–33.
5 Gosudarstvennyi arkhiv Rossiiskoi Federatsii (GARF), f. 5446 [sekretariat Voroshilova], op. 54, d. 3, l. 85.
6 Rossiiskii gosudarstvennyi voennyi arkhiv (RGVA), f. 9 [Politicheskoe Upravlenie RKKA], op. 29, d. 415, ll. 30; 30ob.
7 RGVA, f. 9, op. 29, d. 415, ll. 123; 123ob.
8 Rossiiskii gosudarstvennyi arkhiv sotsial'no-politicheskoi istorii (RGASPI), f. 77 [fond Zhdanova], op. 4, d. 8, ll. 111–129.
9 Stalin 1946, 15-16.
10 Golczewski and Pickhan 1998, 223.
11 Stalin 1946, 10-12.
12 Voss 1998, 47.
13 Litvin 2001, 105–6.
14 Fal'sifikatory istorii 1948, 8–24.
15 Voss 1998, 50.
16 Voss 1998, 48–50.
17 Cf. Nekrich 1995; Markwick 2001, 209–219.
18 Litvin 2001, 105–106. Cf. Voss 1998, 51–53.
19 Davies 1997, 55–58.
20 Davies 1997, 73–75.
21 Litvin 2001, 106–107.
22 Das Ende des Zweiten Weltkrieges 2005, 15.
23 Das Ende des Zweiten Weltkrieges 2005, 4.

References

Das Ende des Zweiten Weltkrieges – der Sieg der Menschheit (1939–1945) (2005). Moscow / Geneva, Ria Novosti.

Davies, Robert W. (1997), *Soviet History in the Yeltsin Era*. Basingstoke, Macmillan.

Dimitroff, Georgi (2000), *Tagebücher 1933–1943*. Berlin, Aufbau-Verlag.

Fal'sifikatory istorii (istoricheskaia spravka) (1948). Moscow, Gospolitizdat.

Glantz, David M. (2004), *The Military Strategy of the Soviet Union: A History*. London, Frank Cass.

Golczewski, Frank and Pickhan, Gertrud (1998), *Russischer Nationalismus*. Göttingen, Vandenhoeck & Ruprecht.

Litvin, Alter L. (2001), *Writing History in Twentieth-Century Russia*. Basingstoke, Palgrave.

Markwick, Roger D. (2001), *Rewriting History in Soviet Russia. The Politics of Revisionist Historiography, 1956–1974*. Basingstoke, Palgrave.

McDermott, Kevin and Agnew, Jeremy (1996), *The Comintern. A History of International Communism from Lenin to Stalin*. Basingstoke, Macmillan.

Nekrich, A.M. (1995), *22 iiunia 1941 g*. Moscow, Pamiatniki istoricheskoi mysli.

Stalin J.V. (1946), *On the Great Patriotic War of the Soviet Union*. Moscow, Foreign Languages Publishing House.

Van Ree, Erik (2002), *The Political Thought of Joseph Stalin: A Study in Twentieth-Century Revolutionary Patriotism*. London, Routledge.

Voss, Stefan (1998), *Stalins Kriegsvorbereitungen 1941, erforscht, gedeutet und instrumentalisiert: Eine Analyse postsowjetischer Geschichtsschreibung*. Hamburg, Dr. Kovač.

Olga Baranova

Collaboration by the Soviet Citizens with the Nazi Occupation Authorities during the Great Patriotic War: How the Issue was Represented and Treated in Soviet, Western and Post-Soviet Russian and Belarusian Historiography

Nazi occupation during the Second World War meant for the peoples of various European countries facing the dilemma of whether to resist and oppose the German forces or try to accommodate and cooperate, in some cases this cooperation took forms of committed collaboration, with the occupation authorities. For the population of the Soviet Union where the occupation was extremely brutal, because there it was motivated not only by economic and geopolitical goals but also by racial ideology, the dilemma of resistance and cooperation was even more pronounced. During the occupation several nations were split, pitching resistance fighters against collaborators in internal conflicts, which profoundly affected post-war history and, in many places such as the Baltic States and the Ukraine to this day influence politics and are the subject of bitter debate. The problem of how to behave toward a foreign occupation force, or toward one's own regime when experienced as tyrannical, is again very acute and worth reevaluating.

In order to understand the growing interest of contemporary historians and politicians in the issue of collaboration by the Soviet citizens with the Nazi occupation authorities during the Second World War it is crucial to review and examine the historiography of the problem.

During the war years a considerable volume of records was produced by both the occupiers and the occupied. Together with the detailed testimonies of the participants of the tragic events these documents became the primary sources and basis for a wealth of historical studies that were undertaken in the post-war period by both Soviet and Western scholars. The enormous interest in the subject of war and occupation can be explained by the fact that the events of the four years period of war profoundly affected the lives of millions of people who were eager to know the truth on what really happened on the occupied territories and to understand the origins of this brutal invasion.

Though the problem of cooperation by Soviet citizens with the German occupation authorities constitutes a coherent and indispensable part of a large historical issue – the Nazi occupation of the Soviet Union, this phenomenon, compared to many aspects of the history of the war, has received less critical attention by scholars and has not been systematically examined. While many other military, political, economic and ethical issues such as achievements of resistance movement, the nature of German occupation policies and Nazi atrocities have received extensive analysis and generated public debate, a moral issue which had such profound human costs – the choice between cooperation and resistance – was ignored or treated rather casually in historical writings for different reason. One of the most probable explanations could be the painful implications of collaboration for scholars native to the countries where it occurred as well as the influence of ideological biases and censorship that prescribed to avoid this "unpleasant" issue, which prevented its impartial objective evaluation. For some other scholars, a more decisive obstacle could be the extreme complexity of the motives and forms of collaboration and changing people's attitudes and sides over time and their transition under the influence of war conditions from collaboration to resistance.

In the 50s–70s Soviet historians produced several multi-volume works on the history of the Great Patriotic war, devoting significant attention to the study of the occupation polices. However, the leading themes in the Soviet historiography were the Red Army operations, the partisan movement, the heroism of the Soviet people and the leading role of the Communist Party organizations in the struggle against the invader. It is important to highlight that from the early 1960s, the partisan movement was increasingly portrayed as a key element in the Soviet victory over the

Nazism. "The concept of the popular struggle in the German rear, where partisans, led by the Party and wholeheartedly supported by the entire civilian population of the Soviet Union, were able to exact a high price from the German forces opposing them became the main statement of the Soviet historiography,"[1] which was largely publicized through a range of memoir literature and specialist historical works. The clearest example of the work that enshrined the notion of the popular resistance movement based on the unity of the Soviet people and their commitment to the regime was the six-volume encyclopedia of *Istoria Velikoi Otechestvennoi voiny 1941–1945* (The History of the Great Patriotic War 1941–1945), published between 1961 and 1965. Another key example of a Soviet monograph on the partisan movement is the work *Vsenarodnaia borba v tylu nemetsko-fashistskih zakhvatchikov* (The Popular Struggle in the Rear of the German-Fascist Occupiers 1941–1944) by Ponkrat K. Ponomarenko, head of the Central Headquarters of the Partisan Movement established in spring 1942. This monograph, despite its considerable potential given to the fact that the author had access to rich archival material and could provide detailed information on the organization and development of the partisan movement, gives little indications on the nature, range and scale of the problems faced by the partisans at the initial stage of the war. Focusing mainly on the achievements of the partisan movement the author, in order to avoid internal censorship and criticism by the authorities, preferred to refrain from discussing such problems as the lack of supplies from the center and the frequent cases of refusal by the civilian population to support the partisans that leaded to initial failures of the Soviet partisan movement. The Soviet accounts presented the development of the resistance movement as a steady uninterrupted process and stated that from the very start of the war "the struggle of the Soviet people in the enemy rear relentlessly grew in strength and with every day it incorporated a wider cross-section of the population."[2] In contrast, the German materials clearly identified a weakening of the fledgling partisan movement during the period of 1941–1942.

Soviet historiography almost completely ignored or deliberately avoided such issues as the nationality question in the republics of the Soviet Union, disaffection of some social groups with the Soviet regime and their possible connection to collaboration with the occupation authorities. During the Soviet era the facts of cooperation between the Soviet citizens and the German invaders were largely neglected and thoroughly hidden for ideological reasons. Whilst doggedly prosecuting and punishing those suspected of "collaboration" as traitors in the post-war period, the Soviet government was reluctant to acknowledge publicly that this war-time phenomenon took place on the Soviet territories during the occupation or sought to diminish the significance of this phenomenon. Since the existence of collaboration could raise the question of the legitimacy of the Soviet regime and also could question the allegiance of the population to the Soviet state, the government refused to divulge the real scale of this movement and to openly analyze its origins and reasons. Thus the Soviet writings, even when briefly mentioned the existence of the problem, sought to explain the reasons and scale of collaboration with the Nazis as the 'traitorous activity of a small group of anti-Soviet elements and betrayers of the motherland'. A key example of such an attitude is the work by Romanovskii *Saudzelniki u zlachynstvah* (Accomplices in Committing the Crimes) published in 1964. It was the only monographic work of the Soviet period that took the issue of collaboration as the main subject of research. The author analyzed the activity and structure of collaboration organizations in Belarus dedicating special attention to the activity of Belarusian nationalists during the occupation and to their post-war fates. However, the author subjected everything connected to the collaboration activities to annihilating criticism without trying to understand the real motives of behavior of those who were working for the German authorities.

Émigré historians, often former collaborators, in their writings, for understandable reasons, preferred to play down the facts of participation of their compatriots and companions in arms in German atrocities highlighting instead their work to secure national independence whilst stressing the limited alternatives that were available to them.

An important feature of the post-war Soviet historiography is that it rarely mentioned the issue of collaboration in Holocaust and in general the tragedy of Jewish population under the occupation. Despite the fact that the heaviest losses had been borne by the Jews, speaking separately of the tragedy of Soviet Jewry was discouraged since it was felt that the Jews who fell at the hands of the Nazis were simply an indistinguishable part of the losses to the Soviet people as a whole. The probable explanation for this can be "the fear of authorities that the special focus on memory of the Holocaust might serve to justify Zionism to the prejudice of the memory of other nations and ethnic groups of the Soviet Union that also suffered and borne huge losses under the Nazi occupation".[3]

Therefore, although many Soviet studies do contain some valuable information, they need to be approached with an understanding of the ideological constraints faced by their authors.

The experience of Western researchers is extremely useful in studying the issue of occupation and particularly the phenomenon of cooperation by the Soviet citizens with the German occupation authorities. Studies of the Nazi occupation of the Soviet Union in the West started almost as soon as the war ended. During the 1950s–60s, historians working for the US military service gained access to German documents of the *Wehrmacht* and the Ministry for the Occupied Eastern Territories captured by the Allied armies. These materials together with interrogations and interviews of survivors in turn became a valuable source for several solid studies.

Several western works specifically on the German occupation of the Soviet territories took the line of an 'alternative occupation policy' and argued that had German policy been more favorable to the civilian population it would have allowed the Germans to mobilize more effectively elements of the Soviet people, particularly various non-Russian groups and the peasantry, against the Soviet regime. The best examples of such approach remain the works *German Rule in Russia 1941–1945: A Study of Occupation Policies* by Alexander Dallin published in 1957 and *Soviet Partisans in World War II* by John Armstrong published in 1964. The works by Dallin, Armstrong as well as those by Reitlinger, Howell and some others produced in the west during the Cold War period, were characterized by an assumption that the Germans could have won the war with the Soviet Union and that they failed only because they committed certain fatal mistakes. It seems that these studies, using the German experience, sought to "draw valuable conclusions from the German defeat in the East and to understand the nature of one of the possible weapons of the opposition to the Soviet Union".[4]

In the 70–80s military collaboration by civilians and POWs with German forces has attracted great interest amongst Western historians. Particular attention has been paid, for example, to the Russian Liberation Army (*Russkaia Osvoboditel'naia Armiia ROA*) headed by General

Andrei Vlasov. Much of the Western literature, based in particular on such primary documents as the Prague Manifesto issued on 14 November 1944, has sought to present the movement as a genuine popular attempt to liberate Russia from 'totalitarianism'. Some Western scholars such as George Fischer, Joachim Hoffman, and Catherine Andreyev have been inclined to regard military and political aspects of cooperation by the Soviet population with the German authorities not as collaboration, but as a struggle for 'liberation' from the Soviet regime, even borrowing the terminology used during the war such as 'Liberation Movement of the Peoples of Russia' and 'Russian Liberation Army' rather uncritically.

Though in the studies conducted in 1950s–80s Cold war bias affected both Western and Soviet historians and forced them to repeat the same generalization supported by isolated examples selected on the base of ideological considerations from a wide range of events and circumstances, which in its turn lead them to make sweeping statements and conclusions and thus to simplify some issues of the Second World War, these works, however, laid a strong basis for future studies.

The end of the Cold War and *Perestroika* era in the USSR were important factors in shaping the historiography of German occupation of the Soviet territories in the late 80s and in the 90s. Since 1991 the issue of cooperation by the Soviet citizens with the German forces has become a subject of intense debate in the independent countries of the former Soviet Union. One of the most important aspects in this process was the opening of the former Soviet archives in Russia, Belarus, Ukraine and the Baltic states, as well as the decentralization of the KGB archives that provided scholars with open access to a wide range of new documents such as military records, reports and propaganda leaflets. All these new materials that were made available not only to Russian but also to Western scholars stimulated substantially studies of the issue and served immensely to improve the understanding of what happened in the occupied territories.

Interestingly that in post-Communist period some Russian historians such as Alexander Okorokov, whilst engaged in a search for an alternative course for the development of the Russian state, have preferred to follow the Cold War Western tradition in portraying collaboration with Nazi Germany as representing a desire to rid the Soviet peoples of the

Bolshevik oppression. However, post-Soviet works advance more critical explanation of collaboration, they acknowledge the complexity of the issue and do not simply suggest that Soviet civilians who cooperated with the German occupation authorities were traitor of the Soviet cause, anti-Bolshevik fighters, nationalists or blatantly only concerned with their immediate survival or material improvement.

The 90s were characterized by the increased interest of historians to individual stories and case studies that stimulated the emergence of new approaches in historiography such as 'microhistory' and 'history from below'. The main examples of these approaches are the works by such scholars as Bernhard Chiari, Martin Dean, and Daniel Goldhagen, which introduced different intentional and psychological issues that were omitted in previous historical studies.

In Belarus after the break-up of the Soviet Union and the proclamation of independence in August 1991, national historiography took off following the road of nationalist history and the possibility of an objective study of collaboration was to some extent outlined. Some attempts in Belarusian historiography of the early 90s were even made to view the issue of cooperation with the occupation authorities from a nationalist perspective and to whitewash the wartime experience of collaboration. Of course, in Belarus the political rehabilitation of collaborators has not achieved such a high scale and has not taken the exaggerated forms that it has in the Ukraine or, especially, in the Baltic states where it was quite obvious in political situation that a monopoly of socialist ideas has been replaced by a monopoly of nationalist ideas and the concept of 'patriotism' has completely changed. As a result, the numerous politicians and historians in these newly independent countries have sought to justify the individuals who collaborated with the German Nazi authorities during the war, and "there was a strong tendency to depict almost any enemy of the Soviet regime as a martyr and fighter for the 'freedom of the motherland'".[5] Nevertheless, even in Belarusian nationalistic historiography, the notion that Belarusian collaborators were the victims of two totalitarian regimes – Stalin's Soviet Union on the one hand and Hitler's Third Reich on the other – and, that they were simply attempting to find their way towards national sovereignty, has become quite popular.

However, the change of political regime in Belarus in 1995 put the brakes on a great deal of research on the history of Belarusian collaboration and many historians had to revert to the old Soviet school, which considered those who supported Germans during the occupation as 'betrayers of the motherland'. This point of view continues to dominate today's Belarusian writings on the war events. Given that defending the Soviet image of Belarus as a partisan republic is seen by many historians and politicians as a patriotic issue, it has meant that whilst the role of the Communist Party may have been played down, in the post-Soviet Belarusian historiography of the war little else has changed. Consequently, in Belarusian post-Soviet writings, despite a wider availability of primary source material, the issue of civilian collaboration with the Germans has received scant attention and little critical analysis, while the "popular character of the partisan movement and its military significance from the beginning of the war has been little questioned and to some extent continues to be exaggerated."[6]

Therefore, in spite of all positive changes in historiography, the history of Soviet collaboration, and its Belarusian as well as Russian aspect in particular, still remains a painful and considerably politicized issue and thus the process of its impartial analyses and reevaluation is far from complete.

Endnotes

1 Hill 2005, 9.
2 *Istoriia Velikoi Otechestvennoi voiny Sovetskogo Sojuza 1941–1945* 1960, 334.
3 Smilovitsky 2000, 37.
4 Mulligan 1988, 25.
5 Kudryashov 1994, 240.
6 Hill 2005, 10.

References

Andreyev, Catherine (1987), *Vlasov and the Russian Liberation Movement.* Cambridge, Cambridge University Press.

Armstrong, John A. (1964), *Soviet partisans in World War II.* Madison, The University of Wisconsin Press.

Chiari, Bernhard (1998), *Alltag Hinter der Front Besatzung, Kollaboration und Widerstand in Weißrußland 1941–1944*. Düsseldorf, Droste Verlag.

Dallin, Alexander (1957), *German Rule in Russia, 1941–1945: A Study of Occupation Policies*. London, Macmillan.

Dean, Martin (1999), *Collaboration in the Holocaust: Crimes of the Local Police in Belorussia and Ukraine, 1941–44*. New York, St. Martin's Press.

Fischer, George (1952), *Soviet Opposition to Stalin. A Case Study in World War II*. Cambridge Mass., Harvard University Press.

Goldhagen, Daniel (1998), *Hitler's Willing Executioners: Ordinary Germans and the Holocaust*. London, Abacus.

Hill, Alexander (2005), *The War Behind the Eastern Front. The Soviet Partisan Movement in North-West Russia, 1941–1944*. London, Frank Cass.

Hoffmann, Joachim (1986), *Die Geschichte der Wlassow-Armee*. Feiburg, Rombach.

Howell, Edgar.M (1956), *The Soviet Partisan Movement, 1941–1944*. Washington (DC) Department of the Army.

Istoria Velikoi Otechestvennoi voiny Sovetskogo Sojuza 1941–1945. (The History of the Great Patriotic War 1941–1945). Volume 2: Iiun' 1941–Noiabr' 1942 (1960). Moscow, Voenizdat MO SSSR.

Kudryashov, Sergej (1994), The Hidden Dimension. Wartime Collaboration in the Soviet Union. In Erickson, John and Dilks, David (eds.), *Barbarossa. The Axis and the Allies*. Edinburgh, Edinburgh University Press, 238–254.

Mulligan, Timothy Patrick (1988), *The Politics of Illusion and Empire: German Occupation Policy in the Soviet Union, 1942–1943*. New York, Praeger Publisher.

Okorokov, Alexander (1997), *Materialy po istorii Russkogo osvoboditel'nogo dvizheniia, 1941–1945 gg*. (Materials of the history of the Russian liberation movement, 1941–1945). Moscow, Graal.

Ponomarenko, Ponkrat K. *Vsenarodnaia borba v tylu nemetsko-fashistskih zakhvatchikov*. (The Popular Struggle in the Rear of the German-Fascist Occupiers 1941–1944). RGASPI, fond 625, opis 1.

Reitlinger, Gerald (1960), *The House Built on Sand. The Conflicts of German Policy in Russia 1939–1945*. London, Weidenfeld & Nicolson.

Romanovskiy, W. F. (1964), *Saudzelniki u zlachynstvah* (Accomplices in Committing the Crimes), Minsk.

Smilovitsky, Leonid (2000), *Katastrofia Evreev v Belorusii 1941–1944.* (Holocaust in Belorussia, 1941–1944). Tel-Aviv, Biblioteka Motveya Chernogo.

Beate Fieseler

The Wounds of War: Experiences of War-Related Disablement in Soviet Feature Films

Introduction

In terms of foreign policy, the Soviet Union emerged as a world power after the Second World War.[1] However, the price for this triumph was monstrous, and reflects the ambivalent nature of victory. As well as the enormous material damage, the war cost a vast number of human lives. The 27 million casualties did not include many millions of war widows and war orphans and approximately 2.5 to 3.5 million officially acknowledged invalids of war.[2]

This contribution focuses on how the official way of remembering the price of victory, particularly how disablement was shown in Soviet feature films from 1944 to 1959. It was after all not clear at first how the war should be remembered. The way the events of war were handled on screen and how the war invalid was represented and interpreted changed according to the political circumstances. Until the Perestroika period in the late 1980s, the Soviet regime determined how the war was depicted. Historiography, journalism, iconography, literature, the visual arts, music and film, were all controlled and censored by the state. The film industry had already been nationalised in 1935, but state influence over film intensified particularly after the war ended in 1945, and all war-related stories and images shown had to conform to the contemporary political climate.

The cinematic portrayal of the Second World War began in the Soviet Union in 1942 and has continued through to the present day. By the end of the war, 48 feature films had been made on the subject.[3] While the suffering of the Soviet soldiers at the front has remained a blank spot in the official depictions of the war, a notably large number of films focus on the misery and suffering caused.[4] The films of the war years showed the brutal murder of civilians by Nazi units, or focused on the forced separation of loved ones. Suffering and loss were however portrayed chiefly in relation to women, children and partisans, while death and injury in the army were hardly touched upon. Nevertheless, a different type of cinema did temporarily come into being which was directly influenced by the reality of war, and which developed images for "sincere" feelings for the first time after the enforced jollity which characterised films and, in particular, comedy musicals, during the 1930s. In the light of the enormous loss and destruction which occurred, this was more than justified.[5]

Here, I shall use the figure of the war invalid as an example in order to examine how this tragic legacy, these "wounds of war" which were inflicted above all (but not exclusively) on men, was portrayed in Soviet films during and immediately after the war, and during the social and political thaw of the 1950s. Despite over 18 million cases of war-related injury and illness,[6] war invalids were relatively rarely shown on the Soviet screen. While this image stands for the high price of victory, it also symbolises the patriotism of the Soviet people who willingly gave up life and limb. This figure therefore demonstrates particularly clearly which of the two aspects prevailed, and whether heroic or tragic elements were included in equal measure. I shall now use three films to show how the treatment of the war and the figure of the war invalid on screen changed according to the political climate. When the cult of the "Great Patriotic War", which focused almost solely on victory and heroism,[7] began to dominate since the late 1960s, the Soviet invalid of the Second World War vanished from Soviet films for nearly two decades.[8]

Six o'Clock in the Evening after the War (1944)

The figure of a soldier with an amputated leg appeared for the first time in 1944, strangely enough in the poetic comedy musical film *Six o'Clock in the Evening after the War* by the acclaimed director Ivan Pyrev.[9] The first, optimistic, half is set before the war, and shows the budding romance between the officer Vasya and the teacher Varya, who must wait until "six o'clock in the evening after the war" before their personal happiness can be fulfilled. Vasya is severely wounded at the front, and is shown on crutches with his leg amputated. Not wanting to be a burden to his bride, he asks his friend to tell her that he has been killed. However, the friend fails to keep his promise, and the lovers Vasya and Varya are happily reunited on victory day – shown in the film as being in 1944 – in the summer sun in Moscow.

In this film, the wounds afflicted by the war were trivialised as being possible to heal. Vasya, who has already exchanged his crutches for a stick, now bears his war injury with full pride like one more medal. The war injury to the female protagonist, who herself served at the front, has left no visible traces. The kiss against the backdrop of the victory fireworks marks the end of the short-term "state of emergency" into which they have both have been forced by the war. He *was* a crippled invalid, and she was a woman in uniform. Now that the war is over, Varya appears wearing a summer dress and holding flowers in her hand, while Vasya is a dashing officer again. When the loving couple is reunited at the end of the film, the summer filled with flowers, music and jubilation symbolises their return to a happy future, in other words, to a state of physical intactness and the normality of the order of the sexes which prevailed before.

The war injury of the male protagonist is not treated as a serious problem. The potential social marginalisation of the war wounded, and the possibility that Varya may cool towards her amputee fiancé, are both ignored. However, the film does show the personal conflict of the war invalid long before the lovers are reunited. This episode has a central place in the film, but only lasts a few minutes. Overall, the film has fairytale overtones which are further underlined by the text, which is recited in verse throughout. In keeping with the aim of the "comedy" genre, the film prepares the audience for the need to integrate millions of invalid war veterans into Soviet society, while offering them relief, reassurance and indeed consolation in the face of this task. At the same time, *Six o'Clock in the Evening after the War* also helps to mobilise the last forces for the final victory now within reach by showing heart-warming images to illustrate the rewards to be expected in the form of the future happiness of the reunited lovers. In the original film script, the lovers are only reunited in the imagination of the dying hero. However, Pyrev, the director, insisted on making changes, and this was exactly what the public wanted to see during the war years. They needed hope and optimism, not tragic stories.[10]

Story about a Real Man (1948)

After the end of the war, millions of people longed for a quick return to normality. In reality, at the start of the Cold War, the partial liberalisation of the war years was reversed. An ideological hardening (*zhdanovshchina*) took hold, with a policy of enforced abstinence from consumerism which had already been implemented during the 1930s. Nobody was spared. The exhausted population, including millions of war invalids, was mobilised for the rapid reorganisation of industry and armaments. It wasn't enough simply to have survived the war. Now, it was far more important that everybody would make heroic efforts and win victories on the reconstruction and production "fronts".[11]

The model of the indestructible war hero strong enough for this task was illustrated in 1948 in the solemn film *Story about a Real Man* by Alexander Stolper, the plot of which was based on the bestselling novel of the same name by Boris Polevoi.[12] Set in the spring of 1942, the film tells the real-life story of pilot Alexei Maresev (known in the book and the film as "Meresev"), who suffered severe leg injuries after his plane crashed in enemy territory. In order to avoid being taken prisoner by the Germans and being branded a traitor, a threat made by Stalin in his infamous Order no. 270 in August 1941,[13] the injured pilot makes the arduous journey back to his own lines. In the film, 18 minutes are dedicated to Meresev's long, extremely painful 18-day trek through the snowy forest. At the last minute, he is discovered by partisans and brought to the field hospital, where he immediately has his legs amputated. After the operation, Meresev falls into deep apathy and depression, feeling that his life has no purpose, lamenting that a pilot without legs is like a bird without wings.

The man in the neighbouring bed, a fatally ill civil war hero (a political commissar), attempts to draw him out of his apathy with the cult novel *How the Steel was Tempered*,[14] but the real turning point (in the 45th minute of the film) comes when the veteran gives him an article to read about a pilot from the First World War who continued to fly even after his leg had been amputated. When Meresev protests that he has lost both legs, the civil war hero counters with "But you are a Soviet Man! Soviet! Soviet!"

Meresev's psychological healing approximately coincides with the death of the political commissar, the "real man" in the title of the film. With his help, Meresev was also able to mature into a "real man" and to understand that heroes do not need legs. From that point on, his healing progresses rapidly. He gains strength by training every day on his new prosthetic legs "created by expert hands, and better than real legs", and is soon well enough to leave the hospital. During his subsequent stay in a sanatorium, he convinces the medical committee that he is capable of returning to the front, he even learned to dance to support his claim. The dramatic climax of the film comes when Meresev succeeds in performing a lively folk dance.

The last 23 minutes of the film show him back in war service, performing so bravely and tirelessly that his comrades at the front don't even realise that he has prosthetic legs. The film focuses on how suffering can be heroically conquered, while at the same time hardly showing this suffering itself, and dwells on the wounded pilot who refuses to give himself up as prisoner, instead limping eastwards. It fails to show shocking images of the mutilated invalid who has had both legs removed. The role of Meresev therefore also fails to reflect the lot of a real war invalid, and the part is furthermore played by Pavel Kadochnikov, a popular screen hero at the time. The film thus consciously refrains from creating authentic images of invalidity. It focuses rather (as in *Six o'Clock in the Evening after the War* discussed above) on Meresev's state of mind, showing him passive, apathetic and lying silently in bed. When he subsequently starts to practise walking, jumping and dancing, the shot is taken from below, making him superhuman in size, indeed, looking like a real hero.

The film thus draws on hero myths which were created in the 1930s, in the novel by Nikolai Ostrovskii *How the Steel was Tempered* (which was later filmed several times), which had secured its place in the Socialist Realism canon for a good twenty years.[15] For this reason, the film is not just an adventure story à la Jack London (as was also thought). It is far more a film designed to mobilise the population for the reconstruction efforts still to come for the fourth five-year plan.[16] The film used cinematic means to convey this message to the audience, as well as the figure of the robust, indestructible hero, Meresev. Again, the *Story about a Real Man* does not present the problem of invalidity and the related physical and psychological stress to the general public. The political conditions of the late Stalinist era, made it impossible to tackle the subject. The population was encouraged to be optimistic, rather than remember the past events of the war and all the traumas resulting from it. From that point, any tragic words (literature) and above all, authentic images depicting the suffering of war were removed from the official Soviet culture of remembrance. The *Story about a Real Man* is therefore a typical film of this era, which after the brief ideological respite during the war years again returned to the heroic myths of the 1930s (which despised the frailty of the human body), while the restitution of manliness again played a dominant role.

Ballad of a Soldier (1959)

As my final example, I would like to consider a film from the thaw period, the Ballad of a Soldier. This film was shown in 1959, three years after the 20th Party Conference and the Secret Speech by Nikita Khrushchev in February 1956. The re-evaluation of the war (alongside the examination of the Stalinist terror) was one of the integral elements of de-Stalinisation, which was at that time initiated but never fully completed.[17] During the late 1950s and early 1960s, artistic life focused to a remarkable degree on portraying the negative aspects of the war, and addressed the issue of the price paid by the population for victory – topics which had become taboo immediately after the war. The film *Ballad of a Soldier* by director Grigori Chukhrai, who had himself served during the war and been wounded several times,[18] tells the story of a young soldier who is granted four days' home leave for being a hero. On the way to his village, he meets and gives help to other people who are suffering. The chance meeting between the soldier and a war invalid is just *one* among various different episodes in the film, but it depicts the disablement caused by war differently than in previous Soviet films. The subject is again a soldier whose leg has been amputated, who has been released from the army and who is on his way home. In contrast to the two films discussed above, this one shows the protagonist with simple wooden crutches – a far more realistic scenario at that time. Victory is not yet in sight, but for this man, the fight is over. He worries whether he should contact his wife, and whether his marriage will be able to withstand his disablement. Here, too, the invalid is played by a good-looking, popular actor, Evgenii Urbanskii, and is a big, strong man. However, the film shows him sleepless and full of anxiety and desperation, while also being comforted by his fellow passengers. After his arrival in his home town, he has to wait for several torturous minutes and almost loses hope before his wife comes hurrying towards him. It is no coincidence that the lengthy reunion scene is similar to *Six o'Clock in the Evening after the War.*

When the war invalid and his wife leave the station together and the wife almost trips over her husband's crutches, it is clear that their relationship will not be an easy one. Both will have to cope with the new situation. The image is of a bitter happiness with an uncertain outcome.

Summary

Although the three films discussed in detail here are so different, none shows the experience of war and the return of the veterans from the perspective of the war injured. In none of the examples given, and to my knowledge, in none of the newer Russian films to date, has the topic of invalidity been treated in any depth. During the war, the issue was trivialised and sanitised, then shown as a challenge for Soviet Man which could be overcome. Only in *Ballad of a Soldier* is disablement a difficult, but primarily individual problem. Despite the approximation to reality during the thaw period, many taboos remained. No Soviet director has yet dared to use a real war invalid to portray the role of the injured protagonist. In contrast to some Hollywood films (such as William Wyler's *The Best Years of Our Lives*, 1946), Soviet cinema avoided portraying invalidity in a radical light altogether.[19] Soviet films avoided showing very young men, blind people, hand or arm amputees or women who had sustained war injuries. Social discrimination, unfair treatment by the authorities and insufficient care were not broached at all. No film tackles the traumas of war or explores the psychological consequences of invalidity for those affected, their families or partners. The war injured are never depicted as outcasts living on the edge of society.

The Soviet films of the 1940s and 1950s entirely ignore the issue of marginalisation or impoverishment, and thus fail to portray the fate of war injured alcoholics, beggars and the homeless. This sanitisation and trivialisation of a difficult topic made it impossible for those affected to identify with the heroes on screen, and spared the audience from having to examine the problem of invalidity at a serious level. For this reason, it is possible to conclude that the aim of the Soviet films (except some during the thaw period) simply to encourage the audience to forget the war, or at least to ignore it. In the war films of the Brezhnev era, the figure of the war invalid vanished completely from the screen. The cult of the Great Patriotic War, which was created in the late 1960s in the Soviet Union, focused unilaterally on war heroes and their acts of bravery. This precluded any war-related experiences of loss and desperation, not only in the official commemoration of the war, but also in the arts.

It is impossible to gauge precisely what effect of the films discussed here had on the audience. However, due to the power of imagery, they presumably characterised their long-term view of invalidity, at least among those who did not experience it either personally or within their family circle.

Endnotes

1 The author wishes to thank the Militärgeschichtliches Forschungsamt (Military History Research Office), Potsdam, Germany, for permission to reprint the contribution: Fieseler 2003, 199–222, in abbreviated and partially revised form.

2 Hildermeier 1998, 615–617; Krivosheev 1997, 91, give the number of people who were released from the Red Army as invalids during the war as 2,756,000. To these must be added those who lay wounded in hospitals at the end of the war, and those who were acknowledged as being invalids during demobilisation and repatriation.

3 Kenez 1995, 166.

4 Zorkaya 2005, 328.

5 Kenez 1992, 204.

6 Krivosheev 1997, 87.

7 Tumarkin 1994, 125–157.

8 The first film, to my knowledge, to deal with the topic of war-related disability in the 1980s was Igor Talankin's *Vremia otdycha s subboty do ponedel'nika*, based on the story *Terpenie* by Iurii Nagibin, from 1984.
9 Domashniania sinemateka 1996, 53; Engel 1999, 89; 336.
10 Engel 1999, 89.
11 Fieseler 2006, 46–61.
12 Domashniania sinemateka 1996, 331; Engel 1999, 338; Polevoi.
13 Der Befehl Nummer 270, 1989, 1035–1038.
14 Ostrovski 1973.
15 Günther 1993, 155–183.
16 Fitzpatrick 1985, 129–156; Fitzpatrick 1989, 37–52.
17 Bonwetsch 2002, 172–175.
18 Chukhrai 2001, 112–128.
19 Etges 2003, 163–172; Gerber 1997, 111–133; Gerber 2000, 70–95; Norden 1994, 160–168.

References

Der Befehl Nummer 270 (1989). In *Osteuropa*, Vol. 39, Issue 2, 1035–1038.

Bonwetsch, Bernd (2002), Der 'Große Vaterländische Krieg': Vom öffentlichen Schweigen unter Stalin zum Heldenkult unter Breschnew. In Quinkert, Babette (ed.), *"Wir sind die Herren dieses Landes". Ursachen, Verlauf und Folgen des deutschen Überfalls auf die Sowjetunion*. Hamburg, VSA, 166–187.

Chukhrai, Grigorii (2001), *Moia voina*. Moskva, Algoritm.

Domashniania sinemateka. Otechestvennoe kino 1918–1996 (1996), Moskva, Dubl-D.

Engel, Christine (1999) (ed.), *Geschichte des sowjetischen und russischen Films*. Stuttgart-Weimar, J. B. Metzler.

Etges, Andreas (2003), The Best War Ever? Der Deutungswandel des Zweiten Weltkrieges in US-amerikanischen Filmen am Beispiel von "The Best Years of Our Lives" und "Saving Private Ryan". In Chiari, Bernhard, Rogg, Matthias and Schmidt, Wolfgang (eds.), *Krieg und Militär im Film des 20. Jahrhunderts*. München, R. Oldenbourg, 163–178.

Fieseler, Beate (2003), Der Kriegsinvalide in ausgewählten sowjetischen Spielfilmen der Kriegs- und Nachkriegszeit (1944 bis 1953). In Chiari, Bernhard, Rogg, Matthias and Schmidt, Wolfgang (eds.), *Krieg und Militär im Film des 20. Jahrhunderts*. München, R. Oldenbourg, 199–222.

Fieseler, Beate (2006), The Bitter Legacy of the 'Great Patriotic War': Red Army Disabled Soldiers under Late Stalinism. In: Fürst, Juliane (ed.), *Late Stalinist Russia. Society between Reconstruction and Reinvention*. London–New York, Routledge, 46–61.

Fitzpatrick, Sheila (1985), Postwar Soviet Society. The "Return to Normalcy" 1945–1953. In Linz, Susan J. (ed.), *The Impact of World War II on the Soviet Union*. New York, Rowman and Allanheld, 129–156.

Fitzpatrick, Sheila (1989), War and Society in Soviet Context. Soviet Labor before, during, and after World War II. *International Labor and Working-Class History*, No. 35, 37–52.

Gerber, David A. (2000), Heroes and Misfits. The Troubled Social Reintegration of Disabled Veterans in The Best Years of Our Lives. In Gerber, David A. (ed.), *Disabled Veterans in History*. Ann Arbor, The University of Michigan Press, 70–95.

Gerber, David A. (1997), In Search of Al Schmid. War Hero, Blinded Veteran, Everyman. In Mitchell, David T. and Snyder, Sharon L. (eds.), *The Body and Physical Difference. Discourses of Disability*. Ann Arbor, The University of Michigan Press, 111–133.

Günther, Hans (1993), *Der sozialistische Übermensch. Maksim Gorkij und der sowjetische Heldenmythos*. Stuttgart–Weimar, J. B. Metzler.

Hildermeier, Manfred (1998), *Geschichte der Sowjetunion 1917–1991. Entstehung und Niedergang des ersten sozialistischen Staates*. München, C. H. Beck.

Kenez, Peter (1995), Black and White. The War on Film. In Stites, Richard (ed.), *Culture and Entertainment in Wartime Russia*. Bloomington-Indianapolis, Indiana University Press, 157–175.

Kenez, Peter (1992), *Cinema and Soviet Society 1917–1953*. Cambridge–New York-Melbourne, Cambridge University Press.

Krivosheev, G. F. (ed., 1997), *Soviet Casualties and Combat Losses in the Twentieth Century*. London–Mechanicsburg, Greenhill Books-Stackpole Books.

Norden, Martin F. (1994), *The Cinema of Isolation. A History of Physical Disability in the Movies*. New Brunswick, Rutgers University Press.

Ostrowski, Nikolai (1973), *Wie der Stahl gehärtet wurde*. Dortmund, Weltkreis Verlags-GmbH.

Polewoi, Boris (1985), *Der wahre Mensch*. Roman–Berlin, Volk und Welt.

Tumarkin, Nina (1994), *The Living and the Dead. The Rise and Fall of the Cult of World War II in Russia*. New York, BasicBooks.

Zorkaja, Neja (2005), Kino in Zeiten des Krieges. Visualisierungen von 1941 bis 1945. *Osteuropa*, Vol. 55 Issue 4–6, 319–336.

Zvi Gitelman

Remembrance of Things Past: Soviet Histories and Jewish Memories

Historical information is generally reported in three ways. One is scholarly, detailed reconstruction and analysis of the past, which some still strive to make "objective," however the post-modernists may scoff. A second is "popular history," that which is less detailed, perhaps more dramatic, intended for general audiences and presented not only in books but also in films, museums, websites and other media. The third is versions of the past transmitted in schools and within families, in informal discussions and reminiscences. It is this last form that shapes and perhaps constitutes "collective memory," or the interpreted history/mythology which all of us absorb at most stages of life.

All forms of historical presentation tend to be parochial and self-serving to one degree or another. Scholars tend to write about areas of personal interest. This is not simply a matter of access to sources and cultures, as these can be acquired. The number of people in France writing about French history is undoubtedly far greater than historians of France in other countries. There is a natural tendency for people to study and write more about themselves.

Interpretations offered in popular history, especially, tend to be parochial. Only an American would write a history of World War Two focused on the United States and called "the greatest generation."[1] Only a westerner, in this case an American, would entitle a book about the invasion of Normandy as *D-Day, June 6, 1944: The Climactic Battle of World War II*.[2] Obviously, a Soviet author would have written about the battle of Stalingrad, and a Polish author would be more likely to write about the Warsaw uprising of 1944 or about the battle of Monte Cassino. Thus, the third type of history, mythologized and transmitted across generations, is almost inevitably parochial and tendentious, for its purpose is socialization. That of popular history is general education, socialization and entertainment, and that of scholarly history is uncovering new facts and developing new understandings – rarely, the confirmation of previous ones.

Information in the Soviet System

Perhaps no modern state gathered more information about its own citizenry than did the Soviet Union. The Soviet system placed great emphasis on the accumulation of information. This included more detailed information about every aspect of economic activity than any other state had ever gathered, and as much as could be learned about the attitudes, beliefs and values of as many citizens. Whether the information was reliable and accurate, and what was done with it, are not our concern here.[3]

In this essay I inquire as to what Soviet authorities knew about the systematic extermination of their citizens of Jewish nationality; what did they do with what they knew, and what motivated them; and how they interpreted some of the information to their own citizenry. Secondly, what did some Soviet Jews know about the same matters, and what conclusions did they draw from their knowledge? My findings are preliminary and await substantiation with further research.

The Holocaust did not figure in Soviet scholarship and did not appear in popular histories of the war. Most likely, it was not part of the private histories transmitted in Soviet families, except for Jewish families. However, the Soviet government knew a great deal about the Shoah (Holocaust) on its territory, and it knew it early in the war. As a prominent official in the Foreign Ministry, Konstantin Umansky, wrote on December 5, 1942 to Foreign Minister Vyacheslav Molotov, "The NKVD has very interesting material about the German annihilation [*istreblenie*] of Jews on the occupied Soviet territories as well as in other countries. This is much more solid information than what Maisky gave to the Jewish organizations in May."[4] This information came to Soviet authorities from eyewitnesses who managed to escape the Nazis, from Soviet agents deliberately left behind in areas occupied by the Axis forces, and, later on, from military investigators and special investigative commissions who worked in newly liberated areas. The latter were known as the *Extraordinary State Commissions for the Investigation of the Brutalities, Acts of Violence, and Other Crimes Committed by the German Armies on the Temporarily Occupied Soviet Territories.*[5]

Military commissions, which preceded the Extraordinary Commissions, entered localities to take testimony almost immediately as those were liberated, and documented German activities in thousands of pages. The Extraordinary Commissions added thousands more.[6] However, this information was used very selectively. I infer that the purpose of gathering it was to amass evidence for trials of Nazis and their collaborators, some of which took place already during the war. The British and Americans had made their intentions clear to have post-war trials and had pressed the Soviets to gather evidence for them. The Soviets were also intent on getting compensation for material damages inflicted by the invaders, as is evident from their detailed documentation of buildings destroyed or damaged, livestock sequestered, and resources despoiled or exploited.

However, this information was reported only to carefully specified audiences, and not for their general edification but for specific purposes. It seems that some of the evidence of Nazi atrocities against civilians was passed on to the Main Political Administration of the armed forces to be used in briefings of the troops in order to arouse them to fighting even harder against the cruel and destructive enemy. Some was reported to specific audiences, such as foreign Jews, who were sent copies of *Einikeit*, the Yiddish newspaper of the Jewish Anti-Fascist Committee whose assignment was to rally support for the Soviet war effort. (Nearly every issue carried the slogan "a thousand tanks and 500 warplanes for the Soviet forces!"). It seems that atrocities against "peaceful Soviet citizens" were publicized to the general public, but the special fate of the Jews was not highlighted or even mentioned most of the time.[7] After the Nazi-Soviet pact of August 23, 1939, there were no Soviet press reports about attacks on Jews in Poland, Germany or elsewhere. After the German invasion of the Soviet Union, "information about what was going on in the occupied territories was still limited" and although "Nazi atrocities against the Jews could not be omitted [...] the truth that they were the only people who faced total extermination, and not the Slavs, was not to be revealed."[8] It was almost only in the context of allied declarations condemning the German mass murders of Jews that Jews were specifically mentioned. Even in the two full pages in *Pravda* devoted to Nazi atrocities following the establishment of the Extraordinary Commissions "[t]here was only one sentence in the whole announcement which said that 100 Jews were shot in the town of Sychevsk."[9] Only once during the entire war, on December 19, 1942, when publishing the Joint declaration of the Allied Countries, did the Soviet press acknowledge the Nazi plan for the annihilation of all European Jews. Nevertheless, there did appear articles by noted Soviet writers Ilya Ehrenburg and Vassili Grossman that addressed the mass murder of Jews.

Thus, information on the Holocaust was assiduously gathered by Soviet authorities as part of their documentation of German atrocities, but it was rarely mentioned in the press, and presumably not in literature, films and newsreels.

Post-War Soviet Historiography

Official histories of the war – there were no others in Soviet times – were carefully developed in order to convey approved images and messages. These latter then became the substance of a mythology of the war, times occupying a place even more prominent than Marxist-Leninist ideology and the mythology of the Revolution in post-war USSR.

The interpretation of the war presented to the Soviet public was that the USSR had won the war because its socialist system was superior to the most degenerate form of capitalism, fascism, and the outcome of the war, which included not only the total defeat of fascism but the expansion of socialist systems to neighboring states, proved the superiority of socialism and its ultimate triumph over capitalism. Second, as Stalin made clear in his famous victory toast in the Kremlin, the war marked the triumph not only of one type of political and economic system over another, but the victory of the Russian people over the Germans and others who had dared attempt the conquest of the motherland of both socialism and the Russian people. On May 24, 1945 in his final toast in the Kremlin to the victorious Soviet officer corps, the Generalissimo said,

> I would like to raise this toast to the health of the Soviet people, and first of all, of the Russian people. I drink first of all to the [...] Russian people because it is the most outstanding nation of all the nations who belong to the Soviet Union [...] because it earned in this war general recognition as the leading force of the Soviet Union among all the peoples of our country. [...] it has a clear mind, steadfast character, and patience [...]. The trust of the Russian people in the Soviet Government turned out to be the decisive force that guaranteed the historic victory over the enemy of humanity – fascism. Thanks to the Russian people for that trust! To the health of the Russian people![10]

Stalin's toast did not ignore other peoples of the USSR, but it placed the Russians in the position of *primus inter pares*, if not higher. What Stalin, historians, propagandists and Party and government officials ignored was the special, perhaps unique, fate of the Jews. They also had difficulty dealing with collaboration with the Nazis by some Soviet peoples, and some individuals. A third issue ignored for decades was the poor preparedness of the Soviet Union for the Nazi onslaught and the catastrophic losses suffered in the first years of the war. Losses were turned into evidence of sacrifice and martyrdom, rather than the results of either miscalculation or cold calculation. The role of the western allies in the defeat of Nazism was not ignored, but it was downplayed, for the same political, psychological and emotional reasons that Britain and the United States focused on their respective roles in the war and, certainly after 1946 or so, soft-pedaled the Soviet Union's place in the victory.

Post-war Soviet books dealing with the war, whether scholarly or popular, did not mention the Holocaust – indeed, the word did not appear in the Soviet vocabulary. While most Soviet writers either ignored the Holocaust or submerged it in more general accounts of the period, none denied it and some did treat it not simply as German atrocities but as a uniquely Jewish fate.[11] But most Soviet works either pass over the Holocaust in silence or blur it by universalizing it. Some works do acknowledge and describe the Holocaust, while others discuss only some aspects of it.[12] For example, a fairly close examination of the six-volume official Soviet history of the war reveals not a single reference to Jews. Nor do the terms "anti-Semitism" or "Holocaust" appear in the index. In the third volume, the Nazi occupation of the USSR is referred to as "a regime of terror and occupation" and the *Einsatzgruppen* are mentioned, as is Babi Yar, but the word "Jew" does not appear in any of these connections.[13] The authoritative *Great Soviet Encyclopedia* acknowledged that anti-Semitism "found its most extreme expression in fascist Germany." It stated succinctly that "the Nazis carried out a policy of mass extermination of the Jews; about six million Jews were murdered in World War II."[14] Thus, Soviet audiences were generally not exposed to even the most elementary details of the Holocaust, though in the 1960s, a few volumes were published that did provide more information. Significantly, at least some were translations from other languages.

Why did the Soviets downplay or ignore the Holocaust? It was seen as an integral part of a larger phenomenon – the murder of civilians – whether Russians, Ukrainians, Belorussians, Gypsies, or other nationalities. It was said to be a natural consequence of capitalism whose most degenerate stage is fascism. Thus, the roots of the Holocaust lay in capitalism. For the Soviets there was no mystery about the Holocaust.

Soviet Jewish Perceptions of the War and the Holocaust

About half a million Soviet Jews served in World War Two – 18.3% of the 3,028,538 Jews in the USSR in 1939. Their casualty rate was very high. If it is true that about 180,000 died, then more than a third of all Soviet Jews in the military (36%) were killed.[15] There were 147 Jewish Heroes of the Soviet Union[16] (of a total of about 12,600,[17] i.e., 1.2 percent of all winners) and 303 Jewish generals and admirals in the Soviet forces.[18] Moreover, as a percentage of the total population of the nationality in the Soviet population, Jewish Heroes ranked third behind Russians and Ossetins. Many Soviet Jews like to point out that in absolute numbers Jews ranked in fifth place in the number of Heroes, whereas they were in eleventh place in the size of their population.[19]

Amir Weiner has observed that, "Memory was a key political arena where the exclusion of certain groups from official representation of the Soviet fighting family, along with the denial of their unique suffering, left those groups politically invisible, without official recognition of their distinct, collective identities."[20] The recovery of history based on memory is vitally important to those who feel that their exclusion from history was deliberate and unjust, as one can see in the ever-growing number of articles and books published on the Shoah in the former Soviet Union (FSU) and in the Soviet Jewish diaspora.

To help recover history, I have collected 225 oral testimonies from Soviet Jewish war veterans in the United States, Israel and Russia. For all its limitations,[21] oral history can nevertheless be useful, especially in establishing perceptions; that is, not so much what happened – though that should not be dismissed – but what people think happened, or *now* think happened *then*. Interviewing Jewish veterans about Jewish aspects of "their war" has the advantage of dealing with a subject that official history and myth-making did not touch, so that there should be less overlay of images, false memories, and purposive conventional understandings that attend more general issues.

The perceptions of the veterans are important because the way they interpreted what happened profoundly influenced their views of themselves, their fellow citizens, and the country in which they lived, and that influenced their descendants quite strongly. World War II was the most important event of their lives, and it transformed them.

Here I shall concentrate only on one issue explored in the interviews with the veterans, motivations for fighting and on how their Jewish identities were affected.

1) The veteran interviewees are very honest about their Soviet patriotism, however mistaken it seems in retrospect. Not a single interviewee says that he or she regrets having fought for the Soviet Union. Not a single one doubts this was a just and justifiable war. The war was just, necessary, and heroic. Yosif Kvasha says: "The war years were the purest years of my life. Before the war, nobody cared about anyone else's nationality. If a person did his job well, he was a good man, and if he didn't he was a bad man, and it didn't matter who or what he was."[22]

2) They seem very honest in reporting the lack of Jewish motivation in fighting. Raya Baranova[23] escaped from the Minsk ghetto on April 28, 1943 and joined a partisan unit. When asked why she fought, she replied "Simply to survive. As Jews and as people. We were fighting for our lives." This interview, free of high-minded phrases, was given by a woman who was 17 when the war broke out, had attended a Yiddish school, always

fasted on Yom Kippur, and lost five of her eight siblings to the Nazis. It seems she was unconcerned with ideology and politics.

Yitzhak Prikupets,[24] a tank man on the Third Ukrainian Front, said he fought because "As a citizen of the Soviet Union, I understood that I had to fulfill my duty to the homeland, because it *was* the homeland." When pressed, "But as a Jew, did you feel that you had to do better, fight harder?" he answered laconically, "I don't recall anything like that in particular." The veterans fought as Soviet citizens, not as Jews. They fought to defend their country, not its ideology and not for its leader. They were patriots more than Communists.

But some recall that their motivations changed during the war. Boris Lvov[25] tried to enlist as soon as the war broke out. The *voenkomnat* official, looking at the near-sighted worker and part-time correspondent for *Komsomolskaya Pravda*, sneered, "So now what? Abram also wants to fight? [...] We found ourselves a Jerusalem Cossack!" Lvov nevertheless became a soldier, shot a German sniper and was awarded a medal. He fought for his country, he says. Nevertheless, when he saw what the Nazis had done to Jews in the occupied territories, it

> had a frightening effect on me. I decided that if I had to take part in hand-to-hand combat, I would not take any prisoners. Why? It wasn't because I hated Germans. In my soul I was an internationalist. Our family, in general was international. We had Jews and Georgians, Russians and Ukrainians and even a Chuvash. But I had lost the ability to approach the question analytically. I did not take any prisoners, even while taking part in group battles.

Abram Galko, who was in the army in 1939 and, as he puts it, "participated in the liberation of Bessarabia in 1940 in the advanced detachments," was a sergeant when the Nazis attacked. He fought because "I considered it my responsibility, my motherland, I had to protect it. But I fought with greater ardor when I learned what the Germans were doing to the Jews," something he heard about on the radio in 1942.

> Then I even read somewhere that Churchill, Stalin and Roosevelt warned the Germans because of it. That there is information that Germans are killing the Jews in occupied territories. [...] That is why

> I hate the Germans to this day. I began hating the Germans [...] in general, I did everything against them. I was taking revenge on them. If I had the opportunity, I would drop the atomic bomb on them, and I would not have any pity. In Kiev, in Babi Yar, on September 29, 1941 were shot: my mother, father, grandfather, my mother's sister-in-law [...] and many relatives. When I came to Kiev I found out that our janitor and his son were arrested later for cooperating with the Germans, that my cousin was turned in by this janitor and was shot. And there were many cases like that.[26]

A relatively small number of the Soviet veterans speak largely or exclusively about revenge as a motivation for fighting. Israel Fuks, who saw combat in the Caucasus, southern Ukraine and Crimea and the Baltics, served in the 51st Army under the Jewish General Yakov Kreizer.[27] Fuks says he learned about Nazi atrocities against Jews from articles by Ilya Ehrenburg.

> Therefore, we fought selflessly and with pleasure and hatred toward those fascists. To be honest, when we saw how we had destroyed the Germans, I got pleasure from it. [...] When I was a battery commander near the town of Krimsk, I got pleasure when I saw how the Germans came running from all sides of the kitchen at sunrise and had no time to eat. We opened fire and destroyed them. That was the kind of hatred I had towards the Germans, towards those who killed our Jews.[28]

Note that none of these people says they fought to defend or avenge the Jewish people. This seems for most to have been a *personal*, not collective, issue. It was not the Jewish nation, the Jewish people, "the Jews" who were being avenged. It was *their* Jews, their relatives.

A more prominent theme in discussions about why the Soviet veterans fought is the desire to show that stereotypes of Jews as shirkers were calumnies. Anatoly Vodopyanov was 17 years old in 1944 and living in Chkalov in the Urals.

> The mind-set was that you are a Jew and you have to be there where it is difficult [...] in order to prove that you are no worse than anyone else and in order to give all you can to your country. That is what prompted me to leave the [Automobile] Institute [...]. It worked for me

> [...] I became the best driver in the army, a master. There were fifteen masters in the whole army."[29]

3) Most of the veterans interviewed report that their sense of Jewishness was changed by the war. Before the war, Jewishness was not denied but was irrelevant. As Lia Kapun says, "You know, before the war when I was in school no one spoke about nationalities, it was not the thing to do [*nie priniato eto bylo*]. Everyone was equal."[30] Alexander Kalish who grew up in Leningrad says that "until the war when I was in school, I myself never even felt I was Jewish," though at the same time he says his parents spoke Yiddish to each other and he recalls the holidays of Purim, Passover, and Hanukkah celebrated at home.[31]

According to the veterans, the feeling of internationalism, or inter-ethnic amity, and of the irrelevance of one's nationality, including Jewishness, carried over to the first years of the war. As Boris Revich puts it,

> Starting with the academy until the end of the war I saw no antagonism between the Jew, Ukrainian, Russian, Belorussian. We really had "friendship of the nations." Now I see that maybe it's not that way. But we were friends, we loved each other. [...] We had a friendship, a friendship of the front. This is not to the credit of Soviet rule, this is due to the camaraderie that is created in difficult circumstances.[32]

Beginning in late 1943, after Stalingrad and the turning of the tide on the Eastern Front, many Jews began to notice that they were not being given the same awards or promotions as fighters of other nationalities. Some were puzzled and others chagrined at what seemed to them a new policy of discrimination. Izrail Kogan, from a small *shtetl* in Belorussia, says that during the war "I didn't notice any anti-Semitism. Even if someone thought something [*kto-to chto-to dumal*] he would be afraid to say it because the other chaps [*rebyata*] would condemn him." But late in the war, after a fierce battle, the regimental commander, also from Belorussia, called him in and said. "Well, countryman, [*zemliachok*] you will get an *orden*, I put you and Davidkin [a Russian] up for an order and sent your name to headquarters [*shtab*] to approve the Order of the Red Star." But when the papers came back, "Davidkin got it and I did not.

About a month later the commander saw me, came up to me and said, 'keep your mouth shut [he put his finger on his lips] but Davidkin got the Order and you did not because you are a Kogan."[33]

Conclusion

Whether as scholarly or popular history, much more needs to be done to establish the record, as it were, on the Holocaust in the former USSR. Some general and monographic works have been published in the post-Soviet period but it is not clear who is reading them, how visible they are and how, if at all, they are affecting scholarship and the kind of history or "collective memory" that becomes part of general culture.[34] There was a witticism in Soviet times that went, "the future is easy to predict; it's the past that is always changing." Indeed it is, and it will no doubt continue to do so.

Endnotes

1 Brokaw 1998.
2 Ambrose 1994.
3 See Dallin and Breslauer 1970; on the trade-offs between coercion and information, see Apter 1965, passim. An early study of public opinion in the Soviet Union is Inkeles 1950, and a recent one is Davies 1997.
4 Letter by Umansky to Molotov, asking him to urgently contact Lavrenti Beria, head of the NKVD, to get them to release information to the Foreign Ministry so that it could be presented to the British and Americans who were pressing for it. United States Holocaust Memorial Museum Archives, RG22.099*01. Original in the archives of the Russian Ministry of Foreign Affairs. Umansky had been ambassador to the United States in 1938 and later was ambassador to Mexico, where he was killed in a plane crash in 1943.
5 The decree establishing the Commissions was signed by AA. Andreev, G.M. Malenkov and A.S. Shcherbakov of the Secretariat of the Communist Party of the Soviet Union and sent to Commissar for Foreign Affairs Molotov on August 20,1942. See RG22.009*01, #3 of 10 microfilms from the Foreign Ministry. The location of the original document in the Foreign Ministry is Fond 06, Opis 4, file 7. When the public *ukaz* (order) creating the Commissions was announced on November 2, 1942, they were called the *Extraordinary State Commissions for the Establishment and Investigation of the Crimes of the German-Fascist Invaders and their Accomplices about the Damages Caused by them to the Citizens, Kolkhozes, Public Organizations, State Enterprises and Institutions of the USSR*. On the Commissions, see Sanders 1995 and Spaeder 1997.

6 According to researchers at the USHMM, researchers from the Yad Vashem Institute in Jerusalem, Israel microfilmed only 27 reels of the Extraordinary Commission reports, and a large amount of the Commission materials remains unexamined in Russian archives. In 2007 Yad Vashem acquired more Commission materials.
7 Arad 2003.
8 Ibid., 200–201.
9 Ibid., 209.
10 Quoted in Vaksberg 1994, 141–142.
11 See Gitelman 2001.
12 For details see Gitelman 1997, ch. 2.
13 *Istoriia velikoi otechestvennoi voiny Sovetskogo Soiuza, 1941–1945 gg* 1962, 438, 442, 443, 446.
14 *Great Soviet Encyclopedia* 1975, 293. There is no "Holocaust" entry in the encyclopedia. On the way Holocaust materials were censored, see Blium 1995.
15 Mark Shteynberg claims that 198,000 were killed according to the records of the Central Archive of the Ministry of Defense of the Russian Federation (Shteynberg 2005, 263). The number of casualties is intrinsically difficult to calculate because of wartime conditions and the inability or unwillingness of Soviet authorities to document every death. One way of calculating would be to go through the eight volumes of the *Kniga pamiatii*, which attempts to account for every Jewish military death on the basis of the Ministry of Defense records.
16 Shteynberg (265–268) argues that some Heroes have been listed as Jews in such places as *Encyclopedia Judaica* when they were not Jewish (e.g., General Ivan Danilovich Cherniakhovsky who, Shteynberg asserts, was Ukrainian). He believes that 136 Jews, including the Polish Jew Julius Hibner, won the award. See Shteynberg 2005, 265–268.
17 Shteynberg says 11,700 won the award, and that includes some civilians. Shteynberg 2005, 222.
18 Again, Shteynberg's figures are different. He counts 216 generals and 9 admirals, of whom 5 were colonel-generals, 29 lieutenant-generals, 182 major-generals, a vice-admiral and 8 rear (*kontr*) admirals. One hundred seventy-five were in active combat, only eleven of them political officers. Most had fought in Spain, the Far East, Mongolia, Finland, or had participated in the invasion of eastern Poland in 1939. Shteynberg 2005, 307-326.
19 According to Shteynberg, 45 Jews got the Hero award posthumously and eight others were killed after receiving it. Several were deprived of the award after the war when they applied to emigrate to Israel, but at least four Heroes had immigrated as of the mid-1990s. See Shteynberg 2005, 224.
20 Weiner 2001, 39.
21 Space does not permit discussion of the pros and cons of oral histories.
22 Interviewed by Elena Perlman, Boston, December 27, 1998.
23 Interviewed by Tatiana Polskaya, Detroit, November 10, 1996. No. 002. (Interviews numbered by the author of this article. They are not publicly available.)
24 Interviewed by Genrikh Schiff, Detroit, November 22, 1996. No. 021.
25 Interviewed by Tatiana Polskaya, Detroit, November 1996. No. 023.
26 Interviewed by Boris Goltser, Ann Arbor, MI, January 3, 1997. Gulko remained in the military and was promoted to Lieutenant-Colonel in 1950 but was denied further promotions.

27 Fuks says he met Kreizer twice. "What a brave, smart and clever person he was. If all the generals in our army had been like him, we probably would have ended the war twice as fast." Interviewed by Lev Paransky, Detroit, November 10, 1996.

28 Similar sentiments are expressed by Moisei Grinblat, from Berdichev. Interviewed in Southfield, MI, November 9, 1996.

29 Interviewed by Maria Mochulski, Oak Park, MI, December 8, 1996.

30 Interviewed in Hannover, Germany by Olena Bagno, December 2005.

31 Interviewed in Southfield, MI by Lev Kupershtain, November 9, 1997. These reminiscences are from Kirovograd in Ukraine, where he was born, rather than from Leningrad.

32 Boris Revich, interviewed in Chicago, by Evsey Tseytlin, September 8, 1997.

33 Izrail Kogan, interviewed by Olena Bagno, December 2005, Hannover, Germany.

34 The most comprehensive work I have seen is Altman 2002a, 538 pps. Altman is also the author of a book designed for use in higher educational institutions, though I do not know where it has been adopted. See Altman 2002b. A scholarly history of the Holocaust in Belorussia is Smilovitskii 2000.

References

Altman, Ilya (2002a), *Zhertvy nenavisti: Kholokost v SSSR, 1941–1945 gg.* Moscow, Fond Kovcheg.

Altman, Ilya (2002b), *Kholokost i Evreiskoe soprotivlenie na okkupirovannoi territorii SSSR*. Moscow, Fond Kholokosta.

Ambrose, Stephen (1994), D-*Day, June 6, 1944: The Climactic Battle of World War II*. New York, Simon and Schuster.

Apter, David (1965), *The Politics of Modernization*. Chicago, University of Chicago Press.

Arad, Yitzhak (2003), The Holocaust as Reflected in the Soviet Russian Language Newspapers in the Years 1941–1945. In Shapiro, Robert Moses (ed.), *Why Didn't the Press Shout? American and International Journalism During the Holocaust*. New York, Yeshiva University Press and KTAV Publishing.

Blium, A. (1995), Otnoshenie Sovetskoi tsenzury (1940–1946) k probleme kholokosta. *Vestnik Evreiskogo universiteta v Moskve*, 2(9), 156–67.

Brokaw, Tom (1998), *The Greatest Generation*. New York, Random House.

Dallin, Alexander and Breslauer, George (1970), *Political Terror in Communist Systems*. Stanford, Stanford University Press.

Davies, Sarah (1997), *Popular Opinion in Stalin's Russia: Terror, Propaganda, and Dissent, 1934–1941*. Cambridge, Cambridge University Press.

Gitelman, Zvi (1997), *Bitter Legacy: Confronting the Holocaust in the Soviet Union*. Bloomington, IN, Indiana University Press.

Gitelman, Zvi (2001), Internationalism, Patriotism and Disillusion: Soviet Jewish Veterans Remember World War Two. In Roth, John and Maxwell, Elizabeth (eds.), *Remembering for the Future: The Holocaust in an Age of Genocide*. Basingstoke, Palgrave, 296–308.

Great Soviet Encyclopedia (1975), vol. 9. New York, Macmillan.

Inkeles, Alex (1950), *Public Opinion in Soviet Russia*. Cambridge, MA, Harvard University Press.

Istoriia velikoi otechestvennoi voiny Sovetskogo Soiuza, 1941–1945 gg (1962). Vol. 3. Moscow, Voenizdat MO SSSR.

Sanders, Marian (1995), *Extraordinary Crimes in Ukraine: An Examination of Evidence Collected by the Extraordinary State Commission of the USSR, 1942–1946*. Unpublished doctoral dissertation, Ohio University.

Shteynberg, Mark (2005), *Evrei v voinakh tysiacheletii*. Moscow–Jerusalem, Gesharim, 2005.

Smilovitskii, Leonid (2000), *Katastrofa Evrev v Belorussii 1941–1944*. Tel Aviv, privately published.

Spaeder, David (1997), *Propaganda and the Politics of Community in the USSR, 1941–1947*. Unpublished doctoral dissertation, Indiana University.

Vaksberg, Arkady (1994), *Stalin Against the Jews*. New York, Alfred A. Knopf.

Weiner, Amir (2001), *Making Sense of War*. Princeton, NJ, Princeton University Press.

Olga Kucherenko

Fiction and Reality of War through the Eyes of Soviet Child-Soldiers

Bellum dulce inexpertis
(War is sweet to them who know it not)
Disiderius Erasmus

We reckoned ourselves heroes. That's why we were longing for a fight, but once we made it to the front... there wasn't much romance in it – there was only blood and dirt!
Recollections of a former child-soldier[1]

In 1943, Vania Solov'iov went to war. The road led the 13-year old 'warrior' to the Black Sea port of Gelendzhik, where he managed to persuade the captain of a motorboat to take him on board as a ship boy. He was issued with a sailor's cap which had to be stuffed with newspapers for a better fit, as well as a pea jacket and a striped vest. Sailors joked that trousers were not necessary, for the oversized vest did the job just fine. Vania's boat was delivering food and munitions to a bridgehead near Novorossiisk, when it came under heavy attack by the *Luftwaffe*. For half an hour the boy desperately tried to evade bullets, screaming for his mother, until the captain seized him by the scruff of his neck and said, "I'll give you your mother! You are damaging the ship's reputation." The little sailor came back from his maiden voyage grey-haired. Despite the shock and his shaking hands, he helped the crew unload the cargo. It was just another day of the war.[2]

Vania was one of thousands of young volunteers in the Soviet Union's struggle against the Axis. Although, with few exceptions, those below the official call-up age of 18 were not mobilised and formally were not allowed at the front, adolescents served with Soviet regular and paramilitary forces throughout the war in a variety of combat roles. There were many reasons that prompted the children to enlist, one of which was a romantic conception of fighting. With individual identities and perceptions forged in the atmosphere of unrealistic heroism and cinematic bravery of the late 1930s, the children regarded war as a time of adventure and participation in it as a rite of passage. The tradition of presenting fictionalised warfare to the young endured well into the Second World War and continued to shape the attitudes of the young on the home front, indirectly encouraging them to join in the fight. When these children finally reached the battlefield, they found reality to be very different from their idealised views. Nevertheless, many pressed on with what they considered their patriotic duty, gradually getting accustomed to the brutality of fighting. If the impulses of adolescence demanded that they be heroes, so did their country.

Born into violent struggle, the Soviet state celebrated warfare and sustained itself on the fear of it. The image of an imminent war and the conniving enemy became indivisible elements in the Soviet patriotic culture of the 1930s. Under quasi-siege conditions, the entire country was turned into a military camp. The prestige of a military career rose considerably, as the army engaged in an extensive marketing campaign to attract recruits.[3] A host of 'defence' films and literature stressed the romanticism of soldiers' daily life and combat training, which excited millions of children throughout the country. Military uniform were quickly adopted by them as the most fashionable outfit,[4] and military themes came to dominate the preferences of the young audiences.[5] At the same time, a comprehensive military-patriotic programme was adopted throughout the educational system. Defence related material now featured in general subjects with persistent regularity and, from 1939 onwards, pre-conscription training was introduced in high schools, whilst younger children were encouraged to acquire military knowledge through war games and defence competitions.

Compared with the 1920s, the number of children's books and films on military subjects markedly increased.[6] These emphasised the glamour and romantic aspects of military life but were not devoid of violence and the depiction of pleasure in actual fighting.[7] Death in battle was particularly honoured "as the highest of all citizens' rights,"[8] and it was a rare Soviet child who escaped a lesson about his civic duties.[9]

Adolescents were allocated a prominent role in the adult world of making war. Many notable writers concentrated on the lives of teenagers and their age-related problems in the revolutionary era. The works of these writers were included in school readers and adapted on screen and stage.[10] They portrayed children not only as witnesses and victims of historic events, but also as active and conscious participants. Hardened in battle, the fictional heroes underwent a process of character development, reaching a mature appreciation of their contribution to the common cause.

Some literary and celluloid works, however, took this idea to an extreme, depicting children as superior to adults in their bravery and devotion to the cause of socialism. In them, patriotic youth paced the front line exhibiting almost inhuman courage and wit, while their adversaries were comical, dim-witted and easily destructible.[11] Packed with adventures, fighting and near escapes, these tendentious examples of revolutionary mythology were, not surprisingly, extremely popular with the young audiences.[12] Presented with such role-models, some children felt insecure about their less than heroic achievements in sport, studies or social work, and regretted, in the words of E. Bonner, "not having been born then and dying with them for the Revolution."[13]

Jingoism in literature and dramatic art instilled Soviet youth with a "devil-may-care attitude towards death" and impatient expectation of coming struggles.[14] The future war was presented to them as an exciting, almost risk-free adventure, and the Red Army as invincible and superior to all other armies. The general principle of pre-war military-patriotic culture was the depiction of a headlong offensive "on the enemy's territory" and the achievement of victory "with little blood." Stimulating literature[15] and cinematography[16] offered a more or less similar pattern of the future conflict: the enemy's invasion – Japanese or German aided by the Poles – is repelled by the technologically superior Red Army, while millions of patriotic Soviet citizens of various nationalities sign up for active duty. As the enemy defences are decimated in a matter of days or even hours, the oppressed workers of the world join forces with the Soviets.

Such an overly optimistic, naïve and romanticised depiction of war and of the ease with which the enemy would be defeated if it dared to invade, created a euphoria of bravado – as some lone voices had predicted[17] – and proved disastrous in the long run, not only for the military planning but also for the self-esteem of young soldiers. So strong was their belief in the army's leadership and technological might that many of them were shocked to see the enemy crashing through the supposedly invincible borders.[18] Nevertheless, the younger ones, listening to the ever optimistic communiqués from the front, still believed that the war was going to be short and victorious, and would end without them having a chance to participate in it. So they made their way to the front.[19]

Not much changed in the depiction of the war when it actually begun. A deliberate policy of concealment and nationalist bravado, together with an initial shortage of resources, contributed to the generally unrealistic perceptions. The real losses and destruction were usually hidden behind endless rhetorical reports that obfuscated and glossed over the facts. The early frontline chronicles rarely reflected the actual fighting, as filmmakers often either used footage of manoeuvres or simply staged artificial battle scenes.[20]

The elevated heroism and naïve self-confidence of the late 1930s continued in feature productions. These noticeably romanticised fighting and in general avoided any hint of horror or failure. Heavily censored popular culture did not dwell on the possibility or depiction of death; instead, suffering was usually reserved either for enemy soldiers, civilians or Soviet prisoners of war, who, after the publication of the notorious Order 270, already had a quasi-illegal status. Just as in the previous world war, the absence of blood – or very little of it – was evident in the information campaigns of the time.[21] As recalled by a cameraman, "senseless destruction of a human life" was rarely recorded, because there was a "strong belief that [artists] should glorify heroism, and heroism, according to the accepted norm, had nothing to do with suffering."[22]

Even though some writers and filmmakers tried to portray war as a "difficult, exhausting, superhuman effort,"[23] realism became acceptable only within certain limits. With few exceptions, those works that dared to dwell on the "existentially discomforting" experience were rejected both by the censor and an audience which craved for escapist entertainment.[24] The epic footage of the Red Army's struggle also avoided the plight of the common soldier. And even when he appeared within its focus, his calm, heroic attitude in the face of danger were magnified to such a proportion that war seemed almost easy. Rather than exposing the effect of war on a soldier's mind and behaviour, artists tried to influence them. The official versions showed real-life people as strangers to crisis, doubt or fear, whilst possessing unshakeable loyalty and ideologically motivated heroism.[25] But even in the folklore of the frontline – at least in that which reached the press – the Red Army soldier was depicted as victorious no matter the dirt, homesickness or the mundane slog of killing.

Similar superficial and romanticised representation of war as an adventure of daring heroes was evident in children's culture and perceptions. No doubt trying to protect children from the tough reality of war, authors avoided "plunging a [young] soul into a bloody nightmare"[26] and instead tried to "exhibit the best that was revealed to us about a person at the front."[27] This usually resulted in the portrayal of war in a rose-tinted and sanitised way, with its hardships glossed over.

As in the previous decade, children came to play an active role in the country's defence. Stories abound of real-life young heroes fighting with the partisans or at the front. The mobilising power of such publications and films cannot be underestimated, as they no doubt inspired some members of the young audience to take up arms to assist their country. "Every lad wanted to be like them and fight the fascists," recalls a former ward of a marine infantry reconnaissance squad, "I wanted to be there, at the front; to be just like those guys they showed in the films."[28]

As it hoped to instil children with a positive attitude towards fighting and the belief in victory, visual and print culture also tended deliberately to undermine the enemy's might and agility. Believing that "he who becomes comical stops being threatening,"[29] Soviet artists sought to cultivate repugnance towards the enemy through laughter.[30] Although soldiers at the front were more realistic in depicting the adversary, they were still prone to boastfulness and mockery, which has always been a traditional attribute of Russian folk culture. With few exceptions, German soldiers were usually represented as docile degenerates and cowards incapable of individual initiative, who attacked civilians and stole women's clothes, and who were terrified of engaging the Red Army or the partisans.[31]

Wartime comedies and children's stories drew sharp caricatures of the Germans and showed that they were easily destructible, even by people of non-military professions or by animals.[32] Portrayed in a comic-book style, the enemy lost his "threatening potential," especially when dwarfed into insignificance by a tall and more Arian looking Red Army soldier or partisan (sometimes a partisan woman). Visual distortions of the adversary's physical appearance made him look pathetic and unreal.[33] By denying humanity to the enemy and representing him as a low form of life incapable of compassion or human interaction, Soviet opinion makers sought to free the young audience from any emotional investment when it came to justifying their desire to kill Germans. Widely used by soldiers and publicists, linguistic variations of the Russian verb to kill – to stitch, to lace up, to crack, to thresh, to wash – had a strong domestic connotation, as well as an element of bravado. Besides neutering the effect of violent acts against fellow human beings, the use of such euphemisms also encouraged a sense of 'ease'.

Anecdotal evidence suggests that children's perceptions of the enemy and the battle followed well-honed stereotypes created by the media, which instilled the children with confidence in their own abilities. "They showed [the Germans] in a much distorted way, as cowards and incompetent soldiers," recalls a former child-soldier, "In reality, at the front, I saw those young, sturdy, handsome lads. [...] They could fight too! And it was very difficult to beat them, and get away from them. Then I changed my views."[34]

While certainly well-intentioned, such depiction of military life and the enemy came to play a highly negative role, when thousands of underage 'heroes' headed for the front unaware of the actual difficulties and dangers this entailed.[35] They soon received a quick and violent introduction to the reality of fighting. When Mirok Tsarikhin ran to the front in 1942 he imagined war "exactly as it was in the movies." However, even though he had observed military exercises at his father's academy on many occasions, he was not prepared for his first bombing experience. As he dodged shrapnel in the midst of screaming people and torn corpses, he "saw the war in a very different light." His perceptions changed even more drastically after the first battle. From then on, he rejected "the illusion of film" and looked at war as an adult, realising that "it was simply very hard work."[36] "When I saw human intestines hanging down the trees," remembers Zhora Vraskov, a ward of the famous 172 rifle division, it became apparent that,

> the war was different from the movies. When there was blood, guts, severed hands and legs everywhere, it turned out to be a totally different business. At first, I felt scared, then indifferent, and after all this, it became just a job to me. That's it! An awful fright at first though… And it was not what I had expected, was it? I thought I would get there, they would take me in, feed me porridge and spam. No way![37]

Gradually the fear faded, as death became a consistent element of child-combatants' everyday existence. For many veterans, this 'habit' remains the most vivid and painful memory. "Before, I used to be afraid of looking at corpses even from afar," recalls one, "but the war hardened my heart somehow. And I was only 12 then."[38] Such indifference towards death, coupled with an adolescent belief in self-invincibility, often led to irresponsible chance-taking. As explained by Mirok Tsarikhin, their fearlessness stemmed from a "childish perception" of danger, which not only "numbed [their] feelings of fear but also allowed [them] to behave foolishly." "It's sheer luck they did not kill [me]," he concludes. Others attribute such "slaphappy courage" to battle exhilaration and attention to duties.[39] Nevertheless, battle stress sometimes manifested itself in prematurely grey hair, temporary loss of eyesight and speech, or crying secretly in the bushes, which one 14-year old "uniformed man" found shameful.[40]

Many years later, veterans speak of their experience with both humour and horror, without any bitterness or self-pity yet, unlike the embellished biographies of Pioneer-heroes, stories of 'ordinary' child-soldiers are filled with harrowing flashbacks of privation, disgust and fear. However, in a culture permeated with heroism and stoicism, personal anguish was not to be made public, and it is obvious that today the veterans do not suffer these reminiscences gladly. Combat-related trauma went unheeded in the Soviet Union, leaving an individual to deal with it in private.[41] As with the tradition of optimism in the 1930s and 40s, post-war official culture generally rejected the "existentially discomforting experience" of war and subjective reflection of an ordinary combatant, substituting them with the idea that eventual victory justifies sacrifice. Long after the war, the veterans' experiences remained a part of their individual memory, if not of the officially constructed collective one. The war they saw and experienced was overshadowed by talk of collective pride and honour, of dedication to the cause and of the necessity to protect the socialist motherland from her enemies. Having been a part of the heroic discourse for more than 60 years, the aged veterans usually wave away inquisitive questions about their war-time experiences, simply saying with parental concern that "you, kids, need not burden yourselves with the horrors of war."[42]

Endnotes

1 Interview with P. Posypaev, Odessa, 23 May 2003.
2 Russian State Archive of Social and Political History (RGASPI), M7/1/6160/15-17.
3 Koroliov 1959, 244. In the period from mid-1939 to mid-1941, *Pravda* ran more than 200 articles about the Soviet military forces. See also *Pionerskaia Pravda* (PP), 20 May, 18 August, 19 September 1940.
4 Interviews with M. Popov, Kursk, 5 July 2007 and N. Tsarikhin, Odessa, 15 July 2006; Aleksievich 2004, 28.
5 Detskomu Fil'mu,' 28; Russian State Archive of Literature and Art (RGALI), 631/2/101/8.
6 Steiner 1999, 158; O'Dell 1978, 151.
7 Ibid, 86, 88, 152.
8 Quoted in Hodgson 1996, 41; also see Tiazhel'nikova 1999, 413–414.
9 See enthusiastic letters from underage volunteers to the authorities in RGASPI, M7/1/4656/2-2ob and M7/1/1270(1)/137.
10 In the period from mid-to late 1930s, a total of nine films and at least three plays were created on the subject of children actively participating in military hostilities (*Sovetskie khudozhestvennye fil'my*, 1961; Zograf 1960, 357; Shpet 1971, 239).
11 *The Little Red Devils* (1928), *Revenge* (1931), *Bomber* (1932) and *Fed'ka* (1938). One critic complained that such films underestimated the hardship of warfare and 'made catching the enemy seem easier than fishing.' Nevertheless, those films that represented the enemy as intelligent and resolute were not allowed on the big screen, lest they compromise the viewer's faith in the mental and physical prowess of Soviet heroes (RGASPI, M1/23/1423/48, 49 and 17/125/71/159).
12 Kalashnikov 1956–59, 103.
13 Bonner 1992, 107.
14 RGALI, 631/2/231/25; Kuleshova 2002, 184.
15 *The Big Day* (1936), *In the East* (1937), *The First Blow* (1939).
16 *The Deep Raid* (1938), *If Tomorrow Brings War* (1938), *The Sailors* (1939), *Squadron no. 5* (1939), *The Tank Drivers* (1939).
17 RGASPI, 17/125/28/2-12; *Kino*, 3 January 1941.

18 RGASPI, M1/32/23/96ob and M1/23/1423/49.
19 Interviews with Yu. Vrazhilov, Odessa, 23 May 2003, G. Belen'kii, V. Kolodko and S. Piatovskii, Kursk, 6 April 2004 and F. Kliuev, Odessa, 15 July 2006.
20 Zolotariov 1996, 98-99, 248, 411; RGASPI, 17/125/71/230; RGALI, 966/2/181/120 and 2989/1/132/14.
21 Jahn 1995, 20–21.
22 V. Mikosha, quoted in Abul-Kasymova 1975, 14.
23 A. Dovzhenko, quoted in Abul-Kasymova 1975, 33-34.
24 Kukulin 2005, 623, 638, 664; Nikolaeva 1991, 11–12.
25 Hodgson 1996, 93; Pushkariov 2002, 325, 330.
26 Tolstoi 1943, 107.
27 Marshak 1944, 151.
28 Interview with Tsarikhin; RGASPI, M7/1/6160/14.
29 *Literatura i Iskusstvo*, 17 March 1943.
30 A.M. Gorky quoted in Akimova 1971, 33.
31 Gusev 1964, 297–298, 140–142, 177–178; Hodgson 1996, 61; Pisiotis 1995, 144; Stites 1992, 111.
32 *Antosha Rybkin, Shveik's New Adventures, The Elixir of Courage* (BK, no.7, 1941), *The Career of Lieutenant Hopp* (BK, no.11, 1942); (1944), Glinskaia 1944, 14–15.
33 Pisiotis 1995, 146; Vaschik 2005, 196, 223.
34 Interview with Tsarikhin.
35 Shpet 1971, 389; Interview with Tsarikhin.
36 Interview with Tsarikhin.
37 Interview with G. Vraskov, Odessa, 15 July 2006.
38 Interview with V. Movzalevskii in *Komsomol'skaia Pravda*, 8 May 1988 in Dossier of N. Sukhoprudskaia, temporary inventory, Museum of the Young Defenders of the Motherland (MUZR).
39 Dossier of A. Prokof'ev, temporary inventory, MUZR. See also an interview with N. Bogdanova in *Komsomol'skaia Pravda*, 30 June 1985.
40 Interview with V. Roshchiupkin in *Komsomol'skaia Pravda*, 8 May 1988.
41 On the absence of psychological trauma in contemporary medical reports, see Merridale 2005, 15, 232–233 and Idem 2001, 304.
42 Interview with E. Makarov, Odessa, 15 July 2006.

References

Detskomu Fil'mu – Khoroshii Stsenarii. Soveshchanie Stsenaristov Detskogo Kino pri TsK VLKSM (1936), *Izvestia TsK VLKSM*, Issue 13, 26–29.

Abul-Kasymova, Khandzhara et al. (1975) (eds.), *Istoria Sovetskogo Kino, 1917–1967.* Moscow, Iskusstvo Vol.3.

Akimova, A.N. et al. (1971) (eds.), *Sovetskaia Detskaia Literatura Perioda Velikoi Otechestvennoi Voiny.* Vladimir.

Aleksievich, Svetlana (2004), *Poslednie Svideteli*. Moscow, Eksmo.

Bonner, Elena (1992), *Mothers and Daughters*. London, Hutchinson.

Glinskaia, Inna (1944), Lesnye Partizany. *Kostior*, Issue 1, 14–15.

Gusev, Victor (1964) (ed.), *Russkii Fol'klor Velikoi Otechestvennoi voiny*. Moscow–Leningrad, Nauka.

Hodgson, Katherine (1996), *Written With the Bayonet: Soviet Russian Poetry of World War Two*. Liverpool, Liverpool University Press.

Jahn, Hubertus (1995), *Patriotic Culture in Russia During World War I*. London, Cornell University Press.

Kalashnikov, Yurii et al. (1956–59) (eds.), *Ocherki Istorii Sovetskogo Kino*. Moscow, Iskusstvo, Vol. 2.

Koroliov, Fiodor (1959), *Sovetskaia Shkola v Period Sotsialisticheskoi Industrializatsii*. Moscow, Nauka.

Kukulin, Ilia (2005), Regulirovanie Boli. In Gabovich, Mikhail (ed.), *Pamiat' o Voine 60 Let Spustia. Rossia, Germania, Evropa*. Moscow, NLO, 623–664.

Kuleshova, Natalia (2002), Bol'shoi Den': Griadushchaia Voina v Literature 1930-kh Godov. *Otechestvennaia Istoria*, Issue 1, 181–191.

Macheret, Aleksandr (1961), *Sovetskie Khudozhestvennye Fil'my: Annotirovannyi Katalog*. Moscow, Gosfil'mofond, Vol. 2.

Marshak, Samuil (1944), O Detskoi Literature Nashikh Dnei. *Novyi Mir*, Issue 3, 149–152.

Merridale Catherine (2005), *Ivan's War. The Red Army 1939–45*. London, Faber and Faber.

Merridale, Catherine (2001), *Night of Stone, Death and Memory in Twentieth-century Russia*. London, Granta.

Nikolaeva, Svetlana (1991), *Deti i Voina: Ocherki*. Moscow, Detskaia Literatura.

O'Dell, Felicity Ann (1978), *Socialisation Through Children's Literature: The Soviet Example*. Cambridge, Cambridge University Press.

Pisiotis, Argyrios K. (1995), Images of Hate in the Art of War. In Stites, Richard (ed.), *Culture and Entertainment in Wartime Russia*. Bloomington, Indiana University Press, 141–157.

Pushkariov, Leonid (2002), Istochniki Po Izucheniu Mentaliteta Uchastnikov Voiny (Na Primere Velikoi Otechestvennoi). *Voenno-Istoricheskaia Antropologia. Ezhegodnik*, 2002, 325–330.

Russkii Arkhiv, Velikaia Otechestvennaia (1996), Moscow, Terra Vol. 6 (1–2).

Shpet, Lenora (1971), *Sovteskii Teatr Dlia Detei, Stranitsy Istorii, 1918–1945.* Moscow, Iskusstvo.

Steiner, Evgenii (1999), *Stories for Little Comrades: Revolutionary Artists and the Making of Early Soviet Children's Books.* Seattle, University of Washington Press.

Stites, Richard (1992), *Russian Popular Culture: Entertainment and Society since 1900.* Cambridge, Cambridge University Press.

Tiazhel'nikova, Viktoria (1999), 'Vy Zhertvoiu Pali v Bor'be Rokovoi...' (Geneziz i Evoliutsia Revoliutsionnoi Zhertvennosti Kommunistov). *Sotsial'naia Istoria. Ezhegodnik*, 1998/99, 411–433.

Tolstoi, Aleksei (1943), Kniga Dlia Detei. *Novyi Mir*, Issue 2/3, 107–108.

Vascik, Claus (2005), Metamorfozy Zla: Nemetsko-russkie Obrazy Vraga v Plakatnoi Propagande 30–50gg. In Gudkov, Lev (ed.), *Obraz Vraga.* Moscow, NLO-OGI, 191–226.

Zograf, Nikolai et al. (1960) (eds.), *Ocherki Istorii Russkogo Sovetskogo Dramaticheskogo Teatra.* Moscow, Akademia Nauk SSSR Vol. 2.

Roger D. Markwick

"A Sacred Duty": Red Army Women Veterans Remembering the Great Fatherland War, 1941–45*

War's Unwomanly Face was the title of a pioneering, albeit censored, collection of interviews with Soviet Red Army women veterans by the Belorussian journalist Svetlana Aleksievich published in 1985, on the eve of *perestroika*. In 2004 a second, uncensored version was published.[1] Since the fall of the Soviet Union, the "unwomanly" mask of the savage fighting on the Eastern Front in the Second World War has begun to be pealed away to reveal more of the faces of the 800,000 women who fought with the Red Army against Nazism. In the past decade or so, freed from the Soviet-era constraints of draconian censorship and the necessity to depict their war against fascism in nothing less than the most heroic terms, women veterans have begun to write and speak more openly about their roles and experiences of the fighting on the Eastern Front. However, even with the demise of Soviet-era censorship, constraints of a different kind remain for Soviet women veterans, not only due to a reluctance to remember the most horrific events of this most horrific war, but also to keep faith with what for many *frontovichki* was a "sacred duty".[2]

Based on memoirs published over the last decade, principally those of former military nurses and snipers, this article looks at what surviving women veterans choose to remember about the war and how, and what they choose to forget or remain silent about. The article also seeks to illuminate shared or disparate collective and individual memory and experiences. A particular objective of the paper is to assess the degree to which these written recollections coincide with or deviate from the

* Research for this paper was supported by an Australian Research Council Discovery Project grant: 'Women, War and the Stalinist State, 1941–45'.

predominant patriotic, heroic, masculine paradigm of the Great Fatherland War and its historiography,[3] which masked other human responses such as fear, cowardice, or collaboration, and ignominious phenomena, such as capture, enslavement, or sexual harassment of women within the Red Army itself. The article seeks to establish what recent memoirs reveal about the female face behind the masculine mask of the Red Army at war and their significance for current Russian consciousness about the Soviet past.

Up until the Khrushchev era personal memories of the war, especially women's, were muted. But Khrushchev's "thaw" saw a flood of military memoirs, including some of the first women veterans' memoirs, which quickened under Brezhnev with the onslaught of the "cult" of the Great Fatherland War, usually under titles explicitly extolling the contribution of women geroiny to the victory of the Red Army.[4] Such memoir anthologies were representative of peculiarly Soviet "collective memoirs" in which individual identity was subordinated to collective identity, creating a "remarkably 'depersonalised' character" located within "a metanarrative of the collective's struggle to win [...]". The result was that "these testimonial texts become stories of heroic and exemplary lives".[5]

Paradoxically, with the fall of the Soviet Union, official remembrance of the Great Fatherland War has become even more intensive, climaxing with the sixtieth anniversary of "Victory Day", 9th May 2005.[6] Increasingly too the role of women in the war has come to the fore. Surprisingly, a 1995 publication could present itself as a "unique" record of the "military exploits of the glorious daughters of our Motherland, which until recent times was virtually unknown to many readers".[7] While women's contribution on the home front, as part of a genderless *narod* [people], had long been recognised; their role on the frontline had received much less recognition. The public image of the war affirmed a clearly gendered division: a masculine fighting frontline defending a predominantly female home front. Men overwhelmingly bore the brunt of the soldiering. But not exclusively, as Soviet readers were reminded in the writings of Vera Murmantseva published in the 1970s, notably *Women in Soldiers' Uniforms* (1971),[8] and then more personally in 1985 with the publication of Aleksievich's remarkable *War's Unwomanly Face*. By 2005 the remembrance of women had peaked in largely celebratory publications and websites.[9]

Volunteers

Memoirs of military medical personnel make up a large proportion of women's memoirs. The Soviet military's view in 1941 that war was not "women's business" led many women who volunteered to take up arms, but were rejected, to seek a more traditional path to the front: through medicine and nursing. However, given the unparalleled savagery of this war, Soviet medical personnel virtually served on the front line, often arms in hand. This searing experience is captured in the memoirs of and recollections about women medical personnel from Kursk, published on the 55th anniversary of the victory, dedicated to *The Fate of Women at War*,[10] and the memoirs of a military nurse, Irina Bogacheva, from Voronezh, *The Paths We Choose*, re-published on the 60th anniversary.[11] Although the degree of their exposure to actual combat varied, common concerns emerge from these memoirs.

Most striking is that almost all the memoirs are written by those who volunteered for the front almost from the beginning of the war, June 1941; that is, they were in that first wave of Komsomol (the Communist Party youth organisation) enthusiasts who genuinely believed it was their patriotic duty as citizens to defend their beloved *rodina* [Motherland]. Rarely do we find memoirs written by those "mobilised" in the second wave of women during the dark days of 1942 when the routed Red Army was haemorrhaging male personnel. Almost all these women volunteers continued to be active members of their veterans' associations, which almost universally initiated publication of these memoirs in a concerted drive to keep social memory of the war alive.[12] Given their provenance, not surprisingly most memoirs still adhere to the patriotic-heroic discourse about the Great Fatherland War. Alleged "cowards" or "collaborators" are unlikely to write memoirs.

Most veteran-memoirists depict pre-war Soviet life as halcyon days, shattered by the Nazi onslaught. Those women who volunteered, and those who later remembered in writing, tended to be among the more educated, and therefore advantaged and literate, Soviet girls. As a cohort, they were the beneficiaries of Soviet industrialisation under Stalin – although his name is strikingly rare in their memoirs. Irina Bogacheva, a maths-physics student at the regional University of Voronezh joined the

Voronezh Volunteer (Communist) Regiment as *medsestra* [nurse] after a one and a half month crash course. For her, university days were the happiest of her life, forging her commitment to Soviet socialism. June 1941, for the volunteers, was the decisive "departure point of the rest of our lives". But Bogacheva also recalls how, like most other young women volunteers, she was rejected by the recruitment office. As a university graduate, it was suggested, she would be more use on the home front, while her mother cruelly suggested she had enlisted only to find a husband.[13] But the Stalin generation of young women believed they had the right to be alongside male soldiers, even if only in a traditional female role, tending to dying and wounded men. Ultimately, Bogacheva believed her role was no less important and only marginally less dangerous than direct combat; indeed, she recalled her last act as a military nurse in 1945 as a "*hymn to life, and to the beauty of human relations*".[14]

Heroines and Heroes

In an overwhelmingly male institution such as the Red Army, military values and virtues, of heroism, self-sacrifice and martyrdom, were inherently "masculine". But such "masculine" values were decidedly affirmed as attributes of Soviet womanhood. Female, as well as male, heroism is central to these memoirs. Furthermore, in this respect, there is no divorce between private remembering and public remembering, suggesting that heroic remembrances of the Fatherland War were not just relics of so-called "totalitarian" indoctrination, but derived from real experiences on the battlefield. To cite but a few heroic instances: surgical operations carried out under "terrible, inhuman conditions" on the front line; a wireless operator whose arm had been amputated appealing successfully to return to the battlefield; field nurses at the Kursk tank battle dragging wounded soldiers with their weapons from the battlefield. For these veterans, these are formative, indelible memories: "as I write these memoirs", laments Evdokiia Pal'onaia, a senior medical officer, "before my eyes arise the images of young nurses, my dear frontline friends [...] no longer alive. It is impossible to forget those days of war".[15] Such memories defined the youthful "front generation".

However, unlike Soviet era memoirs – with their sanitised, bloodless depictions of heroic deeds – suffering, death and dying loom large and are often graphically depicted in these memoirs, especially for nurses, who at a mere 17 to 18 years of age, with a rudimentary six weeks' training, confronted the horrors of war immediately and daily. Overcoming fear of appalling wounds and death, amidst snow, blood, filth and lice, was fundamental to military medicine. More than half a century afterwards the nightmare of fascist atrocities remain, echoing the unwomanly nature of war: the "intolerable and unnatural sight" of "beautiful young girls disfigured by enemy steel",[16] or, in keeping with the lethal misogyny that was Nazism at war, the tortured, "mutilated" corpse of a nurse, a "star cut into her breast".[17] However, these women veterans do not interpret such atrocities against their sex as viscerally anti-female; rather, they were simply another manifestation of fascist barbarism against the Soviet people as a whole. Gender was not in the political lexicon of the wartime generation of women.

Professional Assassins

The Red Army established the world's first sniper school exclusively for women. Women snipers, almost 1500 of whom graduated from the Central Women's Sniper School established in May 1943,[18] had the specific task of premeditated killing; a contradictory vocation for women who believed that nurturing, not killing, was their natural vocation.

Illuminating in this regard are the recently published memoirs of Iuliia Zhukova, *Girl with a Sniper's Rifle*, which detail her path in 1943–44 as an 18-year-old from the Urals factory front to the horrors of East Prussia, where the wounded beast of Nazism lashed out with unbridled fury.[19] In many respects Zhukova's memoirs reflect the general pattern: a Soviet loyalist, initially denied the right to join the military because of her age and sex, Zhukova "dreamed" of going to the front, "envying" the young men who had marched off to battle while she was merely mobilised into the "Labour Front". Zhukova's relentless quest to get to the front reflects the degree to which young women reared in the 1930s Stalin decade were imbued with the expectation that they were just as capable as men of taking up arms in defence of Soviet state and people.[20]

Zhukova's chance to serve came in September 1943 when she was sent to the snipers' school near Podolsk. Military memoirs tend to focus on fighting; the beauty of Zhukova's memoirs is that she depicts the harsh banality of everyday Red Army life, not just the heat of battle. In this regard, refreshingly frank is Zhukova's admission that not all the recruits were heroines in the making. One maimed her hand so as not to be sent to the front; another deserted and was despatched to the front by the military tribunal. But, Zhukova assures us, these were exceptions rather than the rule.[21]

Zhukova provides valuable insights into these young women's strong sense of female self and the depth of their "sacred" commitment to the Soviet cause. Despite the demands of military training, those who survived it eagerly anticipated the 1944 May Day holiday, when they would take their oath and parade in dress uniform, to their delight wearing skirts rather than trousers. "In general, girls remained girls, despite the difficulties", Zhukova affirms. Taking the military oath was a hallowed event; Zhukova "froze with excitement", as the graduating recruits were called one by one to repeat aloud the oath, sign it, and then genuflect to kiss the sniper school's scarlet banner.[22]

The Front

Zhukova "saw the war mainly through the sights of a sniper rifle". Sent to the front only at the end of 1944, she admits she has confused memories of that short but horrific time. This was a war that even in its closing months saw no quarter given. The battles in East Prussia, the "bulwark" of Nazism, were ferocious; each Junker estate a "real little fortress", defended by the "Prussians" to the end. For a rank and file soldier, such as Zhukova, one battle seemed much like another: "Continual battles, transfers, offensives, attacks, the wounded, the dead, the blood [...] At times it seemed this would never end."[23]

Unlike Soviet era memoirs, and unlike most wartime letters and diaries, post-Soviet memoirs are more likely to have recourse to what has been called "battlefield gothic": the gore, horror and stench of maiming, killing and dying.[24] Zhukova witnessed the atrocities of a war without limits: "Thrown onto the street, directly onto a marble staircase, was the violated, mutilated body of a girl in a torn dress."[25] Through such recollections, we begin to understand what steeled Zhukova to fight pitilessly.

Numerous other memoirs, interviews and documents attest not only to the genocidal nature of the *Wehrmacht*'s war but also to its lethal misogyny, directed particularly at "ferocious" Soviet "riflewomen" [*Flintenweiber*].[26] Yet for all the nightmare horror that she depicts, Zhukova seems remarkably untraumatised by it. Her memoirs betray little attempt to wrestle with the psychological aftermath of combat, nowadays referred to as "post-traumatic stress disorder".[27] It is not just the passage of time at work here; it is a Soviet genre of memoir in which personal pain and experience is subordinated to depicting the overriding historical drama of the "war against fascism" and to reaffirming the rectitude of that struggle. There are no regrets about young lives, limbs or minds wasted in vain. Nor are there regrets about killing.

Zhukova definitely recalled her first killing. On the one hand, she was "glad that she opened her fighting account", on the other, "when you kill a human being, even an enemy, it changes you". Such remorse soon passed. When Zhukova "saw the evil wrought by the fascists, then I felt no regret at all for whomever I killed [...]".[28] Revenge was certainly a powerful motive for many women. For sniper Nina Lobkovskaia, revenge for her father's death in action annulled entirely any sympathies for the enemy; her one desire was "to open as quickly as possible" her "military account" by killing a "Hitlerite".[29]

Female Memories

Nothing in these memoirs suggests a "feminist" consciousness either now or 60 years ago. These women fought first and foremost as patriots, for their *rodina*, but not specifically *for* women. But unlike men's memoirs, women's show little or no interest in military feats of arms or weaponry. Rather, they recall experiences that seem specifically female, particularly the human and social dimension of war. Women credited themselves with raising the "cultural level" of male soldiers. Their memoirs often recall the poems they recited and the songs they sang "more than ever" in wartime: "*Zemlianka*" [Dugout] , "*Vecher na reide*" [Night-time raid], and "*Tëmnaia noch*" [Dark Night], ironically the haunting lament of a male soldier for his love on the homefront. Women medical personnel often initiated the social activities so essential to maintaining male military morale. Indeed, military hospitals became "centres of culture" in which women wove the fabric of domestic cultural life: concerts, and readings from popular romance novels, Pushkin's poems, or songs lavishing praise on Stalin.[30] Women, even in the military, were constant symbols and reminders of peace and domesticity – lost but yearned for by the men.

Forbidden Themes

The most striking innovation in contemporary women's memoirs is a hitherto "forbidden theme" in Soviet memoirs: "real love" between men and women soldiers. Much has been written in recent times about the so-called "mobile field wife" or *PPZhe* [*Polevaia pokhodnaia zhena*], based on rumours that *frontovichki* were no more than officers' mistresses. Yet the bulk of women veterans' memoirs assert that relations between men and women within the Red Army were inclined to be paternal and familial – rather than sexual. Sexual relations between *frontoviki* and *frontovichki* undoubtedly has been one of the silences in relation to the Fatherland War. All the more surprising therefore to read in Bogacheva's memoirs of the three days she was sentenced to the guard house for refusing an "order" to attend an evening with a group of "generals": "I won't carry out this order. You will have to shoot me!".[31] Zhukova too writes frankly of the "amorous pretensions of certain officers, of deceived girls and of those contemptuously referred to as *PPZhe*."[32] The willingness of these otherwise ultra-loyal women to confess that relations between men and women within the Red Army were far from perfect may be a reaction against the recent sensationalising of *frontovichki* as little more than "husband hunters" and *PPZhe*.[33]

Silences

Despite some voicing of these "forbidden themes", silences remain. In particular, little is written about the post-war life of women veterans: the official pressure to return to family and working life; the stigma of the *PPZhe*, the fate of women invalids, or those not recognised as heroes. Instead, most memoirs conclude by focussing on subsequent family life, careers – almost invariably made outside the military, or the camaraderie of veterans' life.

All the more remarkable then is the breaking of silence by a veteran who was not hailed as a heroine on her return but stigmatised as a traitor: the posthumous memoir by a Jewish military nurse, Sof'ia Anvaer (1920–1996), *Bleeds My Memory*. It is a harrowing tale. A Moscow medicine student, Anvaer volunteered within 24 hours of the outbreak of war; rebuffed as a soldier she joined a field hospital, only to be captured in late October 1941 and condemned to four torturous years in Stutthof Nazi concentration camp, Poland. Returning home as a former prisoner of war in spring 1945, she was mercilessly subjected to "filtration" by SMERSH (Soviet military intelligence). Although subsequently released she bore the "stain" of suspicion that she was a traitor. Due to her "indelible stain", only after the demise of the Soviet Union could she write of her treatment at the hands of her "own".[34] Perhaps most remarkable about Anvaer's tragic tale is that despite her ordeals, the story she tells is in most respects the same heroic-patriotic saga as those veterans whose stories accorded with the official, sanitized, history of the Great Fatherland War.

Conclusion

Memoirs, it has been said, are an "old self looking back" on "the young self".[35] In the case of memoirs by women veterans it might be asked why they would want to recall? "Even to speak about war …is not women's business", writes Bogacheva. Yet she feels compelled to tell the "tale of the youth of my generation" to the current generation.[36] Whatever doubts might be harboured about the veracity of particular events depicted in these memoirs, in many cases they vividly convey the overall motives, experiences and perceptions of women on the frontline. They can be viewed not only as historical sources, but more so as expressions of the "ways that their authors, as participants in Russian culture, view the world: how they think of their past, and how they connect it to their present [...]"[37] In these respects, women veterans writing their memoirs, like going to the front itself, seems like a "sacred duty", which simultaneously shapes and expresses popular, patriotic consciousness about the war as the collective sacrifice of a generation.

Endnotes

1 Aleksievich 2004.
2 Interview with Irina Rakobol'skaia, Moscow, 8 December 2003.
3 Hösler 2005.
4 Drugovskaia 2000, 10.
5 Liljeström 2000, 81–2.
6 Jahn 2005, 17–19.
7 Fesenko 1995.
8 Murmantseva 1971.
9 For example, Tonchu 2005; http://www.a-z.ru/women_cd2/index.htm.
10 Drugovskaia 2000.
11 Bogacheva 2005.
12 Jahn 2005, 14–15, 18.
13 Bogacheva 2005, 24–5, 80.
14 Bogacheva 2005, 75–6 [original emphasis – RDM].
15 Pal'onaia 2000, 140.
16 Lobkovskaia 1995, 19.
17 Sholupova 2000, 112.
18 Ivanova 2002, 150–51.
19 Zhukova 2006, 11.
20 Krylova 2004.
21 Zhukova 2006, 96–7.
22 Zhukova 2006, 78.
23 Zhukova 2006, 132.
24 Hynes 1997, 26.
25 Zhukova 2006, 96–7.
26 Freitag 2002, 32–3.
27 Talbott 1997, 437–455.
28 Zhukova 2006, 124.
29 Lobkovskaia 1995, 8, 14.
30 Ilina 2000, 11–12.
31 Bogacheva 2005, 54–5.
32 Zhukova 2006, 156–61.

33 Gorbacheva 2000, 166–176.
34 Anvaer 2005, 193–204.
35 Vernon 2005, xiv.
36 Bogacheva 2005, 79.
37 Walker 2000, 329.

References

Aleksievich, Svetlana (2004) (ed.), *U voiny – ne zhenskoe litso*, 2nd edn. Moscow, Pal'mira.

Anvaer, Sof'ia (2005), *Krovotochit moia pamiat': iz zapisok studentki-medichki.* Moscow, Rosspen.

Bogacheva, I. E. (2005), *Dorogi, kotorye my vybiraem: Vospominaniia i razmyshleniia voennoi medsestry*, 2nd ed. Voronezh, Izdo-vo Voronezh. Gos. Un-ta.

Drugovskaia, A. Iu (2000) (ed.), *Voina i zhenskaia sud'ba (K 55-letiiu Velikoi Pobedy).* Kursk, Administratsiaa gorod Kurska.

Fesenko, V. I. (1995) (ed.), *Zhenshchiny na zashchite Otechestva v 1941–45gg.* Moscow, Akalis.

Freitag, Claudia (2002), Trofei 'baba s ruzh'em'. Zhenshchiny-krasnoarmeitsy v nemetskoi plenu. In Jahn, Peter (ed.), *Mascha + Nina + Katuscha, Frauen in der Roten Armee 1941–45.* Berlin–Karlshorst, Ch. Links Verlag.

Gorbacheva, A. D (2000), "O voine khudozhnik obiazan govorit' tol'ko pravdu" (razmyshleniia o fil'me 'Ankor, eshche ankor').In Drugovskaia, A. Iu (ed.), *Voina i zhenskaia sud'ba (K 55-letiiu Velikoi Pobedy).* Kursk, Administratsiaa gorod Kurska, 166–176.

Hösler, Joachim (2005), Aufarbeitung der Vergangenheit? Der Große Vaterländische Krieg in der Historiographie der UdSSR und in Rußland. *Osteuropa*, Vol. 55 Issue 4–5, 115–25.

Hynes, Samuel (1998), *The Soldiers' Tale: Bearing Witness to Modern War.* New York, Penguin.

Ilina, Z. D. (2000), Dukhovno-nravstvenye aspekty adaptatsii zhenshchin … In Drugovskaia, A. Iu (ed.), *Voina i zhenskaia sud'ba (K 55-letiiu Velikoi Pobedy).* Kursk, Administratsiaa gorod Kurska, 9–15.

Ivanova, Iu. N. (2002), *Khrabreishie iz prekrasnykh. Zhenshchiny Rossii v voinakh.* Moscow, Rosspen.

Jahn, Peter (2005),Opora pamiati – vremia pamiati. In Jahn, Peter (ed.), *Triumph und Trauma: Sowjetische und Post Sowjetische Erinnerung an der Krieg 1941–45.* Berlin–Karlshorst, Ch. Links Verlag, 8-19.

Krylova, Anna (2004), Stalinist Identity from the Viewpoint of Gender: Rearing a Generation of Professionally Violent Women-Fighters in 1930s Stalinist Russia. *Gender and History,* Vol. 16 Issue 3, 626–653.

Liljeström, Marianne (2000), The Remarkable Revolutionary Woman: Rituality and Performativity in Soviet Women's Autobiographical Texts from the 1970s. In Liljeström, Marianne, Rosenholm, Arja and Savkina, Irina (eds.), *Models of Self: Russian Women's Autobiographical Texts.* Helsinki, Kikimora Publications, 81–102.

Lobkovskaia, N. A. (1995), Odolevaia smert' i strakh. Fesenko, V. I. (ed.), *Zhenshchiny na zashchite Otechestva v 1941–45gg.* Moscow, Akalis, 5–68.

Murmantseva, V. S. (1971), *Zhenshchiny v soldatskikh shineliakh.* Moscow, Voennoe Izdatel'stvo.

Pal'onaia, E.A. (2000), Eti dni voiny zabyt' nevozmozhno ... In Drugovskaia, A. Iu (ed.), *Voina i zhenskaia sud'ba (K 55-letiiu Velikoi Pobedy).* Kursk, Administratsiaa gorod Kurska, 136–40.

Sholupova, R.M. (2000), Moi boevoi put'. In Drugovskaia, A. Iu (ed.), *Voina i zhenskaia sud'ba (K 55-letiiu Velikoi Pobedy).* Kursk, Administratsiaa gorod Kurska, 110–12.

Talbott, John E. (1997), Soldiers, psychiatrists, and combat trauma. *The Journal of Interdisciplinary History,* Vol. 27 Issue 3, 437–455.

Tonchu, Elena (2005), *Oni pobedili.* Moscow, Izdatel'skii dom tonchu.

Vernon, Alex (2005) (ed.), *Arms and the Self: War, the Military, and Autobiographical Writing.* Kent, Ohio, Kent State University Press.

Walker, Barbara (2000), On Reading Soviet Memoirs: A History of the "Contemporaries" Genre as an Institution of Russian Intelligentsia Culture from the 1790s to the 1970s. *Russian Review,* Vol. 59 Issue 3, 327–352.

Zhukova, Iuliia (2006), *Devushka so snaiperskoi vintovkoi: Vospominanii vypusknitsy tsentral'noi zhenskoi shkoly snaiperskoi podgotovki 1944–1945.* Moscow, Tsentrpoligraf.

Ramona Saavedra Santis

Between Pride and Bitterness. The Fall of Sevastopol in 1942 in the Memory of Soviet Female Prisoners of War and Survivors of the Nazi Concentration Camp Ravensbrueck

It is an undisputable fact that the Second World War and particularly the dearly purchased victory constitute the main components of Russian historical consciousness until today. The experience and legacy of the "Great Patriotic War" – so the preferred Russian term for the German-Soviet hostilities – remain relevant, indeed essential to national identification and to the collective and individual memorial traditions as well.

Over the years an assemblage of predefined and largely euphemised accounts of significant war developments has been generated. The appearance of critical voices as early as in the 1960s notwithstanding, the interpretations sanctioned and exploited by party-state officials persist dominant and binding both for historians and the public. Led on initially by journalists, the "revelations" of Perestroika, and the subsequent scientific step-by-step reappraisal of the history of WWII had provided for new facts, broken old taboos and deleted many of the blind-spots.

But what happened with the memories of those who had once been eyewitnesses of these events? How do these individuals deal with their memories, memories they had over decades adjusted to the official version of the "Great Patriotic War"? What are the interferences between the shaping of individual memories and the dominant historical discourses?

My paper focuses on the statements submitted by female Soviet POW's, survivors of the Nazi concentration camp Ravensbrueck, recalling the events in Sevastopol, in the summer of 1942. By confronting various autobiographical evidences such as memory accounts as well as recent interviews with official Soviet and Russian historiography, I will discuss some strategies and patterns of memorial traditions by these former Soviet inmates of Ravensbrueck.

Defence and Fall of Sevastopol at Summer 1942

Founded 1783, when Russia annexed the Crimean peninsula, Sevastopol emerged as one of the most famous naval citadels in Europe. Since the Crimean war and the siege of the city in 1854/1855 when Sevastopol became a place of collective pride and suffering, it continuously played an important role in national narrations, charged with heroic content.

Its strategic key position in the Black Sea was the crucial criterion why the Crimea had been of primary importance in the Nazi agenda of capturing Soviet territories since 1941. "Entirely cleared" of its non-German population and under the name "Gotenland" this peninsula was to become the "German Gibraltar" as well as "one large German spa", so defined by Robert Ley, chief of the German labour front.[1]

In September 1941 the German 11th army under the command of Field-Marshal Erich von Manstein penetrated the Crimea. After fierce fighting during the winter months, the entire peninsula was subdued by the invaders, except for Sevastopol. The first attacks on Sevastopol were launched by German and Romanian troops by end of October. Having failed to take the city at stride, Axis forces began a siege. The second offensive against the city in December (from 17th to 31st) failed as well. On June 7th under the code-name "*Störfang*" ("Sturgeon-catch") the third storm on Sevastopol began. It lasted four weeks and resulted eventually in the fall of the city.

The Soviet news agency Sovinformbuero reported on July 4th in the newspaper *Pravda* the abandonment of the city as follows:

> On order by Supreme Command of Red Army the Soviet military has left the city of Sevastopol on July 3rd. In the course of 250 days, the heroic Soviet city successfully repelled innumerable attacks of German troops with unequalled bravery and stamina. During the last 25 days the enemy has undertaken obdurate and uninterrupted air-land assaults on the city. Cut-off from over-the-ground communications

> with the rear and being faced with difficulties with ammunition advance and food supply, Soviet infantry and sea-men, commanders and political officers performed wonderworks of valour and combat heroism by defence of Sevastopol. [...]. Although the Soviet military had abandoned Sevastopol, the defence of the city will take its place in the history of the Great Patriotic War as one of its most illustrious chapters.[2]

Pointing out the military and political value of Sevastopol's defence and accounting a detailed catalogue of the heroic individuals and their exploits, this announcement provided a basis for all the forthcoming discourses on this topic. The tale of the hero-city was born. Told over and over again this generally adopted version suggested a happy-end for the survivors of the defence. In 1942 the General Stuff of Red Army stated: "Combatants, officers and wounded were evacuated from Sevastopol". The bitter truth of Sevastopol's fall came to light only as late as 1964, when the Admiral and Hero of the Soviet Union Nikolai Kuznetsov dared to say that the statement that the troops were evacuated from Sevastopol was false. Actually nobody left the city because there was no backing space and no concept for evacuation.[3]

In reality over 95.000 Soviet defenders of Sevastopol fell in the hands of the enemy. A large part of them was injured.[4] Along with the medical personnel caring for them, many female militaries serving as nurses, medical assistants and surgeons were captured. According to evidence given by an eyewitness, the surgeon Nina Kharlamova, approximately 500 women soldiers were taken as prisoners by Sevastopol. Those who were not shot right away or selected by the Special Action groups of Security Police and SD (Security service) to be killed, were sent through several POW's camps. From there they were transferred to Germany after a formal discharge from captivity as forced labourers. The refusal to take up an employment in the German arms industry was the "justification" to admit these women to Ravensbrueck. On February 27th of 1943, over 200 female defenders of Sevastopol – almost all of them belonged to medical stuff – arrived in this Nazi concentration camp.

The Female Defenders of Sevastopol as Inmates in Ravensbrueck and as Repatriated Persons in the Soviet Union

Ravensbrueck, the only concentration camp set up especially for females, existed during the six years between 1939 and 1945. More then 100 000 women, girls and children from over 20 nations were detained there.

The exact figure of Soviet inmates in Ravensbrueck is difficult ascertain because of insufficient and incomplete documentary evidence. By means of the fragmentary preserved transfer-lists, their numbers can be estimated at 23 000 up to 25 000.[5] The overwhelming majority of them consisted of penalised forced labourers, followed by civilians, who were brought straight to Ravensbrueck in the course of Germany's withdrawal from occupied territories. The third, and far less numerous group, constituted female members of the Red Army. According to my previous research their number did not exceed 700.[6] One third of them came from Sevastopol.

On April 30th of 1945, Ravensbrueck was liberated by the Red Army. After being questioned by officers of the People's Commissariat of Internal Affairs (NKVD) or, in the case of former female POW's, interrogated by the Military Security Service "SMERSH", the majority of Soviet survivors – among them the women from Sevastopol – were repatriated to their native places immediately in the aftermath.

Corresponding to the general approach of the Stalinist regime to those Soviet citizens, who were taken prisoners by the Germans, as untrustworthy individuals, all female POW's encountered the suspect of collaboration with the enemy. Thus, regardless of their exploits by defence of Sevastopol, they were stigmatised as cowards and traitors. Already at their first attempts to find a job, they saw themselves confronted with questionnaires inquiring their captivity or "stay in occupied territories". In case they did not succeed to conceal those facts, chances to get the job vanished. Varvara Makovozova, for example, who had served as a nurse on board of the ambulance-ship *Abkhasia* and, after the ship was drowned, in the underground hospital, was not taken back to her pre-war job in the military sanatorium when she returned from captivity. And furthermore she has had difficulties to reinstate in her former office as a nurse.[7]

Only in the mid 1950ies, after the twentieth party convention, charges of treason on the part of the government had been dropped and the written and unwritten provisions concerning these women were reduced. Even if a number of them were subsequently awarded with various orders and medals for their participation in the defence of Sevastopol, they were nevertheless discriminated against in regard to acknowledgment of invalidity on the grounds of captivity or to rights of pensions covering time spans of their concentration camp imprisonments.

The Fall of Sevastopol in the Memory Accounts

In the course of numerous promising developments of the first years of the Thaw, the foundation of the War Veteran Committee 1956 has been extraordinarily important for the former female POW's as well. The establishment of a section dealing with "former concentration camp prisoners and resistance fighters" within this organisation enabled them – at least formal – to equate Red Army veterans.

In the context of activities of the Committee, the first written autobiographical self-reflections referring to their experiences by the fall of Sevastopol were generated by the end of the Fifties.[8] Although those memory accounts have picked out the imprisonment in Ravensbrueck as a central theme, many of them examined the period of the Sevastopol's defence as well. Mainly the last days before the fall of Sevastopol were reviewed. Pointing out the bloody fierceness of the fighting and the desperate heroism of the combatants, they provide additionally a lot of realistic details on the chaotic and tragic developments in Sevastopol on the brink of its fall. Emotive portrayals of the masses of wounded, who were dying in the underground hospital in the Inkerman caves without water and food over days, came along with dramatic episodes about the making attempts to escape the capture by the enemy.

The cadences of the narratives and the style of the presentation of these accounts correspond with the habitual Soviet language use. As regards content, these women place emphasis on the circumstances on their capture. In consideration of the fact, that precisely the captivity has been the real cause for their stigmatisation, in their reminiscences they aver the impossibility to commit suicide. They stress their duty to stay with the wounded or contend that they were unconscious when being captured. By making sense of their having to cope with their hardship, they seemed to cast no doubts on the appropriateness of the decisions made by the military command and by the Soviet government.

Some 30 years passed after these first series of memorial accounts before in the mid-nineties, in the course of Soviet Union's disintegration and reappraising the history of WWII, the public interest in the memories of the former POW's was aroused. In the meantime, their statements appeared in print media and radio, numerous pupil and youth clubs were dealing with their fates, too. They became popular speakers for events in enterprises, schools and various educational and cultural institutions. Along with the debate in the German Bundestag regarding the remuneration of forced labourers and concentration camp prisoners, in unified Germany the interest in them as one group of victims of the Nazi regime was growing. Their memories were sought after. At this time many of the women who once had been participating at the defence of Sevastopol and have survived the concentration camp, were no longer alive and the rest was between the age of 80 and 90. Nevertheless, these female veterans agreed to be interviewed about their war and imprisonment experiences. As a result, I had some ten life stories of the Sevastopol defenders to my disposal. A part of these interviews was made by documentary director Loretta Walz at the Ravensbrueck memorial between 1998 and 2001 and the other part was realised by me last year on the Crimea.

How do these women recall the events in Sevastopol nowadays, in a changed historical situation and at this age?

The changeability and social implications of remembrance have long been paradigms in the research of memory. Originally it was claimed that the retrospect of traumatic, exceedingly impressive and significant events resulted in particular resistance; to date numerous empirical data show that this memory work is also subject to constructive distortions.

From the perspective of their age, these women are now looking back on their entire life-span. Therefore, war, captivity and imprisonment – formerly the central events in their lives – are likely to be clouded by following decades filled with everyday problems. In the course of remembering time of war, some details former omitted were brought up again. So, unlike the early statements, they admit now that not all of them had volunteered for front-line duty but were conscripted. Under the impact of the recently emerged Holocaust discourse in Russia, new details were recalled, dealing with the Jewish comrades and their extermination by the Germans. And last but not least, acknowledging the real situation by the fall of Sevastopol, they provide critical considerations why they did not manage to evacuate themselves and to escape captivity.

Conclusion

As I have tried to show in this overview, the group I have examined, developed in their communication of memory-contents specific strategies of meaning-building. They were being modified according to changes in general discourse on WWII in the Soviet Union and in Russia. Against the background of the practice of stigmatisation and the notorious exclusion from the national memory culture, their statements are dominated by a latently existing leitmotiv of self-justification. As a consequence, the persisting presence of this apologetic motive has caused corresponding elisions as well as recurring and collectively constructed motive-patterns. The frequent public memory presentations have furthermore advanced stereotypes and reductions in the statements which were consolidated in the course of the years and which remain decisive even in the most recent interviews.

Between the two notions, which persisted all along, pride of having taken part in the defence of Sevastopol was one of them and remains all-dominant. The constant emphasising of the daring deeds by the defenders of the city constitutes the other one. Referring to the last days before the fall of the city, in their recent memories the female POW's conveyed yet another notion - a growing sense of bitterness and offence for being abandoned to their fate. However, this understanding is not to be confused with an attempt to challenge the official version of war experience on their part. Because only by identifying themselves with it, they were able to assure their legitimate integration into the community of Red Army veterans and into the Soviet and Russian polity. Thus the slightly exaggerated sounding sentence given by Nina Kharlamova in 1959: "Sevastopol has been the most cherished and powerful time of my past life",[9] applies to all individuals of this group until today.

Endnotes

1 Dallin 1957, 254.
2 Pravda, July 4, 1942, 1.
3 See Vaneev 1995, 248–249.
4 Angrick 1986, 531.
5 Strebel 2003, 149, Note 242.
6 See Saavedra Santis 2004.
7 Ragozin 1963, 132.
8 Kudriavchikova 1959. The second edition of this collection was published in 1961 and the third advanced one in 1966.
9 Kharlamova 1957, 15.

References

Angrick, Andrej (2003), *Besatzungspolitik und Massenmord: die Einsatzgruppe D in der südlichen Sowjetunion 1941–1943*. Frankfurt am Main, Hamburger Edition.

Dallin, Alexander (1957), *German Rule in Russia 1941/1945. A Study of Occupation Policies*. London, Macmillian & co. LTD.

Kharlamova, Nina (1957), *Ot Sevastopolia do konclageria Bel'zena*. Moskva, unedited manuscript.

Kudriavchikova, V. (1959) (ed.), *Oni pobedili smert'*. Moskva, Godudarstvennoe izdatel'stvo politicheskoi literatury.

Kuznetsov, Nikolai (1969), *Kursom k pobede*. Moskva, Voenizdat.

Ragozin, Efim (1963), *Cherez 20 let*. Simferopol', unedited manuscript.

Saavedra Santis, Ramona (2004), *Die fünfhundert Rotarmistinnen – Die Rekonstruktion eines Häftlingstransports in das Frauen-Konzentrationslager Ravensbrück*. http://www2.hu-berlin.de/ffz/dld/saavedra.pdf.

Strebel, Bernhard (2003), *Das KZ Ravensbrück. Geschichte eines Lagerkomplexes*. Paderborn/München/Wien/Zürich, Schöningh.

Vaneev, Genadii (1995), *Sevastopol' 1941–1942. Khronika geroicheskoi oborony. Kniga 2aia*. Kiev, "Kiiv".

About the Authors

Suzanne Ament holds a PhD in history from Indiana University, U.S.A. She currently teaches Russian and world history at Radford University in Virginia. Her research interests include the relationship between music and society in Russian culture. She has published studies on Russian revolutionary songs, World War II music and the genre of bard music. She also regularly performs Russian and other world music.

Olga Baranova has recently obtained her PhD in history from the European University Institute (EUI) in Florence, Italy. Her thesis focuses on forms of interaction between the indigenous population and the German authorities in occupied Belarus during World War II. Currently she is a scientific coordinator at the MAEM/MEMA Association of Mediterranean Universities and Other Academic Institutes in Florence.

Withold Bonner PhD is Lecturer in German Culture and Literature in the School of Modern Languages and Translation Studies at the University of Tampere, Finland. His research areas include the literature of the GDR, memory and autobiographical writing, and migration.

Peter Carrier is a research fellow at the Georg Eckert Institute for International Textbook Research in Braunschweig, Germany, and lectures in Holocaust Studies at Queens University, Hailsham, UK. He has published widely on the impact of language and contemporary arts on collective memory and historical identities, including studies on Holocaust monuments and national memory cultures in France and Germany.

Elisabeth Cheauré is Professor of Slavistics at the University of Freiburg, Germany, and Dean of the Faculty of Philology. Her fields of scholarly interest are the history of Russian culture and literature, German-

Russian cultural transfer, and gender studies. Her most recent project is concerned with gender and national identity in Russia.

Christine Engel is Professor of Russian Literature and Culture at the University of Innsbruck, Austria. Her scholarly interests are in contemporary literature and film connected with questions concerning the changing patterns of cultural orientation. In addition to her published articles in this field, she has also contributed to *The History of Russian Literature* (2002) and edited *A History of Russian Film* (1999).

Liliana Ruth Feierstein obtained her PhD in philosophy from the Heinrich Hein University, Düsseldorf. Currently she is an assistant professor and researcher at the University of Bayreuth, Germany. Her main research focus is on Jewish philosophy, literature and culture, and cultural minorities, racism and education.

Beate Fieseler is Professor of East European History in the Department of History at the Heinrich Heine University, Duesseldorf, Germany. Her main fields of interest are the social, cultural and gender history of Russia and the Soviet Union, and the history of Stalinism. Her latest publications include: "Arme Sieger: Die Invaliden des 'Großen Vaterländischen Krieges' der Sowjetunion, 1941–1991," (forthcoming) and "Arbeiter und Bauern, Feste und Terror im Stalinismus. Ein Bericht über die neuere wissenschaftliche Literatur" (2008, forthcoming).

Liliana Furman was born in Buenos Aires, Argentina. She has a degree in Jewish Education and Psychology (from the University of Buenos Aires), is a graduate of the Senior Educators Program of the Melton Center, Hebrew University (1990–91), and has Magistra Artium in Jewish Studies, from the University of Freiburg (2004). Since 2000 she has worked for the American Jewish Joint Distribution Committee as a Program Director in Germany. Her areas of interest include gender issues in Jewish culture and the construction of identities in Jewish History.

Zvi Gitelman is Professor of Political Science and Judaic Studies at the University of Michigan, Ann Arbor. He received his undergraduate and graduate degrees from Columbia University. Gitelman has written, edited or co-edited fourteen books and many articles on Soviet and East European Jewry and politics. His current research is on post-Soviet Jewish identities and on the Holocaust in the USSR.

Helena Goscilo is Professor of Slavic Studies at the University of Pittsburgh, USA, specializes in gender and contemporary culture. Her most recent publication is *Preserving Petersburg* (2007, with Stephen M. Norris). She has just completed *Fade from Red: the Cold War Ex-Enemy in Russian and American Film, 1990–2005* (with Margaret B. Goscilo) and *Cinepaternity: Fathers and Sons in Soviet and Post-Soviet Film* (with Yana Hashamova). She is currently co-editing a volume on celebrities with Vlad Strukov.

Yulia Gradskova took her PhD in history in 2007, the title of her dissertation being *Soviet People with Female Bodies: Performing Beauty and Maternity in Soviet Russia from the mid-1930 to the 1960s.* Currently she is working at Södertörn University College, Sweden. Her research interests include oral history, Soviet and post-Soviet social politics and gender history.

Kobi Kabalek is a PhD candidate in the History Department at the University of Virginia. He is interested in cultural history and the history of memory in modern Germany and in Israel.

Olga Kucherenko is a PhD student at Cambridge University. Her research in history and military anthropology focuses on the mechanisms and psychological consequences of Soviet state propaganda, and the deployment of Soviet armed forces during World War II.

Kirsi Kurkijärvi, MA, is a PhD candidate in the Department of Russian Language and Culture at the University of Tampere, Finland. Her thesis deals with writing on the Second World War by female authors in Soviet Russia. She is a contributor to *Masquerade and Femininity: Essays on Russian and Polish Women Writers* (Cambridge Scholars Publishing, 2008).

Roger D. Markwick received his PhD from the University of Sydney in 1995, and is currently working in the School of Humanities and Social Science at the University of Newcastle, Australia. He is co-authoring *Women, War and the Stalinist State, 1941–45*, research for which is supported by an Australian Research Council Discovery Project grant.

Serguei Oushakine holds the post of Assistant Professor at the Department of Slavic Languages and Literatures, Princeton, NJ. He is an anthropologist, his main interest being Eurasia. In his forthcoming book, *The Patriotism of Despair: Communities of Loss in Contemporary Russia*, he traces the importance of experienced or imagined traumas for creating post-socialist identities and meanings. His new areas of research focus on the practices of late Soviet consumption, the political mobilization of popular culture in post-Soviet Russia, and socialist nostalgia.

Robin Ostow PhD is a Fellow at the Centre for European, Russian and Eurasian Studies at the University of Toronto, and a Lecturer at Wilfrid Laurier University, Waterloo, Ontario. She has written extensively on museums, memories and national histories. He most recent volume, *(Re)Visualizing National History: Museums and National Identities in Europe in the New Millennium*, was published by University of Toronto Press in 2008.

Katrin Paehler received her M.A. from Philipps-Universität, Marburg, Germany, and her PhD from the American University in Washington, DC. She teaches at Illinois State University. Her research focuses on Nazi Germany, foreign intelligence, the Holocaust, and mass violence/genocide in the 20th Century. She is currently preparing *Making Intelligence Nazi: The SD, Foreign Intelligence, and Ideology* for publication.

Tobias Privitelli has a PhD in contemporary history from the department of History at the University of Berne, Switzerland. His main research interests are Stalin's foreign policy, territorial expansion in Russia and the Soviet Union, the Baltic States in the 20th century, and the Molotov-Ribbentrop Period.

Sveta Roberman is a PhD candidate in the Department of Sociology and Anthropology at the Hebrew University of Jerusalem. Her research interests include memory and commemoration, immigration and post-Soviet diasporas, and post-socialism.

Arja Rosenholm is Professor of Russian Language & Culture and Director of the Russian Studies Programme in the School of Modern Languages & Translation Studies at the University of Tampere, Finland. Her research interests include Russian literary and cultural studies, especially women's writing, autobiographical genres, memory and ecocriticism.

Ramona Saavedra Santis holds a PhD in history and is a lecturer in the Osteuropa Institut at the Freie Universität, Berlin. Her areas of expertise are the history of Soviet Union, World War II, and Soviet and Russian cultures of remembering. For the last few years she has been working intensively with Russian and Ukrainian survivors from the female concentration camp at Ravensbrueck.

Elena Trubina is Professor of Philosophy at the Ural State University in Ekaterinburg, Russia. Her research areas are post-Soviet cultures and subjectivities, social and urban theory, and the politics of memory and emotions.

Aleksanteri Series ISSN 1796-3192

1:2006 Toimittanut Marja Jänis: *Venäjästä suomeksi ja suomesta venäjäksi*. 952-10-2934-X

2:2006 Edited by Hanna Smith: *The Two-Level Game: Russia's Relations with Great Britain, Finland and the European Union*. 952-10-3061-5

3:2006 Toimittanut Jouko Nikula: *Katse Venäjään. Suomalaisen Venäjätutkimuksen antologia*. 952-10-3204-9

1:2007 Toimittanut Kristiina Kalleinen: *Venäjä ja Suomi. Juhlakirja professori Timo Vihavaiselle 9.5.2007.* 978-952-10-3905-8

2:2007 Edited by David Dusseault: *The CIS: Form or Substance?* 978-952-10-4018-4

3:2007 Edited by David Dusseault: *The Dynamics of Energy in the Eurasian Context*. 978-952-10-4019-1

4:2007 Edited by Natalia Baschmakoff, Paul Fryer and Mari Ristolainen: *Texts and Communities: Soviet and Post-Soviet Life in Discourse and Practice*. 978-952-10-4077-1

5:2007 Edited by Maria Lähteenmäki: *The Flexible Frontier: Change and Continuity in Finnish-Russian Relations*. 978-952-10-4093-1

6:2007 Edited by Marjatta Vanhala-Aniszewski and Lea Siilin: *Voices and Values of Young People. Representations in Russian Media*. 978-952-10-4094-8

7:2007 Edited by Markku Kangaspuro: *Constructed Identities in Europe*. 978-952-10-4096-2

1:2008 Edited by Helena Rytövuori-Apunen: *Russia Forever? Towards Pragmatism in Finnish/Russian Relations*. 978-952-10-4095-5

2:2008 Edited by Withold Bonner and Arja Rosenholm: *Recalling the Past – (Re)constructing the Past. Memorizing World War II in Russia and Germany*. 978-952-10-4098-6